Contrastive Analysis

CARL JAMES

LONGMAN

LONGMAN GROUP LIMITED
Longman House, Burnt Mill, Harlow,
Essex CM20 2JE, England
and Associated Companies throughout the world

First published 1980
Second impression 1981
Third impression with corrections 1983

ISBN 0 582 55370 9

Printed in Singapore by
Four Strong Printing Company

Preface

In the heyday of structural linguistics and the pattern practice language teaching methodology which derived insights and justification from such an approach to linguistic description, nothing seemed of greater potential value to language teachers and learners than a comparative and contrastive description of the learner's mother tongue and the target language. If one could juxtapose the structures of the mother tongue against those of the target language, course designers (and teachers and learners) would be better able to plan their learning and teaching; better able to foresee difficulty and consequently better able to husband resources and direct learning and teaching effort. It was on such a basis that the 1960's saw a range of contrastive analyses published (typically between English and other world languages) and a host of language teaching courses made available. Yet, in the 1970's the bubble seemed to burst; contrastive analysis no longer claimed as much pedagogic attention, although, significantly, the decade saw the establishment of major contrastive linguistic projects, especially between English and European languages; German, Polish and Serbo-Croat. What was the reason for this decline in pedagogic interest?

Undoubtedly for two main reasons, one descriptive linguistic and the other, more complex in nature, psycholinguistic-pedagogic. Linguistically, the basis of contrastive description seemed to be unable to withstand the stresses of constantly changing models of analysis and theoretical approaches. If the substance of structural linguistics was called into question, and if the nature of one alternative, say generative syntax, was itself subject to constant emendation and often quite fundamental alteration, how could there be a stable basis upon which to attempt contrastive description? Psycholinguistically and pedagogically, teachers discovered that the contrastive descriptions to which they had been exposed were only able to predict part of the learning problems encountered by their learners, and that those points of potential difficulty that were identified seemed to cause various and variable problems among different learners, and between the production and the perception of language. Language learning, in short, was less predictable from contrastive *linguistic* description than teachers had been led to believe. Partial descriptions of complete systems correlated uneasily with the growing system of the target language in the learner, particularly when teachers came upon idiosyncrasies of language unrelated to either the mother tongue or the target language.

In this atmosphere of a certain unfulfilment it is not surprising that contrastive analysis lost some of its pedagogic impact. We should, however, be careful not to associate the value of contrastive analysis solely in practical language teaching terms. There was always more to contrastive analysis than making claims about learner difficulty. Through the major contrastive projects referred to above, and through journals to which the present author has been a major contributor, contrastive analysis has had much to offer to translation theory, the description of particular languages, language typology and the study of language universals. Because of its closeness, however, to language learning and to the more general concept of bilingualism, contrastive analysis has always been regarded as a major branch of applied, rather than pure linguistics, and hence the appropriateness of this new addition to the *Applied Linguistics and Language Study Series*.

Dr James begins by placing contrastive analysis as an 'inter-linguistic' enterprise which looks on language not merely as form but also as function in context, not merely as system to be described but as system to be acquired: a psycho-sociolinguistic study across language boundaries. In Chapter 2, the author examines the psycho-linguistic bases of contrastive analysis, concentrating on the notion of 'transfer' which has been so powerful an element in its pedagogic appeal. Too simple an association of 'transfer' with behaviourist psychology, and too dismissive an attitude towards behaviourism by applied linguists who regarded it as a total rather than partial explanation of learning, have combined to cast doubt on the psycholinguistic bases of contrastive analysis. It is therefore all the more important that Dr James presents a balanced account in this Chapter. Quite properly, in the light of the extensive literature, it is to the linguistic components of contrastive analysis that the author accords the major sections of the book. Chapters 3 and 4 offer the reader both a theoretical framework and a practical methodology for the activity of contrastive analysis. Taking first a microlinguistic 'code' approach, and concentrating on syntax, Carl James examines the effect on contrastive analysis of alternative descriptive models, structuralist, transformational-generative, case grammar, while using these as means to the isolation of general grammatical categories of unit, structure, class and system, applicable to all descriptive frameworks. '*Microlinguistic Contrastive Analysis*' then follows as a practical Chapter offering a set of principles for contrastive analysis at various language levels.

To this point the discussion has focused in a 'classically' contrastive way, on phonology and morphology and sentence-syntax; Chapter 5 recalls the author's concern in Chapter 1 for language as function in context and focuses on a novel and macrolinguistic approach to contrastive analysis. Here it is possible for those readers concerned with the applications of pragmatics, and those with interests in text linguistics to see a rich potential for contrastive study. In the examination of the research in contrastive text analysis and in the illuminating suggestions for the as yet hardly disturbed ground of contrastive discourse, we begin to see the contribution that contrastive analysis can make to fields as apparently diverse as literary stylistics and social anthropology. At the same time, for those with primarily a language learning and teaching interest this Chapter provides a useful summary of work in textual structure and conversational analysis.

The final Chapters return to the mainstream of the pedagogical exploitation of contrastive analysis, and hence to the historical issues with which this Preface began. The author is rightly sceptical of any plausible, or even possible, direct application of the results of contrastive analysis to the planning of curricula or the design of teaching materials. He stresses rather its implicational value, its role as a source for experimental studies into the predictability of learner difficulty, its major theoretical contribution to current studies into interlanguage, its need to be combined with Error Analysis as a practical classroom research tool for teachers anxious to adjust their teaching to the state of knowledge of their learners. Throughout the book, Carl James has been at pains to present both a theoretical and a practical case for contrastive analysis. In the final Chapter *Some Issues of Contention* he confirms the characteristic applied linguistic position of contrastive analysis, mediating between theory and practice, and, like applied linguistics itself, a bidirectional rather than unidirectional enterprise.

Christopher N. Candlin
Lancaster, March 1980.

TO THE MEMORY OF
ALAN EDWARD SHARP
1922–1979

Acknowledgements

Ten years ago I began my first paper on Contrastive Analysis with an admission that this branch of Applied Linguistics was 'in the doldrums'. That it is slightly less so now than it was then is due to a small group of individuals who persisted in their search for relevance. Of these may I single out a few, and apologise for omitting the others; R. J. Di Pietro, Jacek Fisiak, Rudi Filipović, Eric Kellerman, Wolfgang Kühlwein, Gerhard Nickel, Wolfram Wilß, and Kari Sajavaara.

This book is very much a product of The University College of North Wales, Bangor. Hundreds of students have shared and nourished my enthusiasm for CA over the last decade. My Head of Department, the late Professor Alan Sharp, diligently encouraged this enthusiasm. And the institution itself seemed to work in partnership with The British Council to send me to the important conferences on CA.

Christopher Candlin patiently read several drafts of the manuscript and suggested numerous improvements and Glenda Roberts made a fine job of the typing. I alone have to answer for the book's faults.

Carl James

U.C.N.W.
Bangor, Wales.
11 FEB 1980

I should like to thank in particular Howard Jackson, Eddie Levenston, Manuel Gomes da Torre and Alistair Wood for their constructive criticism of the first edition, which has resulted in an improved third impression.

Bangor
21 AUGUST 1982

Contents

Contents

What is Contrastive Analysis?

1.1 The Place of CA in Linguistics

This book is concerned with a branch of linguistics called Contrastive Analysis, the practitioners of which we shall call 'contrastivists'. The first question that arises is where CA is to be located in the field of linguistics.

The term 'linguist' can refer to the following: a person who is professionally engaged in the study and teaching of one or more languages, usually not his own nor that of the community in which he works; a polyglot, who might work as a translator or interpreter; someone interested in 'language families' or language history; a person with philosophical interests in language universals or the relationship between language and thought or truth; and more. This list is not exhaustive, but is representative. Rather than making a list, it would be better to evolve a way of classifying types of linguistic enterprise. Such a classification will involve three dimensions or axes:

i) Sampson has pointed out (1975: 4) that there are two broad approaches to linguistics, the *generalist* and the *particularist*. "On the one hand, linguists treat individual *languages*: English, French, Chinese, and so on. On the other hand, they consider the general phenomenon of human *language*, of which particular languages are examples". Sampson proceeds to warn against seeing either of these approaches as inherently superior to the other, claiming that it is largely a matter of personal taste which approach one favours. He also states that particularists will tend to be anthropologists or philologers, while the generalists are likely to have more philosophical interests.

ii) Along a second dimension linguists are divisible into those who choose to study one, or each, language *in isolation*, and those whose ambition and methods are *comparative*. The former are concerned to discover and specify the immanent 'genius' of the particular language which makes it unlike any other language and endows its speakers

1

with a psychic and cognitive uniqueness. The comparativist (Ellis, 1966), as the name implies, proceeds from the assumption that, while every language may have its individuality, all languages have enough in common for them to be compared and classified into types. This approach, called 'linguistic typology' has established a classificatory system for the languages of the world into which individual languages can be slotted according to their preferred grammatical devices: so they talk of 'synthetic', 'analytic', 'inflectional', 'agglutinating', and 'tone' languages.

iii) The third dimension is that used by De Saussure to distinguish "two sciences of language": *diachronic* as opposed to *synchronic*. De Saussure (1959: 81) explains the distinction as follows: "Everything that relates to the static side of our science is synchronic; everything that has to do with evolution is diachronic. Similarly, *synchrony* and *diachrony* designate respectively a language-state and an evolutionary phase". In ii) above I mentioned typology: the approach here is synchronic, in that languages are typologically grouped according to their present-day characteristics, no reference being made to - the histories of the languages, not even to their historical relatedness: thus it might happen that two languages, one Baltic, the other Pacific, which could not possibly have ever been genetically related, turn out, typologically, to belong to the same grouping. The diachronic parallel to typology is what is known as philology and is associated with such scholars as Verner, Rask, Bopp and Schleicher. It was Schleicher who 'reconstructed' the Proto-Aryan language or, as Jespersen (1947: 80) called it "die indogermanische Ursprache". Philologists are concerned with linguistic genealogy, with establishing the genetic 'families' of language-groups.

The question we set out to answer was of the nature of CA as a linguistic enterprise. Reference can be made to the above three classificatory dimensions, which are, it must be stressed, overlapping dimensions. We must, then, ask three questions: i) Is CA generalist or particularist? ii) Is it concerned with immanence or comparison? iii) Is it diachronic or synchronic? The answers to these questions, with respect to CA, are not clear-cut. First, CA is neither generalist nor particularist, but somewhere intermediate on a scale between the two extremes. Likewise, CA is as interested in the inherent genius of the language under its purview as it is in the comparability of languages. Yet it is not concerned with classification, and, as the term *contrastive* implies, more interested in differences between languages than in their likenesses. And finally, although not concerned either with language families, or with other factors of language history, nor is it sufficiently committed to the study of 'static' linguistic phenomena to merit the label *synchronic*. (We return to this matter presently *cf.* 1.2.)

CA seems, therefore, to be a hybrid linguistic enterprise. In terms of the three criteria discussed here we might venture the following provisional definition: CA is a linguistic enterprise aimed at producing inverted (*i.e.* contrastive, not comparative) two-valued typologies (a CA is always concerned with a *pair* of languages), and founded on the assumption that languages can be compared.

1.2 CA as Interlanguage Study

We have so far been assuming that any branch of linguistics has as its object of study human languages, or, which is to say the same thing, human language in general. The languages may be extant and vital, or 'dead', and recorded only in written relics, but they are nevertheless viewed as adequate representations of the languages in question. Now, there are other branches of linguistics which are more specialised, and which are concentrated on *parts* of whole languages. Phonetics, for example, is a branch of linguistics which "is concerned with the human noises by which 'the message' is actualized or given audible shape: the nature of those noises, their combinations, and their functions in relation to the message" (O'Connor, 1973: 10). Phoneticians, then, disregard much of what we normally understand by 'language'. Dialectology is another case of such specialisation: a language can be viewed as being actualised in its dialects, and these dialects vary among themselves. There are furthermore three kinds of dialect with respect to any given language – historical, geographical, and social dialects – so a 'social dialectologist' for example, is a linguist who is concerned, not with *the* language,[1] but with the socially marked varieties which, taken together, constitute that language. All that I am saying is that to qualify as a linguist, one need not necessarily be a student of *the* language as a total entity: one still qualifies by studying that entity in part or some aspect of that entity – in our example of the dialectologist, its capacity for variation.

There is a branch of linguistics, which I shall call 'Interlanguage Study', which is likewise not primarily concerned with languages in the conventional sense. This branch of linguistics is interested in the *emergence* of these languages rather than in the finished product. Now, CA belongs to interlanguage study, and, since 'emergence' is an evolutionary concept (in De Saussure's sense), it follows that CA is to be viewed as diachronic rather than synchronic in orientation. However, interlanguage study is diachronic in a slightly different sense of the term than that intended by De Saussure. He was thinking of language evolution in the historical or phylogenetic sense, which pertains to change which spans generations and centuries; I am using the term diachronic in the sense of ontogeny, or change within the human individual. Some examples will make this clear. First, there is the study of language acquisition in infants, summarised recently in Brown (1973). Slobin (1971) entitled an anthology of writings in this field: *The Ontogenesis of Grammar*. Since the child progesses from zero knowledge of the language spoken around him to adequate mastery by the age of five, and since there is only *one* language involved, child language study is not strictly speaking a form of interlanguage study. But the study of second-language or foreign-language[2] learning is concerned with a monolingual becoming a bilingual: two languages are involved, the L1 and the L2, so we have here a true case of interlingual diachronic study. Another branch of linguistics that is concerned with the transition from one language to another is translation theory, or the study of how texts from one language are transformed into comparable texts in another language. Here, however, the focus of interest is not on learning, as in the previous example, but on the process of text-replacement: the process can be enacted inside a bilingual's brain or inside a computer, according to whether one's interest is in human or 'machine' translation.

There are thus *three* branches of two-valued (2 languages are involved) interlingual linguistics: *translation theory* – which is concerned with the processes of text conversion; *error analysis*; and *contrastive analysis* – these last two having as the object of enquiry the means whereby a monolingual learns to be bilingual. Fig. 1 illustrates what I mean by interlanguage studies. Although the point of departure for such studies is the two languages concerned (NL and FL in the case of language learners, SL or 'source language' and TL 'target language' in the case of translation), the focus of attention is on the *intermediate space* between the two. The 'language' which comes into being in this intermediate stage is called by Mel'chuk (1963), in a discussion of translation theory an 'interlingua': it is a system which encompasses, as is desirable for translation, the analysis characteristics of the SL and the synthesis characteristics of the TL text. There is one interlingua for each pair of texts. By contrast, it is suggested by error analysts that the learner, in progressing towards mastery of the FL, develops a series of 'approximative systems' (Nemser, 1971a) or 'transitional dialects' (Corder, 1971), which are successive and intersecting, such that each stage has unique features as well as features which it shares with the immediately preceding and the immediately succeeding approximative system: this is shown by the intersecting circles in Fig. 1.

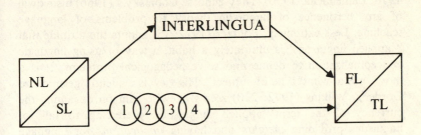

Fig. 1: The field of interlanguage studies

I shall not be discussing further translation theory: the reader is referred to Wilss (1977). But in Chapter 7 I shall be discussing 'translation equivalence' as a basis for language comparison in CA. Also in Chapter 7 I shall explore further the nature of the relationship between error analysis (EA) and CA.

1.3 CA as 'Pure' or 'Applied' Linguistics

In our attempt, in 1.1, to allocate the various branches of linguistics to an overall plan, it seems that one important dimension was overlooked: the distinction commonly drawn between 'pure' and 'applied' linguistics. Since the difference between these two is widely appreciated, I shall not attempt here to define 'applied linguistics', but merely refer the reader to Corder's extensive account of the field (Corder, 1973). It is necessary to point out, however, that in some recent work, including Corder's, doubts have been voiced over the legitimacy of considering the existence of a discipline called 'applied linguistics'. Corder suggests that 'applied linguistics' is not a science in its own right, but merely a technology based on 'pure' linguistics:

"The application of linguistic knowledge to some object – or applied linguistics, as its name implies – is an activity. It is not a theoretical study. It makes use of theoretical studies. The applied linguist is a consumer, or user, not a producer, of theories" (Corder, 1973: 10).

Some, more categorical than Corder, have even questioned the utility of applying linguistic knowledge at all for the solution of pedagogical problems, claiming that linguistics has no relevant contribution to make towards the solution of these problems (Johnson, 1970; Lamendella, 1970). They endorse Chomsky's (1966) disavowal of any pertinence of linguistic theory to problems of language teaching. Less extremely, Politzer (1972: 15) adopts the attitude that "'applied linguistics' is ultimately a habit, a way of using linguistic conceptualisation to define and solve pedagogical problems. It is a 'how', not a 'what' type of subject". His view is evidently germane to Corder's. Wilkins (1972: 220) seems likewise bent on devaluing the currency of the term 'applied' linguistics, preferring to talk of linguistics providing *insights* and having *implications* for language teaching.

I would like to take the opposite view, and to argue that there *is* a science of applied linguistics, so endorsing Malmberg's statement that

"The applications of linguistics can, and should, be looked upon as sciences in their own rights . . . we must be very careful not to mix up practical applications with purely scientific research" (Malmberg, 1971: 3).

Corder, recall, bases his conviction that applied linguistics is not a science on the claim that it does not produce, or add to, theory, but 'consumes' theory. Now a consumer, whether of baked beans or of theories, must be selective: he must have standards against which to evaluate, as a potential consumer, the various alternative theories that are offered to him. Where does he get the standards from but from some theory? His selections are guided by a theory of relevance and applicability.

A further reason why I think it necessary to postulate the existence of a science which is called 'applied linguistics' is slightly paradoxical: applied linguistics is a hybrid discipline, constituted not only of linguistics but also of psychology and sociology. In assessing the relevance of any 'pure' linguistic statement, the applied linguist must assess not only its linguistic validity, but its psychological and/or its sociological validity. In fact, I cannot name one single branch of 'applied linguistics' that relies exclusively on 'pure' linguists: all supplement linguistic theories with insights from the other two disciplines I have mentioned. CA, we shall show in Chapter 2, relies very strongly on psychology. I feel justified in assigning it to a science of applied linguistics for two reasons: first, that it is different from 'pure' linguistics in drawing on other scientific disciplines; and secondly, because linguistics is the science it draws most heavily upon.

It is an undeniable fact, however, that 'pure' linguists, especially during the last decade, have been practising something very much akin to CA. Their interests are not comparative, contrastive, or typological, but lie in the universals of language. The purpose of establishing universals (or what is common to *all* languages) is to achieve economy:

> "Real progress in linguistics consists in the discovery that certain features of given languages can be reduced to universal properties of language, and explained in terms of these deeper aspects of linguistic form" (Chomsky, 1965: 35).

So the linguist is called upon to look at other languages for the confirmation of any tentative universal suggested to him by the deep analysis of any single language. But it is unreasonable to expect any individual linguist to check his tentative universal by looking at *all* the world's languages: the most he can do is to gather confirmatory evidence from the one or two other languages he might know. In so doing he in fact engages in CA. For example, Ross (1969) suggested that, universally, adjectives are derived from NPs in deep structure, as in i). He checked this claim against data from German and French, as in ii) and iii).

  i) Jack is clever, but he doesn't look *it*.
 ii) Hans ist klug, aber seine Söhne sind *es* nicht.
     (*Lit.:* Jack is clever, but his sons aren't [it])
iii) Jean est intelligent, mais ses enfants ne *le* sont pas.

So far, so good: the claim seems to hold, for the pronouns *it*, *es*, *le* certainly refer to the adjectives in the antecedent clause, and so it appears adjectives are 'nominal' in nature. But, as Fedorowicz-Bacz (forthcoming) shows, a CA of the English sentence with its Polish equivalent (iv) introduces conflicting evidence: in the Polish, *taki* is not pronominal, but adjectival.

 iv) Jacek jest bystry, choć na takiego nie wygląda.
     (*Lit.:* Jack is clever, although as this not looks)

What we have here is very reminiscent of CA, but Ross is doing 'pure', not 'applied' linguistics.

Let me make it clear that this book is concerned with 'applied' CA and not with its 'pure' counterpart. I am dealing therefore with what some feel to be the *central* component of applied linguistics, or at least the most obvious component. As Wilkins (1972: 224) says:

> "It is one of the few investigations into language structure that has improved pedagogy as its aim and is therefore truly a field of applied language research."

Politzer (1972) is less explicit, but the fact that CA claims one of the four chapters of his book on pure and applied linguistics speaks for itself: for him, CA is a central and substantial component of applied linguistics.

The answer to the question is CA a form of 'pure' or of 'applied' linguistics? is − of both. But while 'pure' CA is only a peripheral enterprise in pure linguistics, it is a central concern of applied linguistics. From now on I shall intend 'applied CA' whenever I use the term CA.

1.4 CA and Bilingualism

I have characterised CA as being a form of interlingual study, or of what Wandruszka (1971) has called 'interlinguistics'. As such, and in certain other respects, it has much in common with the study of bilingualism. Bilingualism, by definition, is not the study of individual single languages, nor of language in general, but of the possession of two languages. If it is the possession of two languages by a single community we speak of *societal bilingualism*; if we study the person who has competence in two languages we are dealing with *individual bilingualism*: CA's concern is with this second category. Bilingualism refers to the possession of two languages by an individual or society, whereas CA is concerned with how a monolingual becomes bilingual: his bilingualisation, if you like. We can call this difference between the two a concern with *extant* bilingualism on the one hand, and with *incipient* bilingualism on the other (Diebold, 1961).

I shall not attempt to reconstruct the history of CA: Di Pietro (1971: 9) finds an early example of CA in C. H. Grandgent's book on the German and English sound systems, published in 1892. For me, modern CA starts with Lado's *Linguistics across Cultures* (1957). It was, however, two earlier books on the linguistic integration of immigrants to the USA which indubitably gave Lado his impetus: I refer to Weinreich (1953) and Haugen (1956): these are studies of immigrant bilingualism. This is the historical link between CA and bilingualism study.

Some have cast doubt on the legitimacy of this link, claiming that Weinreich's and Haugen's studies are analyses of how the second language (American English) influenced the immigrant's command and maintenance of the NL, whereas CA is concerned with the effects exerted by the NL on the language being learnt, the FL: the *directionalities* are different. Thus Dulay and Burt (1974: 102) support this caveat by quoting Haugen (1956: 370): ". . . it is the language of the learner that is influenced, not the language he learns". In reply, one might note that Weinreich makes no issue of directionality, speaking of ". . . deviation from the norms of either language" and even observing that the *strength* of interference is greatest in the direction NL → FL, which is the concern of CA; he says:

> "It is the conclusion of common experience, if not yet a finding of psycholinguistic research, that the language which has been learned first, or the mother-tongue, is in a privileged position to resist interference" (Weinreich, 1953: 88).

There is a further difference between the two types of study that merits attention: we have already referred to it (p. 4) in terms of the ontogenesis: phylogenesis distinction. CA is concerned with the way in which NL affects FL learning *in the individual*, whereas Weinreich's and Haugen's work studied the long-term effects, spanning a generation, of language contact. CA is concerned with 'parole', their work with 'langue'; CA with 'interference', they with 'integration'. This being so, there does seem to be a substantial difference involved: after all, why would De Saussure have bothered to insist on the langue: parole dichotomy unless it was of fundamental importance for linguistics? My answer is that a necessary dichotomy for linguistics need not be equally valid for 'interlinguistics', to use Wandruszka's term again. In fact, there is a growing body of evidence that interlinguistically the processes that bring about language change in contact situations spanning generations are very similar to those processes determining an individual's acquisiton of a FL in a time-span of weeks. The historical stages in the pidginisation and creolisation of languages (Whinnom, 1965) are similar to those a FL learner undergoes. Initially there is a process of simplification involving loss of inflections, of the copula, and of function words like articles, after which there sets in a process of gradual complication assimilating the interlingua to the target language norm. These matters are discussed by Ferguson (1971) and their significance for FL teaching by Widdowson (1975). I shall return to this notion of interlingua, and to a further distinction drawn in bilingualism study – that between compound vs coordinate bilingualism – in a later Chapter (6) which is devoted to the pedagogical applications of CA. It is now time to turn our attention to the psychological bases of CA.

NOTES

1 *cf.* Fishman (1977: 316): "there can be no dialects unless they are dialects of 'something' . . . and this 'something' may itself be merely an abstraction".
2 The terms 'L1', 'first language', and 'native language' (NL), like the terms 'L2', 'foreign language' (FL), 'target language' (TL) are not synonyms (*cf.* Christophersen, 1973: 39). In the subsequent discussion I shall assume them to be unless otherwise indicated.

2

The Psychological Basis
of
Contrastive Analysis

We have already observed (p. 6) that CA is a hybrid drawing on the sciences of linguistics and psychology. This is inevitably so, since linguistics is concerned with the formal properties of language and not directly with learning,[1] which is a psychological matter. Since CA is concerned with L2 learning, it needs a psychological component.

2.1 Transfer in Learning Psychology

One of the concerns of learning psychologists is the effects of one learning task on a subsequent one. The observation that prior learning effects subsequent learning leads to the hypothesis of *transfer*, which Ellis (1965) refers to as "perhaps the single most important concept in the theory and practice of education". Educationists assume that transfer of training will be pervasive, so that: what is learned in school will be relevant in later life; successive steps in a course will be associated through transfer from earlier to later steps; gains made in one skill, say speaking, will effect gains in other skills, for example writing. Ellis supplies a definition of transfer: "the hypothesis that the learning of task A will affect the subsequent learning of task B". Substitute for 'task A' and 'task B' L1 and L2 respectively, and it becomes obvious that the psychological foundation of CA is transfer theory.

Learning involves the association of two entities: thus, learning the Highway Code means learning to associate the visual sensation of a red light with the need to decelerate or stop the vehicle. The study of this process constitutes Associationism in psychology, a study dating back at least to Aristotle, though Galton was the first modern psychologist to study associations experimentally, as Hörmann shows (Hörmann, 1971: Chapters 6, 7).

The two 'entities' associated in a learning task are a stimulus (S) and a response (R). These labels signal the second strand in the

11

psychology of CA: S-R theory, which is epitomised in Skinner's behaviourist explanation of how language learning is consummated (Skinner, 1957). We are therefore justified in saying that the psychological basis of CA resides in the two psychological enterprises we have mentioned: Associationism and S-R theory.

Now, most of the experimental investigation of transfer undertaken by psychologists concerned very primitive learning tasks performed – frequently by animals – under laboratory conditions. Where the intention was to study language learning by humans, the tasks were similarly very much simplified in comparison with the real-world processes of language learning: the favoured technique was (and still is) the learning of sets of nonsense-syllables. The question must arise of whether observations from such simplified settings and types of learning can validly be extrapolated to serve a theory of real language-learning. One defence of such extrapolation is that a fundamental assumption of the philosophy of science is that it is, and it is on this basis that progress is made in science. Secondly, there is evidence of a strong link between experimental and real-life learning, as far as transfer is concerned. This was recognised by Underwood (1957) and by Underwood and Postman (1960). Furthermore, the study of bilingualism corroborates many of the experimental findings concerning transfer effects. Thus Weinreich is able to write of interference as ". . . those instances of deviation from the norms of either language which occur in the speech of bilinguals as a result of their familiarity with more than one language" (Weinreich, 1953: 1). There remain, nevertheless, certain differences and certain problems, which deserve some attention.

2.2 Some Problems of Definition

i) In non-verbal learning involving the 'conditioning' of certain responses, that is, their association with certain stimuli, the responses are assumed to be available to the learner, already part of his repertoire: it is not these as such that he has to learn, but their association with a S. In L2 learning, the responses themselves – by which I mean L2 utterances – have to be learnt as well as with which S they are to be associated.

ii) CA is concerned with teaching rather than learning. The former involves the predetermination and conventionalisation of what Ss and Rs are to be associated, whereas the latter does not: the decision can be quite arbitrary. Thus, from the point of view of learning it is immaterial whether 'green' or 'red' is to be associated with 'stop' – no appeal is made to convention; but from the driving instructor's point of view it matters a great deal, of course. In other words, the responses of L2 learners have to be appropriately associated to set stimuli.

iii) What constitutes a S or a R in L2 learning? S is the least elusive of definition. It is best to assign to it a prelinguistic definition, as does Jakobovits (1970), and, indeed, as did Bloomfield (1933: 24) in his parable of Jack and Jill taking a walk. Jill, feeling hungry (the S), 'responds' by asking Jack to pick her an apple. Jakobovits sees S as constituted of ". . . the environmental conditions that are antecedent to linguistic utterances". I would add ". . . and mental conditions" to cover non-observable and personal or affective stimuli to speech and to satisfy mentalists' complaints about empirical accounts of behaviour: Jill might have been not hungry, but greedy. A S, then, is what Richterich (1974) has called a 'communicative need', or *besoin de communication*.[2]

One might be tempted to include the language to be used in the definition of S, arguing that Jill realises that Jack will only pick her an apple if she asks in English – assuming Jack is monolingual in English. I think it preferable to reserve the language to be used for defining the R, for two reasons. First, there is no element of choice in Ss: one either is, or is not hungry or greedy, whereas adding the language would introduce an element of choice. Second, a point to be amplified in Chapter 7, it is desirable to formulate language-neutral definitions of S so that they can serve as a basis for interlingual comparison, a *tertium comparationis* as it is called.

A further problem in defining S is that language behaviour is a two-way process: not only do we produce utterances: we also receive them. In Bloomfield's example, Jill's speech (her R) becomes in turn a S to Jack, on the basis of which he picks an apple. So we must, if we are to accommodate language perception, include *purely* linguistic Ss. Jakobovits' definition of S will not serve perception, so we are faced with a dilemma. There are suggestions in psycholinguistics which could resolve it though, in the form of the notion 'analysis by synthesis'. This is an attempt to explain our understanding of sentences through a process of resynthesising what we hear: I understand what you say because I am capable of saying it myself. However, this notion is not without its weaknesses, as has been pointed out by Thorne (1966). I shall propose an alternative solution presently, when discussing the 'paradigms'.

iv) A 'response' in language behaviour is the utterance itself, the study of which is the proper concern of linguistics. Before utterances are described, however, they are subjected to a process of abstraction which converts them into sentences: as Corder (1973: 162) says: "Linguistic descriptions which aim at accounting for language as a system ... deal with sentences, not utterances". There is a one-to-many relationship between sentences and utterances: one sentence (St.) underlies many concrete utterances such as Utt. i–n below:

St.	Pron.	Aux.	V.	NP Object
Utt. i)	He	can	make	cake.
ii)	We	shall	sing	songs.
⋮				
n	You	should	send	flowers.

A concern with sentences reflects a preoccupation with *form* and a nonchalance over *substance*. Sapon (1971) draws two conclusions from this: the first is that linguists have no right to dabble in psychology, since *form* concerns itself with the *product* of psychological processes, and not with the psychological processes themselves. His caveat refers to the psychological unreality of linguistic descriptions, to which we return in detail below. Sapon's second misgiving is that while linguists may be equipped to describe both form and substance, they can make *predictions* only about form: "Given a fragment of an utterance such as 'What I really want to do is –' a linguist can make a prediction that the next fragment ... will belong to a given form-class. He is utterly unprepared to specify which member of the form-class called 'verbs' is likely to appear" (Sapon, *op. cit.*: 77).[3] Therefore, in specifying Rs in language we must limit ourselves to their abstract form, as sentences, rather than their substance as utterances, and we must beware of suggesting the nature of the psychological processes antecedent to the production of Rs.

2.3 Transfer Theory and CA

CA is founded on the assumption that L2 learners will tend to transfer to their L2 utterances the formal features of their L1, that, as Lado puts it "individuals tend to transfer the forms and meanings and the distribution of forms and meanings of their native language and culture to the foreign language and culture" (Lado, 1957: 2).[4]

Osgood (1949) summarised two decades of research into the phenomenon of transfer in the three 'paradigms' of Fig. 2.

Paradigm	Task 1	Task 2	Task 3	T-value
A	S1 – R1	S2 – R1	S1 – R1	+T
B	S1 – R1	S1 – R2	S1 – R1	–T
C	S1 – R1	S2 – R2	S1 – R1	–T

PROACTION   RETRO-ACTION

Fig. 2: Osgood's transfer paradigms

Osgood envisaged three learning tasks being set in sequence: notice that for each paradigm (A, B, C) task 1 and task 3 are identical. When considering the effects on task 2 of having already done task 1, or "the effect of a given specifiable prior activity upon the learning of a given test activity" we speak of *Proaction*, whereas *Retroaction* is concerned with "the effect of a specifiable interpolated activity upon the retention of a previously learned activity". In fact, there are only *two* learning tasks, not three: 'task 3' is in reality a performance task. CA is concerned with proaction of course, seeing 'task 1' as the learning of L1 and 'task 2' as the learning of L2. Retroaction is of potential interest to CA in two ways: first, it could handle effects of L2 upon performance in L1, or what Jakobovits (1969) vividly terms 'backlash'. Secondly, it is concerned with forgetting, or 'oblivescence', as Baddeley (1972: 41) observed. It would have to be invoked in any attempt to explain why L1 is not usually forgotten when a L2 is learnt.[5] Here, we shall only be concerned with proaction.

In the paradigms, Ss and Rs carry subscripts: these refer to the identity or non-identity of Ss and Rs in consecutive tasks. Note that Osgood assigns Transfer values (+ or –) to each paradigm: +T is 'positive transfer' or 'facilitation' while –T is 'negative transfer' or 'interference'. The *amount* of +T or –T generated by each paradigm will depend, of course, on how similar Ss are with identity of Rs or how similar Rs are with identity of Ss: "where stimuli are functionally identical and responses are varied [paradigm B], negative transfer and retroactive interference are obtained, *the magnitude of both decreasing as similarity between the responses increases*" (Osgood, *op. cit.*: 135).

Let us take each paradigm in turn and state its relevance to CA: in each case, we have at our disposal two types of behavioural interpretation, one a model of language production, the other of language reception. That is, we may view Rs as *utterances* fitting some communicative intent, or Rs as *meanings* (or interpretations) assigned by the learner to utterances (Ss) produced in the L2 by his interlocutor. In the first case, S and R issue from the same person, while in the second two persons, a speaker and a hearer, are involved.

Paradigm A

L1	L2
S1 – R1	S2 – R1

In production by the learner, Rs are utterances with certain formal characteristics, by which I mean such linguistically-specified formal devices as: Subject-Verb inversion; equi-NP deletion; reflexivisation of object pronouns, and so on. Paradigm A obtains where L1 and L2 employ the same formal device, but to serve different communicative purposes in L1 and L2. L1 could be English, L2 Welsh, and the formal device is Auxiliary-Subject order in the clause: in English it signals a question, while in Welsh it marks statements, *e.g.*

(English): Is she speaking German?   (Aux-Subj-V-Obj)

(Welsh): Mae hi'n siarad Almaeneg.   (Aux-Subj-V-Obj)
        (*Lit.*: is she in speak German)

The English L1 speaker is familiar with this device, so will not have to learn it, but can transfer it to L2. His problem will be to associate it with a new meaning in Welsh. The magnitude of the problem reduces as the functional or semantic discrepancy between identical formal devices in L1 and L2 decreases, until we reach a position of absolute L1:L2 identity for both Ss and Rs: L1 (S1 – R1): L2 (S1 – R1).

Turning now to the L2 learner's comprehension of utterances (Ss) produced by a native speaker, we identify formal devices within S, and 'meanings' (assigned) in R. Our English/Welsh example can serve again. Upon hearing the Welsh *Mae hi'n siarad Almaeneg* as a S, the learner's response must be 'not question, but statement'. If he produces an appropriate, secondary, verbal response it will have to be an assent or dissent, *not* an answer.

Paradigm B

L1   L2

S1 – R1   S1 – R2

For production, this paradigm defines translation-equivalence: that is, in L1 and L2 there is sameness of meaning accompanied by difference of formal devices. An example is where L1 and L2 use different formal devices for questions. German uses Subject-Verb inversion, while Polish uses an interrogative particle *czy*:

R1 (German):   Kennen   Sie   ihn?

               (Verb   Subj   Obj)

S: Question

R2 (Polish):   Czy   pan   go   zna?

     (*Lit.*:   If   you   him   know)

     (Part   Subj   Obj   Verb)

For comprehension, Rs are assigned meanings paired to the L2 S, which is now the formal device used by the L2 in expectation of a different meaning-association from that associated in the learner's L1 by the 'same' device. Now *czy* in Polish means the same as *if* in English, in different contexts, so the English learner of Polish will be tempted to 'hear' Polish *czy*-clauses as if they were English *if*-clauses (conditionals): this misunderstanding is the result of his L1-interpretation interfering with his L2 interpretations.

Once again, when L1 Rs and L2 Rs are identical, we have the condition (L1) S1 – R1; L2 (S1 – R1) which, as we have seen, can also be accommodated, as an extreme case, under Paradigm A. This condition is what is known in learning psychology as 'ordinary learning' or 'practice': it is a paradoxical label, since in effect NO learning needs to take place. The L2 structure itself, and the meaning with which it is to be associated, are the same in L2, and so are already known: it is a case of "what he [the learner] already knows because it is the same as in his native language" (Lado, 1957: 7). A bizarre conclusion from this claim is that, since all languages have something in common – the 'linguistic universals' – each of us knows at least parts of languages we have never even heard or read. This is however a *reductio ad absurdum*, not to be taken seriously. It is not to be interpreted as implying that no teaching is necessary of those parts of the L2 which fit the 'ordinary learning' sub-paradigm. Teaching and learning, as I said above (p. 12) are not coterminous, and the learner will at least need to gain *confirmation* that the L1 and L2 structures are identical: he needs to experience positive transfer personally if relevant learning is to take place. We shall return to Paradigms A and B presently.

Paradigm C

L1	L2
S1 – R1	S2 – R2

This paradigm is of little interest to CA, because of the non-identity of *both* Ss and Rs in the two languages: where there is *no* constant, only variables, there are no grounds for comparison. What would be the purpose of executing a CA of, say, issuing commands by inversion in L1 with interrogation by intonation in L2? I mention Paradigm C here both for comprehensiveness, and because it might provide an explanation for Lee's (1968) claim that 'different' or 'exotic'[6] languages may not be difficult to learn. He remarks on the absence of L1 interference during his learning of Chinese, which he attempts to explain by suggesting that L1 and L2 were so very different that no false associations, and therefore no interference, were possible. I suggest he might have been operating in Paradigm C and producing Chinese utterances that were at the same time not adulterated by English (R1 ≠ R2) AND did not mean what he thought they meant (S1 ≠ S2): he noticed the nonidentity of Rs, but only his Chinese interlocutors could have spotted the effects of the nonidentity of Ss.

2.4 A Scale of Difference

Let us return to the paradigms, adding a further complication. Instead of talking of identity or non-identity of Ss and Rs in L1 and L2 as if it were always a clear-cut yes-or-no decision, we shall consider *degrees* of similarity. To simplify somewhat, I shall illustrate by reference only to production of L2 utterances within Paradigm B: the reader may extend the exemplification to the other modality and the other paradigm.

As we have seen, 'ordinary learning' is the case of greatest similarity (or identity) of Ss *and* Rs in L1 and L2. An example is the use of Subject-Verb inversion in German and French as the formal device used to ask questions.

R L1 (German): Sprechen Sie deutsch?

S (L1 and L2): Question

R L2 (French): Parlez-vous français?

At the other end of the scale, we have maximum *difference* of Rs in L1 and L2. Our Polish/German example of word-order question as opposed to particle question (*cf.* p. 17) was a case in point.

Somewhere intermediate between these extremes we have cases of *partial* similarity of Rs. Among languages which signal questions by use of particles are those which position them sentence-initially (Polish) and those which have them in sentence-final position, such as Japanese:[7]

Kore wa hon desu.   → Kore wa hon desu *ka*?

(*Lit.*: This Subj. book is   This Subj. book is Q)

(This is a book)   (Is this a book?)

Russian alternative questions also utilise a particle [li], which is optional (Bidwell, 1969: 99). Its position is different from that of the Japanese and Polish particles in that it occupies the second slot in the clause, between the finite verb and the Subject, as in:

Работаете ли вы на фабрике?
(Do you work at the factory?)
Rabotaeti li vi na fabriki?
Finite verb-Part-Subj-Adverbial

In other words, Russian has both the Verb-Subject order of German, and a particle for questions: it must lie somewhere on the scale between German and Japanese/Polish. Even English fits into this scheme, if we care to classify the special auxiliary *do* as, among other things, a type of question particle. *Does John play often*? could be analysed: Q-Particle + Subject-Verb-Adverb. English, like Russian, therefore, has a 'particle' *and* since this particle carries a concord inflection and is therefore 'finite', we could say that it has interrogative clauses with the finite element inverted with the subject, like German. We might place these observations on a scale as follows:

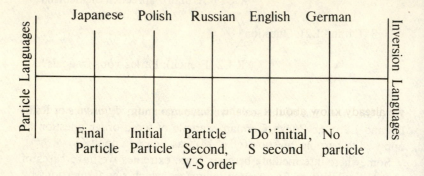

The point to be made is that we must be prepared to quantify, in as precise a way as possible, *degrees* of difference between Rs in the two languages under CA. This is the linguist's task. A further task, which falls to the contrastive analyst, is to establish the relationship between degree of linguistic difference and degree of learning difficulty. We shall return to this problem in Chapter 7 when assessing the status of CA.

2.5 CA and Behaviourist Learning Theory

The psychological basis of CA, then, is Transfer Theory, elaborated and formulated within a Stimulus-Response (Behaviourist) theory of psychology. As Corder puts it:

> "One explanation [of L2 errors] is that the learner is carrying over the habits of his mother-tongue into the second language .. . .. Clearly this explanation is related to a view of language as some sort of habit-structure" (Corder, 1971: 158).

In the '60s and '70s we have witnessed something of a 'revolution'[8] both in linguistics and in psychology: just as taxonomic linguistics has yielded to generative grammar, so Behaviourism has been supplanted by Cognitive psychology. The turning-point, as far as theories of language learning are concerned, is marked by Chomsky's (1959) review of Skinner's *Verbal Behavior* (1957).[9] The question inevitably arises: have the psychological foundations of CA been undermined? Some insist that they have; witness Slama-Cazacu (1971: 59): ". . . in present scientific psychology transfer is considered a 'controversial' and hypothetical concept". This is an overstatement: a perusal of the psychological literature on Transfer reveals, not rejection of the concept, as Slama-Cazacu claims, but rather attempts to refine it (Martin, 1971: 314–32), or to include it under some broader notion: *e.g.* Postman's (1959) term 'response selection mechanism' which accommodates Transfer under Gestalt 'set'. Indeed, we find Corder, in a later article, easily accommodating Transfer within Cognitive psychology; he refers to "Piaget and other learning theorists . . .", then continues: "the sense we make of our environment depends on what we already know about it . . . the relevant existing cognitive structures may be those of the mother tongue" (Corder, 1975: 411). If the Whorfian hypothesis can be expressed in cognitive psychological terms, so can the CA hypothesis.

Rather than reject the psychological apparatus which serves CA, we should, I think, be aiming at an elaboration, not of the psychological component, but of the structural specifications of language: this, of course, is the linguist's contribution. As Crothers and Suppes (1967: 20) put it: "A richer characterisation of structure seems essential to any account of more complex learning", and "these issues will not be resolved by any facile shift from the behaviouristic language [terminology] of conditioning to the mentalistic language of cognition". We must, in other words, beware of confusing shifts in terminology with more fundamental shifts which really offer alternative explanations of observed phenomena.

Let us examine two recently proposed putative alternative explanations for what the contrastive analyst would consider to be L1 transfer: H. V. George's mechanism of 'Cross-Association', and Newmark and Reibel's 'Ignorance Hypothesis'.

2.5.1 *Cross-Association*

This mechanism is proposed by George (1972). He reconstructs the mental processes of induction and generalisation which the L1 German learner of English seems to be subject to. First, he learns that *woman* means 'female human adult': on this basis he equates *woman* with *Frau*. Now *Frau* has the other meaning 'female spouse', and on the basis of the association set up *woman* attracts this second meaning of *Frau* also, so the German says the inappropriate:

*The man met his woman and children in the park.

George gives several examples of this process at work, none of which any contrastive analyst would object to, until he says (p. 41) that this ". . . underlies what is usually meant by mother-tongue interference", and further (p. 45): "direct interference from the mother-tongue is not a useful assumption". George prefers to invoke the redundancy of the L2 as the *direct* cause of such errors: the fact that English has two words – *woman* and *wife* – for the one German word *Frau*. Surely, though, this redundancy of English will only constitute a learning problem if the L1 does not show a corresponding redundancy. The German learner of French is familiar with the 'redundancy' of having two words for 'know' in his L1 (*wissen/kennen*) and so will be unperturbed by the identical redundancy of French *savoir/connaître*: indeed, it would bother him if French did not have it.

2.5.2 *The Ignorance Hypothesis*

This is another cognitivist alternative to L1 transfer. It was proposed by Newmark and Reibel (1968) to explain L2 learners' errors: "The adult can want to say what he does not yet know how to say [in the L2], and he uses whatever means he has at his disposal . . .. This seems sufficient explanation of how interference comes about, without the unnecessary hypostatisation of competing linguistic systems . . . taking pot shots at each other". Selinker (1972: 219) has revived the notion of ignorance and given it a cognitivist aura of respectability by referring to it as a precondition for a learner applying a strategy when: "the learner realises . . . that he *has no linguistic competence* with regard to some linguistic aspect of the TL".

A moment's reflection on these excerpts will reveal that ignorance is not an alternative to interference, but at best a precondition for it: if L1 and L2 formal devices for a particular function are identical – the 'ordinary learning' subparadigm – the learner will merely successfully transfer the L1 item to L2 use. It is only when they are different, and he nevertheless transfers the L1 item, that interference – and with it, error – accrue.

That ignorance and interference do not refer to, or explain, the same phenomena can easily be demonstrated if either can be shown to work without the other – as they can.

Ignorance-without-interference was a possibility seen by Duškova (1969: 29), who, discussing Czech learners' errors in L2 English, observed of one particular English construction that it ". . . will not present problems on the production level simply because hardly any learner will spontaneously use it". They will instead employ what has since come to be known as an 'avoidance strategy' (Schachter, 1974; Kleinmann, 1977). Learners who have had bad experiences of failure or of tenacious difficulty over some L2 structure will not go on committing error, but will avoid the structure in question by resorting to paraphrase, or to some near-equivalent. Learners of Welsh are likely to find the preterite morphologically difficult, so will use the simpler perfect for all types of past-time reference, even though it is not quite the same functionally: they will, in Levenston's (1971) terms, 'overindulge' b) while 'underrepresenting' a)

a) Canodd Siôn yn yr eglwys.

    (*Lit.*: Sang John in the church)

                                               John sang in church.

b) Mae Siôn wedi canu yn yr eglwys.

    (*Lit.*: Is John after sing in the church)

Interference-without-ignorance also frequently manifests itself, much to the chagrin of L2 teachers. It often happens that students are drilled in a particular L2 pattern until their performance is error-free: they have learnt it 'to criterion'. They are no longer ignorant of the pattern. Nevertheless, two minutes later they produce errors over that very same pattern. Not that they are ignorant of the pattern: they can easily self-correct when the teacher expresses his dismay.[10] The errors will often have clear indications of L1 transfer – without ignorance.

Recall that Osgood's paradigms also cater for backward interference: from L2 to L1. Now, since no native speaker can properly be said to be ignorant of the central structures and lexis of the L1, any interferences in L1 from L2 will normally have to be accepted as constituting interference without ignorance. Wilss (1977: 265), in a treatise on the theory and practice of translation, documents such a case. Germans, translating the English L2 lexical item *backbreaking labour* into L1, used *rückenerlähmende/rückgratbrechende/ rückenbrechende Arbeit*, but NOT the 'natural' German equivalent *Schindarbeit*, of which few Germans are ignorant. Without ignorance, these translations were selected under the spell of the L2.

The ignorance hypothesis is vulnerable in other ways. I shall list three major weaknesses:

i) Interference theory predicts that if a learner is called upon to produce some L2 form which he has not learnt, he will tend to produce an erroneous form having its origin in his L1. Now consider how this situation is viewed from the standpoint of the ignorance hypothesis. Kellerman (1977: 73) suggests that "the learner assesses his knowledge with respect to a particular TL feature and finds it lacking": he is "ignorant by self-evaluation". This decision on the learner's part comes before he resorts to the L1, before he utters an (erroneous) word. So 'ignorance by self-evaluation' involves the learner deciding he is ignorant of a L2 form, so incapable of producing it. But how can he make this decision? Who supplies the particular L2 form for him to assess his ignorance of it? If he can supply the form himself – which we must assume he can – then how can he be said to be ignorant of it in the first place? We are in a logical impasse here.

ii) It is possible for different learners to be equally ignorant of a given L2 structure; as is often the case where the two learners have different L1s. For example, the L1 Spanish and the L1 German learner of L2 Russian each enquires about identity in ways different from the Russian:

> *L1a* (Spanish): Como se llama?
>
> (*Lit.*: How himself he calls?)
>
> *L2* (Russian): Kak evo zovut?
>
> (*Lit.*: How him they call?)
>
> *L1b* (German): Wie heisst er?
>
> (*Lit.*: How calls he?)

Each learner is ignorant of the Russian pattern, yet their learning difficulties and errors are likely to be different. We can differentiate their respective difficulties only by invoking interference theory.

iii) Those proposing the ignorance hypothesis conceive of learners being called upon to produce L2 patterns of which they have no knowledge. When this demand is made the learner cannot but use "whatever means he has at his disposal". But this predicament is not one into which any mildly conscientious teacher ever places his learners. No language-teaching theory to my knowledge has ever envisaged asking learners to perform *specific L2 items* before giving them some reasonable access or 'exposure' to the L2 item in question. Kellerman seems to be analysing L2 performance that is elicited without such exposure, and studying learners induced to perform in the L2 without being induced to perform *particular* predetermined repertoires. He is concerned with L2 *acquisition* but not L2 *learning*, the distinction between which has been made by Krashen (1976). 'Acquisition' takes place in naturalistic, untutored settings, whereas 'learning' implies teaching. The CA hypothesis rests on the observation that with equal degrees and intensities of teaching (of whatever kind), the learner gains control of some L2 items more easily than of others, although he was equally ignorant of them all at the outset.

'Transfer' is the psychological cornerstone of CA. I have shown how it is manifested in L2 learning. The concept of transfer originates in behaviourist psychology, which has been superseded by cognitive psychology. It appears that attempts to accommodate CA under cognitivism are not very profitable: thinking in terms of a "strategy" of transfer seems to add little to our understanding of the mechanisms involved.

The contrastive analyst is not, and need not aspire to become, a psycholinguist. It is the contrastive analyst's duty to chart the linguistic (structural) routes in L2 learning. His findings and those of the psycholinguist will be complementary, but their instruments and methods must be different. It is for this reason that the psychological basis of CA should be as simple as possible, and for this reason that we now turn to the linguistic component of CA.

NOTES

1 This is not strictly true. In Chomsky's writings we can trace a growing concern with grammars as learning models. In *Syntactic Structures* (1957: 50) he suggests that a theory of grammar "... must provide a practical and mechanical method for actually constructing a grammar". He has in mind the linguist's 'discovery procedures' for grammar. In *Current Issues* (1964: 26) he elevates 'discovery procedures' to the status of 'learning model': "The learning model B is a device which constructs a theory . . . as its output on the basis of primary linguistic data . . . as input". Then, in *Aspects* (1965: 58), this 'learning model B' becomes personified in a child learning the language of its environment: the 'model' has come to be known as the LAD or 'language acquisition device'. Whether the same LAD is operative in L2 learning is a question I shall discuss in Chapter 6.

2 Some lists of such 'communicative needs' are to be found in Wilkins (1976: 29–54). He divides them into three types of 'meaning': i) conceptual or propositional meanings, ii) modal meanings, and iii) meanings by use. Other labels currently applied are 'notions' and 'functions'. They are discussed in Wilkins (1976).

3 Sapon's example is not ideal: the *nouns* 'carpentry' 'embroidery' etc. could fit. But it is true that no individual word can be uniquely predicted.

4 Notice that Lado includes the transfer "of meanings": we shall assume that this inclusion is meant to refer to reception of language.

5 *Cf.* Dodson (1967: 90): "It is only possible to teach a second language by direct-method techniques at the expense of the first language, and it is sheer hypocrisy to claim that the final aim of such teaching philosophies is bilingualism."

6 This term 'exotic language' is an inherently contrastive one, since no language viewed in isolation can be so labelled: a language can only be 'exotic' vis-à-vis some other language.

7 "Questions are expressed in Japanese by adding the interrogative particle *ka* at the end of the sentence" (Kuno, 1973: 13).

8 Somewhat less sensationally, we could use Kuhn's (1962) notion of scientific revolutions involving a change in 'paradigm' or theoretical and methodological orientation. Osgood's (*op. cit.*) use of this term is less ambitious.

9 Though MacCorquodale's (1970) review of Chomsky's review is less well-known.

10 Although they are self-correctable, I would not agree with Corder (1967: 167) that they should be viewed as 'mistakes' [of Performance] rather than 'errors' [of Competence].

3

The Linguistic Components
of
Contrastive Analysis

Contrastivists see it as their goal to explain certain aspects of L2 learning. Their means are descriptive accounts of the learner's L1 and the L2 to be learnt, and techniques for the comparison of these descriptions. In other words, the *goal* belongs to psychology while the *means* are derived from linguistic science. It is in fact this demarcation of goal and means, through their allocation to two different sciences, which disqualifies CA from becoming subsumed under the rubric of the hybrid discipline called 'Psycholinguistics'. I shall argue later (*cf.* Chapter 7) that some of the misunderstanding surrounding CA has arisen from the mistaken view that CA *is* a form of psycholinguistics. Let me merely reiterate at this point that CA is a form of linguistics.

In Chapter 1 we saw that there are many forms of linguistics, and drew a number of crucial distinctions. It is now necessary to draw a further distinction, that between *microlinguistics* and *macro-linguistics*. With certain notable exceptions (Firth, 1951) modern 20th century linguistics has seen as its goal the description of the linguistic code, without making reference to the uses to which the code is put, or how messages carried by this code are modified by the contexts in which they occur: modern linguistics has taken the microlinguistic approach. Consequently, CA has also taken this approach. There has recently however been increasing attention to contextual deter-mination of messages and their interpretation, a growing concern for macrolinguistics. This is not the place to explain this shift of emphasis, but we may point out that it coincides with a growing interest in semantics, sociolinguistics, discourse analysis, speech-act theory and ethnomethodology. In this chapter and the next we shall perpetuate the microlinguistics bias, returning to the broader perspective in Chapter 5.

First and foremost, CA owes to linguistics the framework within which the two linguistic descriptions are organised. By 'framework' we mean three things. First, CA adopts the linguistic tactic of dividing up the unwieldy concept "a language" into three smaller and more manageable areas: the *levels* of phonology, grammar and lexis. Secondly, use is made of the descriptive categories of linguistics: unit, structure, class, and system. Thirdly, a CA utilises descriptions arrived at under the same 'model' of language. We shall now consider each of these in turn.

3.1 Levels of Language

Imagine meeting an octogenarian who is the sole surviving speaker of a language. As a linguist it is your moral duty to preserve some account of this language in the form of a set of descriptive statements. Here are some of the descriptive statements which might be made:

  i) This language (L) uses the sounds [θ], [β], [ɫ] etc.
  ii) L has four words for 'cousin', depending on whether the cousin is male or female or on your mother's or your father's side of the family.
  iii) L shows plurality of nouns in four different ways, each involving addition of a consonant to the end of the noun in its singular form.
  iv) To ask a question, take the finite verb (which is in initial position in declarative sentences) and transpose it to sentence-final position.

No one of these descriptive statements encapsulates a total description of L, of course: but the more there are, the fuller the description becomes. Notice that each statement restricts itself to some *aspect* of L, and does not pretend to cover several aspects of L simultaneously. So i) says a little about the sound system of L; ii) says something about its lexical stock; iii) describes an aspect of word-formation, or morphology of L; while iv) talks of the arrangement of words in L, the syntax. In other words, linguistic descriptions are approached observing the principle of 'division of labour', each statement – or grouping of statements – being aimed at one of the *levels* of language. The four descriptive statements of our hypothetical last-surviving native-speaker is each made on a different *level*:

  i) on the level of *phonology*
  ii) on the level of *lexis*
  iii) on the level of *morphology*
  iv) on the level of *syntax*

3.1.1 *Procedural Orientation*

Two further points should be made concerning the observation of linguistic levels for description. First, there has been a traditional 'procedural orientation' which has dictated that, in the course of producing a total description of a language, the phonology has been described before the morphology, and the morphology before the syntax. This 'direction' of description seems to have been dictated by two things: the linguist's perception of feasibility, and a conviction that the phonology of a language is somehow 'basic' and merits priority in description. The idea of feasibility derives from the fact that the sound-system (phonology) of a language is more finite, more of a 'closed system' than the grammatical or lexical systems and therefore more amenable to exhaustive description. There is much truth in this: Stockwell and Bowen (1965b: 116) are able to say with little fear of contradiction: "Spanish has nineteen consonants including two semivowels ... English has twenty-four, including two semivowels". By contrast, no linguist would claim to know how many syntactic patterns or how many lexical items there are in any particular language: at best he would hazard approximations. The claim that phonology is somehow more 'basic' is less easy to justify. It is true that every utterance in a language must employ the appropriate phonological segments if it is to be understood: but likewise every utterance has to have some syntactic structure to qualify as an utterance of the language in question. The fact that any given phoneme has a greater probability of occurrence in speech than any one morpheme or any one syntagm is not an index of the basicness of phonemes, but of their limited number, the fact that they comprise a small closed set. It is an undeniable fact, however, that the procedural direction of describing the phonology first has been observed by structural or 'descriptivist' linguists, frequently to the relative or total neglect of the other descriptive levels.

3.1.2 *Mixing Levels*

The second repercussion emanating from the observance of levels of description has been the injunction that they should not be 'mixed'. In other words, it was a regulation within structural linguistics that the description of, say, the level of phonology should be carried out without reference to the other linguistic levels. To invoke grammatical factors to facilitate the description of the phonology of a language or vice versa, was viewed as illegitimate and this 'mixing of levels' was ruled out of court. Nowadays mixing is allowed, and sometimes found to be necessary to account for some fact of language. Hetzron (1972), for example, in a paper entitled "Phonology in Syntax", shows that it is necessary to invoke phonological factors to explain why, of the following Russian sentences, i) and iii) are grammatical, while ii) is not.

i) mat' rodila doč':   'mother gave-birth-to-fem daughter'
ii) * doč' rodila mat':   'daughter gave-birth-to-fem mother'
iii) etu doč' rodila mat': 'this-Acc. daughter gave-birth-to-fem mother'

Hetzron concludes (p. 253): "Initial object is possible when the accusative marker is not homonymous with the nominative ... The reshuffling of SVO → OVS is blocked when such a homonomy would result". 'Homonomy' is a phonological feature, determining, in these examples, syntactic possibilities: to explain why ii) is ruled out one *must* mix levels.

CA likewise observes the principle of linguistic levels,[1] and in the next chapter we shall be discussing in turn phonological, lexical and grammatical CAs. Now, any CA involves two steps: first, there is the stage of description when each of the two languages is described on the appropriate level; the second stage is the stage of juxtaposition for comparison. In the first stage the observance of levels can be adhered to, but it will frequently be necessary, at the comparison stage, to cross levels. Indeed, the degree to which it is necessary to cross levels at this stage is a useful measure of the degree of interlingual non-correspondence (contrast) between L1 and L2. Let me give some examples of what I shall call *interlingual level shifts*

i) He wanted to escape: Il voulait s'échapper
    He tried to escape: Il a voulu s'échapper

ii) We knew where it was: Sabiámos donde estaba
    We found out where it was: Supímos donde estaba

iii) I don't lend my books to anyone: Je ne prête pas mes livres à n'importe qui
    I don't lend my books to anyone: Je ne prête mes livres à personne

iv) Vi znajiti gdje magazin: You know where the shop is
    Vi znajiti gdje magazin?:   Do you know where the shop is?

In i) and ii) what is a lexical distinction in English is expressed through a grammatical, or more precisely, a morphological contrast within

French and Spanish respectively: we have an interlingual level shift from lexis to grammar. In iii) the two English sentences are differentiated through intonation, a device operating on the phonological level, whereas French uses two distinct lexical items to convey the same difference: we have a level shift from phonology to lexis. In iv) we see that questions are distinguished from statements in Russian by intonation, and in English by the grammatical device of *do*-insertion: a phonology-to-grammar level shift. We can plot these level shifts on a grid:

L1 / L2	Phonol.	Lexis	Grammar
Phonol.		iii)	iv)
Lexis	iii)		i) ii)
Grammar	iv)	i) ii)	

3.2 Categories of Grammar

Consider again the 'descriptive statements' pertaining to our imaginary moribund language on p. 28. Besides restricting itself to one of the levels of language we may note that each makes reference to various grammatical entities or concepts. Thus i) refers to sounds or '*phones*'; ii) refers to a *class* of *nouns*; iii) to four different ways of marking a noun as plural, four *allomorphs* of the *morpheme* 'plural'; and iv) refers to two sentence-types, which it differentiates on the basis of the relative order of their *word-classes*. In other words, linguistic descriptions are organised within a framework of categories. Halliday (1961: 247) suggests that there are four such fundamental categories: *unit*; *structure*, *class*, and *system*. Moreover, these four categories are universal: they are necessary and sufficient as a basis for the description of any language – which adds to their attractiveness for the contrastive analyst. Only these four are required, no more and no fewer: "because language is like that – because these four, and no others, are needed to account for the data: that is, to account for all

grammatical patterns that emerge by generalisation from the data"
(Halliday, *op. cit.*). Let us consider these four categories in turn.

UNIT   The units of grammar which enter into the description of
English and any 'related' language are: sentence-clause-phrase-word-
morpheme. Here they are arranged on a scale from 'largest' to
'smallest', which implies that any unit consists of one or more
instances of the next lower unit, and *vice-versa*, that any unit is a
direct constituent of the next higher unit: sentences consist directly of
clauses, clauses directly of phrases, and so on. This order of direct
inclusion in turn implies a scale, which is called the *rank scale*.

In traditional CA, as in traditional linguistics, one does not analyse,
nor, in the case of CA, juxtapose, units larger than sentences.[2] A single
sentence in L1 will always correspond on a one-to-one basis with a
single sentence in L2: the main difference is that some languages have
to be more explicit than others. Note how explicit English is compared
to Russian in the following translationally-equated pair of sentences:

> ix povitaskal: I've finished dragging them out in all directions
> one at a time.

CA is therefore concerned with the possibilities of, and limitations on,
maintaining 1:1 correspondence of units at ranks below that of
sentence. In the following sentence-pair

> The pupil (who has fallen asleep) is Peter.
> Der eingeschlafene Schüler ist Peter.

the English version consists of two clauses, whereas the German
version is a one-clause sentence: at clause rank there is a 2:1
correspondence, or, as we shall term it a 2:1 *interlingual rank shift* is
called for. A more complex set of shifts is exemplified in the following
Russian/English pair:

	S.	Cl.	Phr.	Wd.	Morph.
Ona dočitala etu knigu	1	1	2	4	10
She has finished reading this book.	1	1	2	6	8

The two sentences are unit-identical (isomorphic) down to the rank of
phrase: now they begin to diverge, the Russian sentence employing
four words, the English six. This imbalance is reversed when the
morphemes are counted for each sentence, as follows:

> (Russian): on/ a/ do/ čita/ l/ a/ et/ u/ knig/ u = 10
> (English): She/ has/ finish/ ed/ read/ ing/ this/ book = 8

STRUCTURE This category is the one most familiar to language teachers who have adopted a 'structural' approach. "A structure is thus an arrangement of elements ordered in 'places'" (Halliday, *op. cit.*: 255). The 'elements' making up the structure of the unit *clause* in English are the Subject, Predicator, Complement and Adjunct, as in: *'The cat(s) caught (P) a mouse (C) last night'* (A). A nominal group such as *'the green shed outside'* has the structure D E H Q: Determiner (*the*), Epithet (*green*), Headnoun (*shed*) and Qualifier (*outside*), each of which is a word. Morphemes, being the smallest units on the level of grammar, have no grammatical structure, of course: they are composed of phonological units. On the level of phonology one would say that the words [strit] and [æktə] have the structures CCCVC and VCCV respectively, where 'C' means consonant and 'V' vowel.

CAs have traditionally focused on the category structure, in this sense of the possible linear arrangement of units into clauses, phrases, and words. Typical CA structural statements are implicit in the following:

My father, *who plays chess*, is very patient.
Mein Vater, *der Schach spielt*, ist sehr geduldig.

In English relative *clauses*, the finite verb occupies second position, before the complement and after the subject pronoun: Spron. + Vfin. + Comp. In German the order is Spron. + Comp. + Vfin.

La porte étroite . . .: The narrow door . . .

(Il) écrira (une lettre): (He) will write (a letter)

In French, adjectives tend to be postnominal, while they are usually prenominal in English: N + Adj vs. Adj + N. In French, future is marked by an inflection suffixed to the verb stem, while in English a pre-verbal auxiliary *will* is used for this function: Vb + Suff vs. Aux + Vb.

Past participles: gespielt: played

Noun plurals: Apfel-Äpfel: apple-apples

Contrasts in word-structure are here exemplified from German and English. Past participles are composed of a prefix + verb-stem + suffix, in German, while in English only the suffix is used. German nouns are frequently pluralised by vowel-rounding, indicated by the writing convention of the 'Umlaut', whereas in English sibilant-suffixation is normal.

CLASS   There are restrictions on which units can operate at given places in structures. There is one class of the unit phrase which can fill the Predicator slot in the clause: this we call the 'verb phrase'. '*Thursday next*' exemplifies a unit phrase which typically occurs as Adjunct: this we may call an instance of the class 'adverbial phrase'. An interlingual class contrast at clause rank is exemplified in:

> *V Londone* tumano: *London* is foggy

In Russian, a locative prepositional phrase can occupy Subject position, but not in English:

> * In London is foggy.

A second example, this time distinguishing classes of elements acting as modifiers of nouns, is:

> ... eine unter meinem Wagen schlafende Katze ...
> ... a cat sleeping under my car ...
> *cf.* * a sleeping under my car cat ...

In German the complex modifier (m^c) can occur as epithet before the noun, whereas this is ruled out in English, where it must follow the modified noun: the m^c element belongs to the e (epithet) class in German, but to the q (qualifier) class in English.

SYSTEM   And finally, each language allows its speakers choices from sets of elements which are *not* – unlike the class-choices exemplified above – determined by the place which the element is to occupy in the structure. 'Choice' here means "the selection of one particular term at one particular place on the chain in preference to another term or other terms which are also possible at that place" (Muir, 1972: 10). For example, we must use a nominal class phrase to fill the Subject slot in the clause: but we are free to choose between a singular and plural nominal phrase. When we come to the slot P, we must use a verb phrase, but we are free to choose between past and present tense forms, and simultaneously between perfect or non-perfect, as well as between progressive and non-progressive forms in English: there are in English three simultaneous two-term systems from which choices must be made. Systems operate over the domains of units: there are systems of sentences, of clauses, of groups, of words and of morphemes. Typical systems at clause rank are *mood, transitivity, theme,* and *information* (*cf.* Muir, *op. cit.* 119). The mood system offers a choice between indicative and imperative; if the speaker selects indicative, a second choice is open to him, between declarative and interrogative, and so on. It is likely that all languages operate the system of mood: but they are liable to differ in the formal characteristics of the 'exponents' as they are called, of any option chosen. We know, for example, that the German who chooses simultaneously the imperative option from the mood system and the polite option from the deference system will commit himself to the exponent *Kommen Sie morgen*, which has a PSA structure, whereas a Frenchman, making the same two selections from the same two systems (mood and deference) will produce a PA structure such as *Venez demain*.

Languages may differ, not in demanding different structural exponents of identical system or system-combination choices, but in offering different ranges of options. For the system *number* we normally recognise two terms in English: singular vs. plural, whereas in some languages, like Arabic, there is a third term, dual. Similarly, English operates a two-term system of *case*, the terms being common and genitive. In Russian, by contrast, there are six cases: nominative, accusative, genitive, instrumental, prepositional and dative (Bidwell, 1969: 23): a language like Finnish uses even more.[3]

In this section we have seen the value of having available a fixed set of categories of language under which one organises descriptions. CA hinges on the notion of contrast, which we might define as "difference seen against a background of sameness". Difference is the variable which CA is concerned with. It will be most clearly evident when all other concomitant factors are not variables, but constants. A further opportunity to achieve a constant is by utilising the same *model* of analysis for L1 and L2.

3.3 Language Models for CA on the Grammatical Level

Two linguists, in total accord about the levels and categories of language description can still produce different analyses of the same language data. When this happens, it is probably the case that each linguist is using a different model of language. To take a familiar example: the word 'took' (/tʊk/) can be analysed in either of two ways.

    i) /tʊk/ = /teik/ + (/ei/ → /ʊ/), which is to be read as: "/tʊk/ consists of the present tense form /teik/ with the medial dipthong /ei/ replaced by the vowel /ʊ/".

    ii) /tʊk/ = /t-k/ + /-ʊ-/. or "/tʊk/ consists of the discontinuous root /t-k/ with /ʊ/ inserted to mark past tense"

i) is based on an item-and-process (IP) model, while ii) exemplifies the item-and-arrangement (IA) model, as Hockett (1954) terms them.

There are as many models for use in CA as there are descriptive models. Here we shall mention four: the structuralist or 'taxonomic'; the Chomskyan 'Standard T-G'; Krzeszowski's Contrastive Generative Grammar and Fillmore's Case Grammar. Since this book is not an introduction to general linguistics, I shall not attempt to render exhaustive accounts of these four models, but shall instead concentrate on their relative merits for the practice of CA.

3.3.1 *Structural or 'Taxonomic' Model*

CA was elaborated by the structuralists Fries (1945) and Lado (1957), and the earlier volumes of the University of Chicago CA Series (ed. Ferguson), namely the German/English (Kufner, 1962; Moulton, 1962) and Italian/English (Agard and Di Pietro, 1966) volumes, were based on the structuralist model. It is the model expounded by Bloomfield (1933) and elaborated by Harris (1963). In fact Harris himself, in an article entitled "Transfer Grammar" (1954) claimed that the model could be used for comparative purposes: "The method outlined here enables us to measure the difference in grammatical structure and to establish what is the maximum difference (or the maximum similarity) between any two language systems."

The analytic technique developed by the structuralists is known as Immediate Constituent (IC) analysis. The claim is that any grammatical construction which is not 'simple' (which does not consist of only one element) can be reduced to pairs of constituents: so a construction like *disgraceful* is analysed into *disgrace + ful*, while the seemingly identical *ungraceful* reduces to *un + graceful*. In other words, given a construction made up of the parts ABC, it will be analysable as either AB + C or A + BC. The same procedure applies to larger constructions: thus while *nice old woman* splits into *nice + old woman* (A + BC), *very old woman* has the two ICs *very old + woman* (AB + C). The sentence

John is the nicest boy who speaks French.

has two ICs, the main clause and the dependent clause. The main clause breaks down into the Subject (*John*) and the Predicate (*is the nicest boy*) while the dependent clause is likewise constituted of the Subject (*who*) and the Predicate (*speaks French*). We now proceed in similar manner, to analyse each Predicate into the Verb and the

Complement. We are left with the Complement object of the main clause – *the nicest boy*, which is an ABC construction having the two ICs *the* and *nicest boy*. And finally *nicest boy* has the two ICs *nicest* and *boy*. The total analysis of our sentence is thus shown in our IC branching diagram:

John is the nicest boy who speaks French.

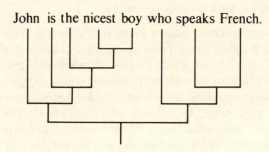

Each horizontal line demarcates a construction, while each vertical line indicates the two ICs of that construction.

In such an analysis no reference is made to the *meaning* of the constructions or of the putative ICs, some of which are constructions in their own right. The whole process of analysis hinges on the notion of *distribution* or what naturally 'goes with' what. For example, the phrase *light house keeper* is capable of two analyses (AB + C or A + BC) and the decision which analysis is appropriate is determined by what goes with what, whether we are talking of marine navigation or about domestic help. The decision for *rather nice girl* is made on the basis of omissibility: if I omit *nice*, I am left with the non-construction *rather girl*, whereas omission of *rather* leaves the grammatical *nice girl*. In other words, $Adj + N$ being a construction in English, but $Adv + N$ being a non-construction suggests that such phrases be analysed as i), *not* as ii):

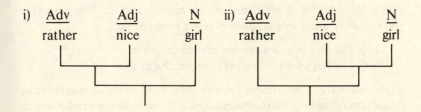

i)   Adv   Adj   N   ii) Adv   Adj   N
    rather   nice   girl   rather   nice   girl

This type of analysis presupposes that language is structured on two axes, a horizontal axis delineating construction-types, and a vertical axis defining sets of possible fillers for each position: the *syntagmatic* and *paradigmatic* axes respectively (Lyons, 1968: 70 ff). Take the following sentence:

He gave her a lovely *x* yesterday.

The *x* is not specified, but we know that since it is in the environment following a determiner (*a*) and an adjective (*lovely*), it is going to be a noun. We don't know which noun – no reference is made to meaning – but we can propose a list or 'paradigm' which might include *present, watch, dress*, etc. If the adverb were *for her birthday*, we could narrow the list even more, to exclude *shock* or *fright*. The principle of syntagmatic and paradigmatic determination of linguistic choices is of course exploited in L2 teaching through the substitution table (Dakin, 1973).

The structuralist model obviously makes full use of the four categories of language discussed above (*cf.* 3.2): unit, structure, system and class. Thus the noun phrase (a *class* of a unit) *the clever boy* has the *structure* Determiner + Adjective + Noun. Given the incomplete Det + Adj – we know that it will be complemented by the insertion into the slot of a *class* of word called Noun. And, as we also saw above, these categories lend themselves well to interlingual comparison, to CA. There are, however, certain weaknesses in the model. Consider the following:

i) She is a *beautiful* dancer.
ii) The *clever* boy missed the prize.
iii) John is *easy/eager* to please.

Each of i) and ii) contains an ambiguity which is not, unlike that in *light house keeper*, resolvable by drawing an IC boundary. Was she a *beautiful* girl to behold, or was she an ugly girl perhaps, who danced beautifully? Did the boy miss the prize because he was clever, or didn't his cleverness play a part in his missing it, being merely incidental? In other words, does ii) relate to iia) or iib)?

iia) The boy who was clever missed the prize.
iib) The boy, who was clever, missed the prize.

In iia) we have a restrictive relative clause, in iib) a non-restrictive clause: no redrawing of IC boundaries in ii) can tell the reader which type of clause the adjective before *boy* is related to. In iii) we have two sentences, each containing an adjective. But it seems that the selection of either one has grammatical repercussions for the rest of the sentence, as the following paraphrases show:

iiia) John is easy to please = It is easy to please John.
iiib) John is eager to please = *It is eager to please John.

These examples show that identity of position or 'distribution' is no guarantee of identity of function: as Fowler (1971: 11) puts it: "in [iia)] *John* stands in an Object-Verb relation to *please*; in [iiib)] *John* is in a Subject-Verb relation to *please*." Observations made on the basis of relative position in the structure refer to the surface structure; observations concerning the functional relations between constituents refer to the deep structure. Structural models confine themselves to observations about surface structure. We shall return to this matter of deep and surface structure in CA presently. First let us see how one could proceed with a structuralist CA.

Fries (1952), writing an account of English sentence structure defines grammar in true structuralist vein as "the devices of form and arrangement". 'Arrangement' refers to the relative order of elements in constructions; formal devices operating at the level of grammar are of three kinds: morphological markers, such as *-keit* and *-ness* in the words *Sauberkeit* and *cleanliness*, marking these as nouns; function words, such as articles, conjunctions, prepositions, which signal what classes of elements are likely to precede or follow; and supra-segmentals, the devices of stress and intonation which indicate to the hearer whether an utterance is a question or statement, a word is a verb or noun (*cf.* 'conduct: con'duct), or whether a Russian noun is genitive singular or nominative plural (*cf.* d'oma: dom'a), 'of house': 'houses'.

To conduct a CA, we first enquire whether the two languages employ the same four devices. Usually languages show preferences for the use of some formal devices rather than others – hence the distinction between so-called 'analytic' and 'synthetic' language types. Turkish is an agglutinating language: its words are made up of formatives which, unlike the 'function words' of English for example, cannot occur alone (Jespersen, 1947: 375). Jespersen cites a set of Turkish words: *sevmek* – 'to love'; *sevilmek* ('to be loved'); *sevdirmek* ('to cause to love'); *sevdirilmek* ('to be made to love'); *sevishmek* ('to love one another'), etc. Some languages make extensive use of the pitch suprasegmental: these, which include Chinese, Thai, and Chagga are called 'tone' languages. So much for these typological statements. Returning to CA and to *pairs* of languages, we are likely to discover that L1 carries a certain meaning by one device, while L2 conveys the same meaning by another device. Thus in English, direct object nouns are differentiated from indirect objects by the latter coming before the former: the sentence structure is S + V + IO + DO., as in

She gave the cat a rat.

German exploits morphology to achieve the same ends: indirect objects are marked by dative case endings, direct objects by accusative inflections:

Sie gab der Katze (IO) eine Ratte (DO).

Another example: English uses function words called articles: *the* to signal definiteness, and *a* to signal indefiniteness; Russian achieves the same contrasts through word order:

i) *A* woman came out of the house: Iz domu višla *zhenshina*.
ii) *The* woman came out of the house: *Zhenshina* višla iz domu.

(Catford 1965: 28)

In Russian, indefinite subject nouns occur late in the sentence while definite ones are in initial position. These examples are reminiscent of the cases of 'level shift' discussed earlier: the difference is that the shifts we now have in focus are viewed as occurring within the level of grammar. We have now identified three ways for talking about how pairs of languages can differ: level shifts, rank shifts, and now, *medium shifts*. In the use of such concepts as shifts we are defining language contrast operationally, that is, in terms of what operations, if applied to L1 constructions, would convert these into L2 constructions.[4] We are in fact using Hockett's IP (item-and-process) model.

So far we have considered grammatical contrasts emanating from the preference by each language for a different *medium* of grammar. Lesser contrasts result when the two languages use the same medium but different items. A simple case is illustrated by the German/English sentence-pair:

Wer kam?: Who came?

Information questions in either language are signalled by a Subject-Verb word order, the Subject being one of a class of interrogative pronouns: moreover, these pronouns are *W*-words, although the W-element is pronounced differently in each language. All the learner need do is learn the new items to be fitted into the pattern with which he is already familiar in his L1. In the Spanish/English pairs

Singular:	Plural:
The car runs	The cars run
El coche corre	Los coches corren

the matter is more complex. Both languages mark number concord between the Subject and Verb by morphology: the medium is the same. Moreover, the /-s/ suffix marks noun plurals in both cases. Here the similarity ceases however, since Spanish has no marker of 3rd person singular on the verb, while English does (*corre*: *runs*); and conversely, Spanish marks the verb for 3rd person plural, while English does not (*corren*: *run*); and Spanish has a plural article while English does not (*los*: *the*). So we have a case of: same medium, partially same items; but these items being differently distributed.

3.3.2 *Transformational-Generative Grammar*

Transformational-Generative Grammar (T-GG) was elaborated by Chomsky in his *Syntactic Structures* (1957) and his *Aspects of the Theory of Syntax* (1965). The salient features of such a grammar are: that it recognises a level of deep structure and a level of surface structure, the two being related by sets of transformations; the syntactic component of the grammar is 'generative', while the semantic component is 'interpretative'. The term 'generative' has been explained by Lyons (1968: 155) as combining two senses: i) 'projective' (or 'predictive') and ii) 'explicit'. Such a grammar is 'projective' in that it establishes as grammatical not only actual sentences (of a corpus) but also 'potential' sentences: in other words, a T-GG is a grammar that sets out to specify the notion of and the limits of grammaticality for the language under its purview; a major tool which it uses in this enterprise is that of transformation – it defines the grammatical boundaries of the language in question in terms of the transformational relations between the sentences of that language. A T-GG is generative in being explicit: it says which sentences are possible in the language by specifying them: ungrammatical sentences are by definition omitted from the grammar. The reader of such a grammar therefore is not given the job of deciding which sentences are grammatical and why they are: the grammar does this for him.

One reason for using T-GG in CA is the same as that for using it in unilingual description – its explicitness. For each step in deriving surface from deep structures an explicit rule must be formulated. Other reasons are particularly attractive to CA: first, it has been claimed that deep structures are 'universal' or common to all languages, so we are provided with a common point of departure for CA: the so-called Universal Base Hypothesis; secondly, the transformations applied to deep structures are taken from a universal stock, which Chomsky calls the 'formal universals', so we have a second criterion for comparison or 'tertium comparationis'. Some have gone so far as to claim that a T-GG is a *sine qua non* for CA, for example König (1970: 45): "Certain differences between English and German can only be observed if a transformational grammar is adopted as theoretical framework for one's statements". Let us take some examples of doing CA in this framework.

It is standard T-G practice to derive attributive adjectives from predicative adjectives contained in relative clauses: the relative clause itself is derived from an independent clause. Three transformations are therefore involved in passing from deep structure (DS) to surface structure (SS): relativisation, (a), whiz-deletion (b) and adjective shifting (c):

> *DS* I have an apple + The apple is red →
>
> a) I have an apple which   is red →
>
> b) I have an apple   red →
>
> c) I have a red apple. *SS*

It is possible to posit exactly the same input and transformational history for analogous German strings,

> *DS* Ich habe einen Apfel. Der Apfel ist rot →
>
> a) Ich habe einen Apfel, der rot ist →
>
> b) Ich habe einen Apfel – rot – →
>
> c) Ich habe einen roten Apfel. *SS*

The only differences are: in the names we might give to the corresponding transformation b) – not *whiz* deletion, but '*dist* deletion' perhaps; and in the final German string we must have a transformation to add the masculine accusative case ending -*en* to the attributivised adjective. The analogous French, Spanish or Welsh strings differ from the English and German ones in frequently dispensing with the adjective preposing transformation: attributives normally follow the modified noun in these languages: *le moulin rouge, la casa blanca, tŷ newydd.* By the same token, those exceptional cases of Noun + Adj. order in English (*the president elect, the heir apparent, the only river navigable* . . .) can be catered for by dispensing with the preposing rule.

A further bonus in this approach is that it provides for the two languages identical means for explaining in an explicit fashion the nature of sentential ambiguities. We suggested above that attributive adjectives can be ambiguous: Chomsky's own example is *The industrious Chinese dominate the economy of S.E. Asia.* The subject NP is ambiguous in that it can refer either to *all the Chinese* or to just *those Chinese who are industrious.* The ambiguity is simply accounted for by deriving one reading from a deep structure with a restrictive relative clause, and the other from one containing a non-restrictive relative. The same technique is equally applicable to German:

The industrious Chinese $\leftarrow \begin{cases} \text{The Chinese who are industrious.} \\ \text{The Chinese, who are industrious.} \end{cases}$

Die arbeitsamen Chinesen $\leftarrow \begin{cases} \text{Die Chinesen}^{\#}\text{, die arbeitsam sind.} \\ \text{Die Chinesen, die arbeitsam sind.}^{5} \end{cases}$

Similarly, in German *Maria ist eine schöne Tänzerin* is ambiguous in the same way as the English translation-equivalent: one reading derives from the adjectival relative clause deep structure, the other from a deep structure in which *beautiful* is an adverb in a relative clause.

Mary is a beautiful dancer $\begin{cases} \text{Mary is a dancer(,) who dances beautifully.} \\ \text{Mary is a dancer(,) who is beautiful.} \end{cases}$

Reference to deep structure can *explain* different surface-structure possibilities between languages. Why is it, for example, that German typically admits attributive modifiers in prenominal position which are patently of clausal complexity and origin? Such a modifier is seen in:

Der *in Berlin seit langem bekannte* Author . . .
(*Lit.*: *The in Berlin since long known* author)
Der *den ganzen Nachmittag unter dem Wagen schlafende* Hund . . .
(*Lit.*: *The the whole afternoon under the car sleeping* dog . . .)

It is equally clear that English does *not* allow such modifiers before nouns:

> *The *for a long time in Berlin known* author ...
> *The *all afternoon sleeping under the car* dog ...

König's (1971) explanation of this difference between English and German relies on two observations, made by other linguists. In 1963 Fillmore formulated the generalisation that only clause-final adjectives or participles may be pre-posed; and in 1962 Bach proposed that the basic or deep-structure element-order of German sentences ought to be the one having the finite verb in final position: in other words, the order found in German dependent clauses. So let us compare the German and English relative clauses from which we derive (or, in the case of English, fail to derive) the complex modifiers exemplified above.

> Der Hund, der den ganzen Nachmittag unter dem Wagen schlief ...
> The dog(,) which slept under the car all afternoon ...

Notice that in the German sentence the verb, which is the source of the participle *schlafende*, is in clause-final position: when this is fronted to prenominal position it can take with it all that precedes it in the same clause. There is NOTHING before *slept* in the English sentence, so nothing can be taken with this verb (destined to be converted into a participle) to the position before the noun. The grammar of English allows a choice here: either prepose only the verbal element or prepose nothing: compare;

> The sleeping dog under the car ...
> The dog sleeping under the car ...

Another virtue of the approach through T-GG is that the contrastive analyst is receptive to the significance of linguistic phenomena which he would otherwise tend to overlook as trivial. The TG grammarian Ross has pointed out that in differential comparative constructions there appear elements which we normally expect only in negative or interrogative constructions: *ever*, and the modal *need* in English, *jemals* in German:

> Bill is more polite than you *ever* were.
> Bill was crueller than he *need* have been.
> Fritz ist heute schon geschickter als es sein Bruder *jemals* war.
> (*Lit.:* Fred is today already more clever than it his brother ever was)

From this it is inferred that the deep structures of such comparatives must contain a negative constituent sentence: John is *taller than Bill* derives from something like *John is taller than Bill is NOT tall*. Not only have we some internal motivation for this claim, but it is further supported by those languages – French and Welsh being cases in point – which actually retain this trace of negation quite clearly in the surface structures of their comparatives:

> Il est plus puissant que vous *ne* croyez.
> Oedd hi'n hynnach *nac* oeddwn i'n feddwl.
> (*Lit.:* Was she older not was I think)

And finally, the T-GG approach provides the contrastive analyst with some kind of measure of degree of difference between compared constructions in L1 and L2. We have suggested that deep structure is common to all languages, and that languages differ most in their surface structures. The degrees to which they differ is determined by *where*, in their derivational histories, the compared constructions begin to diverge. As Di Pietro (1971: 26) puts it: ". . . the differences between languages must come at various levels of intermediate structure", while Whitman (1970: 40) justifies the contrastivist's reference to these 'intermediate structures': "If deep structures are what we fed into the transformational component, and surface structures are what came out, then one can usefully talk about intermediate structures as well". The difference, therefore, between the Structuralist and this approach in CA is that instead of looking for surface-structural correspondence, we look for correspondence between transformational rules (Nickel and Wagner, 1968).

When a rule of L1 corresponds perfectly with a rule of L2, no contrast results: to be perfect correspondents, rules of L1 and L2 must, according to Marton (1968):

   i) operate on the same base string or intermediate string
   ii) involve the same 'operation': deletion, insertion, or reordering elements
   iii) (This follows from i) and ii)) result in congruent structures of L1 and L2

We saw such a case above: English *whiz-deletion* and German *dist-deletion* are corresponding rules.

The contrastive analyst is more interested in how rules *differ* in their applicability to congruent deep structures (or intermediate structures) of two languages. There are several types of difference in rule application:

i) One of the languages applies the rule, whereas the other either does not, or does so less generally. For example, there is a rule involved in generating *that/daß* clauses in English and German which applies to German but not to English: this is the OBJECT-VERB permutation rule which transforms 1 into 2 in the German derivation below.

S1	S2	S1	S2
I know it + They see him		Ich weiß es + Sie sehen ihn	
1 *Embed S2 in S1*			
I know that they see him		Ich weiß, daß Sie sehen ihn	
2 *O-V permutation in S2*			
(Does not apply)		Ich weiß, daß Sie ihn sehen.	

A rule which is more restricted in scope in French than in English is the adjective preposing rule: it is normally the case that English adjectives precede their nouns, but normally the case in French that they follow.

ii) In L1, the rule is obligatory, but in L2 it is optional (or vice versa). By 'optional' we mean that the grammar generates equally correct sentences irrespective of whether the particular rule is applied. For example, the rule of Object Relative Pronoun insertion is optional in English but obligatory in German: compare:

That was the film (which) I saw.
Das war der Film, DEN ich gesehen habe.
*Das war der Film ich gesehen habe.

Another example (Stockwell et al., 1965) concerns the deletion of *and/e* with coordinated adjectives in English and Spanish. In English, retention of the coordinator is optional: in Spanish it is obligatory:

an attractive, intelligent girl
    or
an attractive and intelligent girl
una señorita atractiva y inteligente
      but not
*una señorita atractiva inteligente

iii) Transformations are 'extrinsically ordered', or apply in a certain fixed order (Chomsky, 1965: 133). In English Reflexivisation is a rule that can only be applied after pronominalisation: i), then ii) are the steps leading to iii):

    i) John shaves John. (the two 'Johns' being coreferential)
    ii) John shaves him. (= John)
    iii) John shaves himself.

In German, the Passivisation rule must apply *before* the rule of Equi-NP deletion (Huber and Kummer, 1974: 302), as the following show:

    i) Fritz wünscht, daß Paula ihn küßt.
    ii) Fritz wünscht, daß er von Paula geküßt wird.
    iii) Fritz wünscht, von Paula geküßt zu werden.

iii) is derived from ii) by deleting the pronoun *er*, which is the same case as the subject *Fritz*; this process cannot apply to i) (before Passivisation) because in i) the pronoun coreferring to *Fritz* is in the accusative case, which is a difference great enough to block equi-NP deletion.

    Some contrasts between languages can be attributed to differences in rule-ordering. Halle (1971) demonstrates how different rule-orders can account for differences in accent-placement in several Slavonic languages. For English, Jacobs and Rosenbaum (1968: 31) show the necessity of applying the Reflexivisation rule before the Imperative rule, since the reverse order would first generate *wash you*, to which

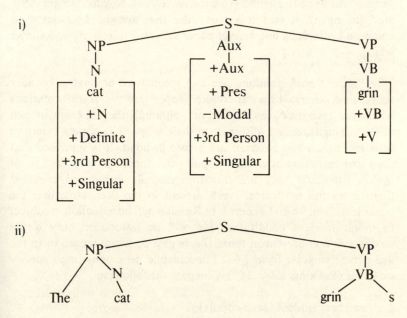

Reflexivisation cannot apply, the two-coreferential-NPs condition for the latter transformation not being met. In German this strict order of rule application is not necessary. Thus, to *Sie₁ waschen Sie₁* we can apply the Imperative rule to get *Waschen Sie Sie*: this does have two coreferential NPs, so Reflexivisation does apply, to yield *Waschen Sie sich*. Another contrast between two languages that is explicated by postulating different orders of rule application concerns the verbal agreement transformation and the copula transformation. The former copies the person, number, and tense features of the auxiliary segment on to the verbal, then deletes the auxiliary, ultimately to yield ii) from i).

Now, the deep structure of *The cat is black* does not contain a copula, so the copula transformation must apply first to provide one for the surface structure. If this is not done, the verbal agreement transformation will delete the auxiliary node and affix its person, number and tense features to the adjective, to yield the ungrammatical **The cat blacks*. There are a number of verbs in Russian, however, which require a rule ordering where the verbal agreement rule is applied without the effects of a previously-applied copula insertion rule: these verbs include the following (Pul'kina, 1975: 280): *belet'* (to be white), *krasnet'* (to be red), *zheltet'* (to become yellow), *bogatet'* (to get rich), *zret'* (to ripen). It was this rule-order that allowed Lermontov to compose his famous line *belejet parus odinokoj* (a solitary sail shows white).

iv) Some transformations are less specialised, or have a broader scope, than others. It may therefore happen that two transformations which are recognised as 'the same', although they operate in two different languages, are different in their scope. The copula-insertion rules of English and Russian are a case in point. It is supposed that deep structures do not contain copulas (*i.e.* forms of *be* in English, of *byt'* in Russian[6]): they are transformationally introduced provided there is no full or 'lexical' verb present in the deep structure: the condition is simple and general. In Russian *byt'* introduction is subject to more stringent conditions: *byt'* will be introduced only if the auxiliary is non-present in tense (*i.e.* is past or future tense), or in the 3rd person singular form (*jest'*) in scientific definitions or to specify existence (Pul'kina, *ibid.*: 242). Compare the following:

moj brat student (zero copula)
(My brother [is a] student)

moj brat byl/budit studentom
(My brother was/will be a student)

Prjamaja linija jest' kratchajšje rasstojanije mezhdu dvumja
tochkami:
"A straight line is the shortest distance between two points." (a
scientific definition)

U menja jest' bratja i sjostri: "I have (*Lit*: to me exists) brothers
and sisters" (an existential sentence)

v) A fifth advantage of the T-GG approach is that it yields
'significant generalisations': this happens when two different areas of
the grammar call for the application of one and the same transformational rule. König (1972: 57) exemplifies this. He points out that
English and German relative clauses containing adverbs or prepositional objects exhibit certain differences: in English the preposition
can either precede the relative pronoun or appear at the end of the
relative clause, as in i) and ii) respectively:

i) The problem *about* which John thought . . .
ii) The problem which John thought about . . .

whereas in German the second option is not allowed.

iii) Das Problem, über das Hans dachte . . .
iv) *Das Problem, das Hans dachte über . . .

Consider now *interrogatives* with prepositions in these two languages:
exactly the same difference obtains, English allowing two possibilities,
German only one:

v) About what is John talking?
vi) What is John talking about?
vii) Über was (Worüber) spricht Hans?
viii) *Was spricht Hans über?

König rightly claims that what is called the 'Pied-Piping' rule accounts
for both of these phenomena: in German, the whole of the
prepositional phrase must be fronted, whereas it is possible in English
for the pronoun (relative or interrogative) to be fronted alone, without
luring the preposition with it. What would otherwise have been two
unrelated statements can thus become, in a CA based on the T-GG
model, a significant generalisation.

vi) Not only do some transformational rules strictly precede or follow others, as we have seen: some rules *imply* others. This is something which a CA must take into account. König (*op. cit.*: 61) shows how the rule which is known as Raising generates structures which can undergo passivisation in English. 'Raising' applies to a structure like that of i) to yield the accusative-with-infinitive construction ii): this latter, having a direct object NP 'John', can be passivised to yield iii):

    i) They believe that John is a clever boy.
    ii) They believe John to be a clever boy.
    iii) John is believed (by them) to be a clever boy.

As König says, a structure like ii) is "practically non-existent" in German. The English learner of German will, however, tend to produce German forms analogous to ii). And moreover, since forms like ii) are readily passivisable in English, he will tend to assume that this can be done also with the German forms resembling ii) he produces: he will produce the non-existent

    *Hans wird geglaubt, ein kluger Junge zu sein.

This sequence of linguistic events shows clearly how learners tend to transfer transformational potential from L1 to L2, with resultant errors. There are seemingly definite advantages in conducting CAs within a T-G model.

3.3.3 Contrastive Generative Grammar

So far we have been assuming a procedure whereby each of the two languages (or parts thereof) involved in the CA has been analysed independently beforehand, after which the two resulting analyses are juxtaposed for purposes of comparison. The CA would seem therefore to involve two phases, the first being that of independent description, the second that of comparison. Obviously, this two-phase approach is not wholly satisfactory: the descriptive phase seems to be a mere preliminary to CA rather than an integral part of it; and the comparative phase seems to be determined by input, in the form of two independently executed descriptions, which lies beyond its control. A more satisfactory procedure would be one whereby L1 and L2 structures were generated from some common base, and were compared and contrasted *during* this process of generation – a single-phase CA in fact. This is what Krzeszowski (1974, 1976) attempts with his Contrastive Generative Grammar (CGG).

According to Krzeszowski, 'classical' CAs of the kinds we have been discussing are essentially '*horizontal*' in nature. Since the respective phenomena have been analysed in advance of the CA, the only way in which the CA can be effected is through cross-referencing or "movement from L1 to L2 and vice-versa" (Krzeszowski, 1976: 59). It is the analytic procedures that are 'horizontal'.

Horizontal CAs are limited to statements of three kinds of interlingual relationship: those existing between i) L1 and L2 *systems*, or ii) *structures*, or iii) *transformational rules*. This we have already witnessed to be the case in this chapter. Now, systemic and structural categories, as well as rule configurations are potentially language-specific, and so there is very much that one must take on trust if one decides to compare, say, noun-modification structures or rules of equi-NP deletion in two languages. One can never be wholly sure that one is comparing comparables. And in fact, it is in cognisance of the potential incomparability of systems, structures or rules of two languages that 'classical' CA has resorted to the security of independent prior description, in a sense shelving the problem of comparability.

Krzeszowski's alternative, manifest in CGG is a *vertical* CA. Its two defining characteristics are:

i) It is not based on the confluence of two *monolingual* grammars, as classical CA is, but is a single *bilingual* grammar. Krzeszowski attempts to justify this preference with the argument that the function of a CA is precisely this: to render an account of the intuitions of an 'ideal' bilingual about the relatedness of his two languages. I think this claim that a psycholinguistic model of a bilingual and a model for CA are one and the same thing is very dubious. As pointed out in Chapter 1, CA is not so much concerned with extant bilingualism (which is a 'fait accompli') as with certain forces that prevent a person from becoming a bilingual: the term I used there was 'bilingualisation'. Certainly if by 'ideal' bilingual, Krzeszowski means *balanced* bilingual, that is, one whose command of two languages is equal, then there would seem to be little of relevance in such an individual's intuitions about L1 and L2 relatedness. To be a balanced bilingual is to have solved the problems of L1:L2 mismatch and of the dominance of one of these languages over the other; in other words, to have solved the very problems that CA addresses itself to.

ii) CGG proceeds in its derivations from universal semantic inputs to language-specific surface structure outputs in five stages:

v) Post-lexical → OUTPUTS
    ↑
iv) Lexical
    ↑
iii) Syntactic
    ↑
ii) Categorial
    ↑
INPUTS → i) Semantic

STAGE 1: The level of category-neutral INPUT, of "a universal *semantic* or conceptual input consisting of configurations of elementary primitive notions such as Agent, Patient, and all sorts of specifications of location in time and space" (*ibid.*: 69). The accent here is on language-neutrality, so no language is excluded, since none is included. Krzeszowski claims that standard T-G does not satisfy this requirement of language-neutrality, since its base component contains many non-universal categories closely connected with the surface-grammar categories *of English*: copula, manner adverb, article for instance.

STAGE 2: Each language *categorises* the configurations introduced at Stage 1 in ways that are characteristic of, but not necessarily all unique to it: some categories may be universal, others shared by language types, some unique.

STAGE 3: *Syntactic* rules apply now, arranging the categories into permissible orders in actual sentences. Function words are introduced here: Krzeszowski calls these 'minor lexicalisations'.

STAGE 4: In accordance with language-specific possibilities lexical entries from the dictionary are inserted into the syntactic frames specified at Stage 3. This is 'major lexicalisation'.

STAGE 5: Here, post-lexical or 'cosmetic' transformations are applied, providing outputs with inflections and word boundary markers.

CGG AND LEARNER-STRATEGIES. Selinker (1972) proposed that L2 learners' language takes on the form it does because five "central processes" are at work. These five processes are: 1) L1 transfer; 2) Transfer of training from the L2; 3) Overgeneralisation of L2 rules; 4) Strategies of communication; and 5) Strategies of L2 learning. Krzeszowski's contention is that while 1), 2), and 3) can be attributed to the horizontal processes, 4) and 5) cannot, "since they do not involve any transfer either from the source or from the target language". These two 'strategies', contributing to the form interlanguage takes are, he suggests, best accounted for in terms of the 'vertical' processes which CGG is designed to explain.

Here we must pause a moment to consider Krzeszowski's reasoning. It seems that he has taken a conceptual double-leap. His original formulation of the term 'horizontal' in the context of CA took its name from the procedure whereby the contrastivist moved to and fro' between L1 and L2 descriptions. But now the horizontal movement is ascribed not to the analyst, but to the *learner*. Horizontality, originally a characteristic of procedure, is now suddenly a learning strategy – or indeed three. This kind of double-think, however isolated, must inevitably undermine one's confidence in Krzeszowski's whole CGG.

Several applied linguists (Ferguson, Corder, Widdowson) have recently drawn attention to the fact that learners tend to produce *simple versions* of the language they are learning. These 'simple codes' as Corder calls them, have universal characteristics, inasmuch as all learners, irrespective of their L1, and irrespective of which L2 is being learnt, 'reduce' this latter in about the same way. We have, Corder suggests, intuitions about simplicity to which we resort when we talk to foreigners, to children, to our loved ones, and also when faced with an L2 learning task. The result is a kind of learner pidgin.

Learners initially reduce the L2 to its bare communicative essentials, therefore. No matter what language it is, the bare essentials are the same. The L1 seems to play no part in this. But once they have reduced the L2, learners embark on the long process of re-elaboration: they gradually cut out reduction and *add* to their interlanguage the specific features of the particular L2. Which they add first, and with what success, is to a large extent determined by the degree of matching that exists between L1 and L2. It is here where L1 transfer, and with it CA, comes back into the picture.

Krzeszowski (1976) claims that his CGG can account for both of these processes of simplification and re-elaboration: *Simplification*, he claims, is a relative term, and CGG provides a five-point scale on which to locate any manifestation of it. Foreign learners who must communicate are prepared to abandon linguistic conformity: this they do by resorting to forms of utterance which are "less elaborate by being closer to the 'basic' form". Since this 'base' in CGG is language-neutral, we have already some explanation for the universality of simplified codes.

Native speakers' utterances have, by definition, passed through all five stages of CGG. The *degree* of simplicity of learners' codes can be stated in terms of which of the 'later' stages have been left out. Krzeszowski cites 'premature lexicalisation' as the essence of simplification. Since natives 'lexicalise' at stage four, for this operation to be premature it must precede stages 3) or 2). Utterances in the absence of any linguistic categorisation would not, I feel, qualify as instances of language: we can disregard these. But utterances to which no obligatory language-specific syntactic transformations have applied do occur among learners. They are those singled out by Ferguson as typical of pidgins, *e.g.*

> Me Tarzan, you Jane (no copula)
> Me see thief (no article; no tense; no case system for pronouns).

Elaboration is likewise dependent on some kind of scale – such as that provided by CGG – for its description. The point is that L2 elaboration will frequently be achieved by L1 means: at stage 3 English requires article-insertion (a minor lexicalisation), whereas Russian at the same stage will require 'corresponding' word-orders to be fixed, and the Russian learner of English is likely to substitute *his* means for English ones.

There is no denying that CGG can accommodate many of the facts that are being discovered about learner language. But this is not a very impressive claim to make. It would only be impressive if CGG could *explain* these phenomena: this it seems incapable of achieving. The exaggerated claims of its author, and the logical inconsistencies of the kind we have uncovered make it necessary for the time being, at least, to approach CGG with caution.

3.3.4 *Case Grammar*

It has been proposed (Birnbaum, 1970) that there are two sorts of deep structure: on the one hand there is what Birnbaum calls 'infra-structure' which underlies the surface structure of a particular language and may be invoked to explain instances of ambiguity and synonymy between pairs of sentences in that language; the other deep structure is called 'profound structure', and is assumed to be universal. The former, being language-specific, is more complex and diverse than the latter, which is simple in its basicness. The putative existence of the latter is the "universal base hypothesis", defined by Peters and Ritchie (1969: 150) thus:

> "There is a version of the theory of transformational grammar in which there is a fixed base grammar B which will serve as the base component of a grammar of any natural language."

If this is indeed the case, then this base will be an ideal starting-point for CA. As Di Pietro (1971: 3) says: "the assumption that there are universal constraints on language is basic to the implementation of

CA", since without it, CA can be no more than a listing of language idiosyncrasies and a random itemisation at best. The existence of some universal set of basic categories will allow the pairing of the respective idiosyncrasies of L1 and L2, since they can be matched by reference to the same underlying category. Even the statement that there is nonoccurrence of a certain surface category in a given language – for example, saying Russian has no articles – is vacuous without the recognition of some deep category which is realised by different surface phenomena in different languages. In other words, we specify what 'notions' articles express in English, then enquire how these same notions are expressed in Russian: we find that, at least in part, the Russian system of verbal aspect serves as a vehicle for the notion of definiteness (*cf.* James 1969: 93). We shall return to this issue.

I have been using the label 'notions' to refer to these linguistic universals. Two other types of universal have been posited by linguists: the 'formal' and the 'substantive' universals. To talk of *formal* universals is to claim, among other things, that all grammars employ transformations, which, as we saw in the previous section, are ordered and may be cyclically applied. The substantive universals are seen as a common set of linguistic categories such as Noun, Verb, Noun Phrase, Subject, and so on. When we refer to 'notions' however, we allude to the theory of semantic universals. This theory, according to Chomsky (1965: 28), "... might assert that each language will contain terms that designate persons or lexical items referring to *certain specific* kinds of *objects, feelings, behaviour*, and so on" (my italics). The linguist credited with having developed the theory of a universal semantic base of languages is Fillmore, and his model is known as Case Grammar (Fillmore, 1968). Significantly, the most substantial monograph on CA since Lado's – Di Pietro's *Language Structures in Contrast* (1971) – adopts Fillmore's framework.

The 'Case Grammar' approach proposes that the 'profound' deep structure of any sentence in any language must be of the form:

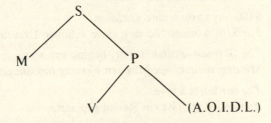

That is, a sentence (S) consists of a proposition (P) and its modality (M). P is the 'content' of the sentence, while M embraces such features as negation, tense, mood, aspect and speaker's attitude: these are the features which Chomsky, in the quotation above, loosely refers to as 'feelings'. P is made up of a lexical verb (*cf.* Chomsky's 'behavior') and one or more nouns, which are differentiated according to case: *A*gentive, *O*bjective, *I*nstrumental, *D*ative, *L*ocative. These case relationships comprise, as Fillmore (1968: 24) puts it:

> "a set of universal, presumably innate, concepts which identify certain types of judgments human beings are capable of making about the events that are going on around them, judgments about such matters as who did it, who it happened to, and what got changed."

Verbs can be classified according to which combinations of case-specified nouns – or what Fillmore calls 'case-frames' – they can occur with. Some verbs can occur in more than one case-frame, *e.g.* *open* in i)–iv).

  i) The door *opened*. (– O)
 ii) John opened the door. (– O + A)
iii) The wind opened the door. (– O + I)
 iv) John opened the door with a chisel. (– O + I + A)

Notice that in these four sentences only one of the case-specified NPs occurs with a preposition: *chisel* in iv) is governed by the preposition *with*. Compare this with *the wind* in iii): this noun is, like *a chisel* in iv) in the Instrumental case, but, since *the wind* is the (surface structure) subject of the sentence the preposition is deleted. It seems that subjectivisation of an NP in English has the consequence of deleting the case-marking preposition from the noun phrase. In German, by contrast, subject NPs are more likely to retain their prepositions; compare the following, (*cf.* Zimmermann, 1972: 175–177):

Cancer kills many people.
An Krebs sterben viele Leute.

$100 buys you a nice vacation.
Für $100 können Sie sich einen schönen Urlaub machen.

The German–Polish Treaty begins a new era.
Mit dem deutsch–polnischen Vertrag beginnt eine neue Ära.

The car burst a tyre.
An dem Wagen ist ein Reifen geplatzt.

In the same context, Nickel (1971a: 13) points out that German, since it is able (unlike English) to subjectivise a *Locative* NP, differentiates between the following pair.

   i) Der Ofen ist warm. (to the touch)
      The stove is warm.

   ii) Im Zimmer ist es warm. (the atmosphere of the room)
      (*Lit.*: In the room is it warm)
      The room is warm.

The important thing about the German–English sentence pair ii) is that, despite their surface-structure difference, they reduce to the same (deep) case-configuration, namely:

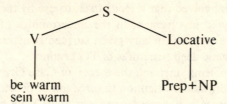

Di Pietro (1968) demonstrates how two sentences with even more widely divergent surface structures derive from the same case configuration: the two sentences are *I like tea* and its Italian translation *Mi piace il tè*. This deep structure is approximately

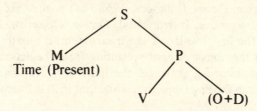

The Italian realisation rules reshuffle the three constituents of P to the order [D + V + O] "and realise O as subject and D as indirect object" when the verb is *piacere*, while for English [D + V + O] where V is *like* selects D as subject and O as direct object:

cf. {
Indirect Obj + V + Subject   Subject + V + Direct Object
Mi piace il tè   vs.   I like tea
D + V + O   D + V + O
}

Case Grammar would appear to be a model ideally suited to exploitation for purposes of CA. First, its finite universal array of categories provides us with a common point of departure for any pair of sentences we wish to compare structurally; indeed the fact that a pair of structures of L1 and L2, in spite of their superficial differences, can be traced back to a common single case configuration is a justification for comparing them in the first place – this case-structure identity is the *tertium comparationis*. Secondly, since surface structures are derived from deep case configurations by transformations, all the advantages of the transformational approach (as discussed in the previous section), especially the feasibility of tracing *sentential* derivations through 'intermediate structure' apply equally well. And thirdly, the machinery of deep case configurations is so simple and uninvolved that it lends itself to use by the applied linguist wishing to avoid involvement in the uncertainties of what syntactic deep structure to posit for any given surface structure, as is the case with the syntactic deep structures of TG grammar.

Certain problems surround the theory of Case Grammar, however: Boas (1977) draws our attention to three major problems. These are i) How many cases is it necessary to posit? ii) How can the cases be defined? and iii) How can one explain, in their framework, "the differences in subject selection possibilities of equivalent lexical items in different languages permitting the same array of cases" (Boas, *op. cit.*: 23). Since we have already raised this third issue, we need dwell only on the first two.

The original theory (Fillmore, 1968: 24) posited six cases, as we saw above: Agentive, Instrumental, Dative, Objective, Locative and Factitive. The first five labels are transparent: the sixth (Factitive) is the case of the object or entity resulting from the action of the verb. Thus in the following sentences the italic NPs are surface structure objects, that in i) being Objective, while that in ii) is Factitive:

    i) John painted *the old kitchen chair* red.
    ii) Sutherland painted *a controversial portrait of Churchill.*

As the theory has developed, need has arisen to add more cases, Fillmore himself positing the cases of Experiencer, Source, Goal, Time, Path and Result, while others have suggested the need for Comitative and Reciprocal, as in the following:

John and Mary are going out tonight.

The subject NP here, consisting of two conjoined Proper Nouns, implies that John is going *with* Mary and she *with* him: Comitative.

Hans und Maria schreiben einander seit Jahren.
(*Lit.*: John and Mary write (to) each other since years)
John and Mary have been writing (to each other) for years.

In this sentence the action of writing has been reciprocated by each party, so the subject NP may be said to be in the Reciprocal case. The fact that more and more cases have to be postulated as the theory develops detracts from its original appeal, for applied linguistic consumption at least, and Fillmore's promise of an inventory of universal case relationships "defined once and for all for human languages" (Fillmore, 1971: 247) seems a little empty. One solution to the dilemma, for the contrastivist, might be to relinquish the claim to a *universal* set of case categories, satisfying himself with an inventory which is necessary and sufficient for the two languages under contrast. But by so doing, there arises a conflict between the abstractness of these case categories on the one hand, and their specificity (in being valid for only two languages at a time) on the other hand. Assembling an inventory of cases for a given pair of langauges is certainly open to the charge of being 'ad hoc', and it is an expediency which offers to CA no prospect of a universally valid 'modus operandi.' One way out of the apparent impasse, suggested by Boas (*op. cit.*: 25) might be to give up the claim that all cases are unanalysable primitives and represent some of them as consisting of two or more components. But we shall not pursue this suggestion further here.

In this chapter we have attempted, while avoiding the temptation to give the reader an overview of linguistics (many of these are now available) to outline the major components of linguistics which impinge on CA. We have in so doing singled out three aspects of linguistics of which the contrastivist must be conscious and cognisant: the organisation of linguistic descriptions by *levels*; the necessity for a set of linguistic *categories* to provide the basis and the vocabulary of CAs; and the need to select a *model* of linguistic analysis so as to yield comparable accounts of the two languages involved in the CA. In this context of 'which model', I should point out that my account is not exhaustive: I have, for example, not mentioned Pike's Tagmemic model, Halliday's Systemic model, or Lamb's Stratificational model, any one of which is a plausible candidate for CA. This should not be taken as a dismissal of these models. I have concentrated on the three models outlined in Section

3.3 for two reasons: first, because the greatest volume of publication in the field of CA has utilised these three models; and secondly, because they are the best-known models in contemporary linguistics.

We have now laid the theoretical bases for CA, both psychological and linguistic, and are in a position to move forward to more practical considerations. Accordingly, in the next chapter, we shall exemplify the execution of sample partial CAs.

NOTES

1 The *Contrastive Structure Series* edited by C. Ferguson and published by The University of Chicago Press has produced CAs – of Spanish, Italian and German with English – in paired volumes, one of which treats the phonologies, the other the grammars of the two languages under contrast.

2 In Chapter 5 we shall render an account of CAs which *do* transcend the sentence: Text CAs.

3 I am aware of claims made by the protagonists of Case Grammar that in deep structure cases are a universal fixed set: *cf.* 3.3.3: Here I am concerned with surface structure.

4 *Cf.* Harris (1954: 259); who defines language difference as "... the number and content of the grammatical instructions needed to generate the utterances of the one language out of the utterances of the other."

5 Since it is a German orthographic convention to place a comma after the antecedent NP irrespective of whether the clause is restrictive or not (unlike English) I have indicated by a # sign the pause observed before *spoken* non-restrictives.

6 The conditions for *be* insertion in Russian are similar to those for Arabic (*cf.* Ferguson, 1971: 142).

4

Microlinguistic
Contrastive Analysis

In this chapter and the next we shall be concentrating on the practical matter of executing CAs. In the first chapter we shall focus on the traditional practice of microlinguistic or 'code-oriented' CAs on the three levels of Phonology, Lexis, and Grammar. In the second, we turn our attention to the broader perspective of macrolinguistic analysis, which represents a relatively new departure in 'pure' and Applied Linguistics, and offers considerable scope for new work in CA. Microlinguistic CA is a well-explored, yet still controversial, territory, so any account of it runs the risk of appearing 'déjà vu', while the account of the 'new' directions in macrolinguistic analysis runs the equally obvious risk of appearing over-tentative and programmatic. Nevertheless, these two chapters will at least counter-weight each other, perhaps yielding a balanced view of current practices in the discipline.

Notice further that the title of this chapter treats CA as a mass noun. Although I myself am guilty of not consistently adhering to this principle, it is nevertheless one worth upholding. The principle is that doing CAs of a global and exhaustive nature is neither feasible nor desirable. Such CAs are infeasible simply because Linguistics is not yet in a position to describe a language 'in toto', so there are no pairs of total descriptions for input to CA. They are undesirable because it is inconceivable that a learner could gain access to, or be exposed to, the whole of the L2 in an instant: to suggest that he can is to subscribe to what has been called the 'blindingflash fallacy' (Sciarone, 1970). In fact there has been no global and exhaustive CA published to date. The volumes of the Chicago series (Ferguson, ed.) carry titles suggesting a claim to be global,[1] but they turn out to be superficial sketches of the major areas of the grammar they set out to describe. The publications emanating from the various European CA Projects[2] do not even attempt to be global, but consist of anthologies of studies concentrated on selected areas of the grammatical, phonological and lexical systems of the pairs of languages concerned. It is, I think, salutary to think in terms of doing some relevant *bit* of CA rather than to set out to do *the* CA of two selected languages as wholes.

The practice adopted for CA of executing partial differential descriptions of selected systems and structures of L1 and L2 has, however, attracted criticism. Contrastivists, especially those working within the Audiolingual movement of foreign-language pedagogy, attempted to execute CAs which would serve the principles of selection and grading advocated by that movement: they singled out areas of L1:L2 contrast which would present major learning obstacles in the early stages, but would become less difficult as the learner's knowledge of the L2 increased. For this they have been criticised for perpetuating a naive view of L2 learning. Lee (1968: 192) objects to their practice of piecemeal CA, and protests "A language is not a collection of separate and self-sufficient parts. The parts are mutually dependent and mutually determinative". In similar vein Newmark and Reibel (1968: 161) condemn contrastivists for their assumption that humans ". . . learn a new language . . . one bit at a time". These critics seem to overlook the facts of descriptive expediency, that it is the conventions for stating points of interlingual difference which give the false impression that CA endorses an atomistic view of language and of language learning.[3] It is impossible to say how two complex systems such as languages contrast without first reducing these systems to manageable subsystems. As Halliday, McIntosh and Strevens (1964) observe: "There can be no question of, say, comparing English and Urdu. . . . One may be able to compare, for instance, the nominal group of English with the nominal group of Urdu, or English clause structure with Urdu clause structure; but one cannot generalise from these two comparisons." Furthermore, since most CAs are destined for eventual pedagogic use, it is expedient, even at this prepedagogic stage, to prepare the ground for the sequencing and grading implied by pedagogy. Even if an L2 is not learnt atomistically, that is no reason for not making it *available* for learning "one bit at a time".

In what follows, therefore, I shall not apologise for failing to demonstrate how *full* CAs are executed: we shall content ourselves with doing some bits of CA, and pointing to the general principles guiding this practice.

4.1 General Principles

Before suggesting how CAs are executed on the various levels of language, it will be useful to outline the *general principles* of the procedures: since repetition will be avoided by so doing, a measure of economy will be gained.

Executing a CA involves two steps: *description* and *comparison*; and the steps are taken in that order. These two procedures cannot be said to characterise CA uniquely, however. Indeed, Corder (1973: 144 ff.) sees the whole of Applied Linguistics as involving a first, a second, and a third 'order of application', and talks of *description* and *comparison* being the first and second of these.[4] The same view is implicit in the following much-quoted statement of Fries (1945: 259) claiming that ". . . the most effective materials (for teaching an L2) are those based upon a scientific description of the language to be learned, carefully compared with a parallel description of the native language of the learner." Note what CA consists of: descriptions of L1 and L2, and comparison of the two. Furthermore, the two descriptions need to be 'parallel'. What does this mean?

The minimum requirement of 'parallel description' is that the two languages be described through the same model of description: "im Rahmen der gleichen Theorie und mit denselben Notations-konventionen" (Schwarze, 1972: 20). We have discussed alternative syntactic models in the previous chapter. We shall presently meet alternative models for phonological description. Why, we may ask, must the two descriptions be framed in the same model? There are several reasons: First, different models can describe certain features of language more successfully than other models. We saw instances of this in the previous chapter: T-G grammars can effectively account for native speakers' intuitions that certain construction-types are somehow related (Active and Passive sentences, for example) and that certain others are ambiguous (*e.g. She's a beautiful dancer*); Case Grammars, on the other hand, provide apparatus for explaining the semantic affinity between a pair of sentences like

This key opens that door
and
That door opens with this key.

Now, it follows that if the 'same' data from L1 and L2 are described by two different models, the descriptions are likely to highlight different facets of the data. When this happens, the subsequent comparison will be unnecessarily difficult, and, what is more serious still, the analyst will be uncertain of the status of the contrasts he identifies: are they linguistic contrasts, in representing differences between the L1 and L2 data? Or are they reflections of the use of two different models, *i.e.* description-induced rather than data-induced contrasts? It was for this reason that Harris (1963: 3) insisted that comparable descriptions of two languages will only be guaranteed if identical 'methods' of description are used for description of the two: "since any differences between these descriptions will not be due to differences in method used by the linguists, but to differences in how the language data responded to identical methods of arrangement".

Linguistic typology tells us that human languages fall into several types according to which grammatical, phonological or lexical features they show preferences for. If some models are better at describing certain features, it must follow that some models will describe certain languages better than others. It is possible that T-GG, a product of American Linguistics, describes English better than it describes other languages. It seems that Applicative Generative grammar, a model devised by the Soviet linguist Shaumjan (1965) is eminently better suited to describe Russian, a language with a complex morphology, than it is to describe English. Obviously, distortion would result if we did a CA of Russian and English using a model which favours one of these languages at the expense of the other: the descriptions, while being 'parallel', would be unequal.

We seem to be faced by a dilemma, then: on the one hand, there are good theoretical reasons for using the same model for yielding the descriptions of L1 and L2; on the other hand there are equally cogent practical reasons why this is undesirable. There would seem to be two ways out of the dilemma.

i) Describe L1 and L2 data independently, using the models which yield the fullest descriptions of either language, and then translate these two descriptions into a form which is model-neutral. There is a precedent for this in Translation Theory, where use is made of an artificial 'étalon language' (Melchuk, 1963: 62) which is a neutral intermediary between L1 and L2: in fact it is a composite of the two, or 'supralingua', in containing the features both of the L1 construction and of the L2 construction. Catford (1965: 39) illustrates this convention (see page 65) in comparing an English and a Russian sentence which are translationally equivalent.

Note that the English construction selects from the *etalon* features 1, 3, 5 and 6, while the Russian selects 1, 2, 3, 4, 5 and 7. These sets of features are those which a good grammar of English and Russian would specify, but which no grammar of either language would generate all seven of.

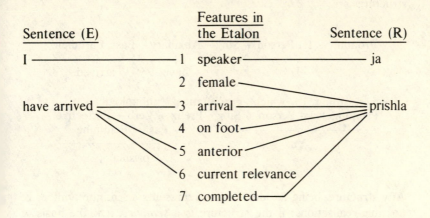

ii) A second solution would be to abandon the requirement that the two descriptions need to be equally exhaustive, or, to use Halliday's term (1961: 272) 'delicate'. A number of contrastivists have suggested that a CA should indeed show a descriptive imbalance, in favour of the L2. Sciarone (1970: 126) points out that "If both languages are described beforehand, too much, *i.e.* superfluous work is done for the sake of CA." He suggests that less attention needs to be paid to the L1 than to the L2, since it is the latter which must be learnt. Slama-Cazacu (1971) suggests a "procedural adjustment" of CA which she terms 'contact analysis': we should be more concerned with what the learner does *with the L2* than with what linguistic knowledge (the L1) he enters the learning situation. Filipović (1975: 15) openly asserts that his CA of Serbo-Croatian (L1) and English (L2) has been descriptively biassed toward the latter.

So much, then, for description. Let us move to the second step, comparison. Here again we encounter a number of theoretical problems, mainly surrounding the issue of criteria for comparison, or the *tertium comparationis*: we postpone our discussion of these to Chapter 7, and concentrate here on *how* to compare rather than *on what basis* to compare. Admittedly, this is a somewhat arbitrary approach, since the 'how' and 'why' are inextricable.

We compare 'types' rather than 'tokens': that is, to refer again to Catford's example above, we do not compare these two sentences as strings of sound or graphic substance, but their structures. Their structures are:

Pronoun + 1st Person + Sing – Auxiliary – Past, Participle

I   have   arrived.

and

Pronoun + 1st Person + Sing – Prefix + Verb + Perfective
                                          + Past + Feminine

Ya

prishla.

Any structure, being an idealisation, represents an infinite number of possible realisations: if the structure is a *sentence*, it is the basis of many *utterances*, as Lyons (1968: 176) points out. He explains the difference by reference to de Saussure's famous distinction between *parole* and *langue*:[5] "Utterances are stretches of *parole* produced by native speakers out of sentences generated by the system of elements and rules which constitute the *langue*."

From the premise that CA compares abstract elements rather than their concrete realisations it follows that each of its statements has very broad coverage of potential utterances. We shall now illustrate how CA utilises parallel description and comparison of types in L1 and L2.

4.2 Grammatical CA

Grammatical CAs are carried out on comparable systems of the two languages concerned. We shall postpone to Chapter 7 our discussion of the question of criteria of comparability, which remains an issue of contention in CA. In the following example I shall attempt to produce a step-by-step algorithm (Levelt, 1970) for the execution of a representative CA.

4.2.1 *Copula Sentences Designating Profession in English and Brazilian Portuguese*

This data is taken from Di Pietro (1971). The steps involved are:

STEP 1:   Assemble the data exhibiting the relevant systems in each language, *viz*:

English	Brazilian Portuguese
i) He's a teacher	Êle é professor
ii) He's a good teacher	Êle é um bom professor
iii) They are teachers	Êles são professores
iv) They are good teachers	Êles são uns bons professores

There are in fact several grammatical phenomena (systems) manifested in each of these sentences, in addition to the system that is the focal point of the present CA: the systems of personal pronouns; the existential copula, *be* in English, corresponding to a choice in Portuguese between *ser* and *estar*; the system of word order in the clause, which happens to be Subject + be + Complement in each language. We disregard these other systems for the moment and concentrate on the article and modifier systems operating over the Complement noun phrase in such sentences.

Notice that the English and Portuguese sentences are translations. While it is a procedural convenience to work with translationally equivalent sentences, it is not necessary to do so: obviously, the same grammatical systems would have been brought into play if the English sentences had been about 'a skilful engineer' and the Portuguese about 'um bom professor'. As we observed earlier, CAs aim to be generalised statements about systematic correspondence, and we should bear in mind continually that the utterances in the corpus are merely concrete representations of the underlying regularities. An obvious danger of working with translation equivalents is that of chance correspondence (or non-correspondence) being mistaken for the norm. For example, a French/English CA based on the translation-pair *a pretty girl/une belle fille* would lead to the erroneous generalisation that attributive adjectives occupy prenominal position in both languages, which is manifestly untrue.

STEP 2:   For each language, state the realisations of each grammatical category pertinent to the CA being done. In the present instance, the pertinent categories are: indefinite article and attribute. This means that in each of our two languages these two categories accompany the predicate head noun in sentences identifying individuals by profession: this is the *constant* across the two languages. Since we are concerned with differences rather than constants, we are as contrastivists on the lookout for any co-occurrence restrictions imposed by either language on the ways in which the two categories are realised. As we shall see presently, the variant realisations of the category 'indefinite article' are determined by two factors: whether an attributive adjective co-occurs in the NP, and whether the head noun is singular or plural.

Although this is essentially the descriptive phase of the CA, it will be convenient to anticipate the third, contrastive, phase by listing the descriptions in two parallel columns. Each statement made at this stage is a 'rule' in the sense of being the explicit formulation of a regularity of the language.

Rules

English	Portuguese
1) Indef. Article $\rightarrow \begin{cases} \text{a/--(Adj) N. sing.} \\ \emptyset\text{/--(Adj) N. pl.} \end{cases}$	Indef. Article $\rightarrow \begin{cases} \text{um/--Adj N. sing. m} \\ \text{uns/--Adj N. pl. m} \\ \emptyset\text{/--N} \end{cases}$

Rule IE (English) states that the indefinite article is realised in one of two ways: as *a* before a singular noun, irrespective of whether that noun is premodified; and as zero ($\emptyset$) before a plural noun, premodified or not. The brackets on (Adj) are a convention for stating that the adjective is optionally present.

Rule PI (Portuguese) states that the indefinite article has three possible realisations: *um* before a singular masculine noun modified by an adjective; *uns* before a modified masculine plural noun; and zero before any unmodified noun, irrespective of the noun's gender or number.

The adjective rule is stated as follows:

English	Portuguese
2) Adjective $\rightarrow$ base form/--N.	Adjective $\rightarrow \begin{cases} \text{bom/--N. sing. m} \\ \text{bons/--N. pl. m} \end{cases}$

2E states that the form of the adjective is invariant in English, irrespective of the number of gender of the head noun. 2P states – reflecting the finite data on p. 67 that the adjective has two realisations in Portuguese: *bom* before a masculine singular noun, *bons* before a masculine plural.

Notice the caution with which these descriptive statements are made: they are accounts of the data upon which they are based, and do not transcend it. This is why in both Portuguese rules, we take the trouble to specify that the nouns involved are masculine in gender. At this point we say nothing about the forms articles and adjectives assume in the context of feminine nouns, simply because there are no feminine nouns in the corpus. This points to the *third* step for the contrastivist to take:

STEP 3: Supplement the data: since our interest has been aroused for the ways in which feminine head nouns in such sentences in Portuguese influence the forms of the article and adjective, we add two further sentences to our corpus, together with their translation equivalents:

English	*Portuguese*
v) She's a kind nurse	Ela é uma enfermeira bondosa.
vi) They are kind nurses	Elas são (umas) enfermeiras bondosas.

Having done this, we perceive the need to expand the Portuguese rules to accommodate the new data. The reader is invited to rewrite rules 1P and 2P. We move on to the fourth and final stage of the CA, namely:

STEP 4:   Formulate the contrasts which have been identified by the analyses of Steps 2 and 3. This then, is the contrastive phase proper; and it is here where we face a number of procedural problems. The foremost of these concerns the formulation of contrast: whether contrast is best stated in terms of imbalanced equations or in terms of operations. It is a decision which will, in the main, be dictated by the 'model' of grammatical description one has chosen. We have already discussed linguistic models for CA, in Chapter 3. The decision that has to be made can conveniently be referred to in terms of Hockett's (1954) distinction between IP (item-and-process) and IA (item-and-arrangement) models for monolingual description. We have also mentioned that Harris (1954) in an article entitled "Transfer Grammar" nominated the IP model for comparative purposes. Harris' suggestion is that it is possible to formulate a set of instructions which, when applied to the grammar of one language, will yield the grammar of another. Let us consider what form these 'instructions' would need to take to deal with our Portuguese/English data.

   For the indefinite article we start from the position that English allows the option between overt *a* and zero, the choice being determined wholly by whether the head noun denoting profession is singular (a) or plural (∅). To show the relationship between English ∅

and Portuguese Ø we have to add two instructions to the 'transfer grammar'. The first is to relax the singular vs. plural condition; the second is to introduce a condition that the head noun may not be premodified. The two transfer (TR) rules will therefore be as follows:

TR1. Indef. article → Ø/–N $\boxed{\begin{array}{l}\text{(sing.)} \\ \text{(pl.)}\end{array}}$ M

We introduce a convention of including within a box labelled 'M' (for 'modification') the crucial feature of the transfer rule, *i.e.* the feature that carries the specific contrast.

TR2. Indef. article → Ø/– $\boxed{\text{-Adj}}$ M N.

Here again the crux of the contrast appears in a box labelled 'M' to indicate that for Ø to occur the Portuguese noun must *not* be premodified: note the minus sign.

Similar transfer rules will have to be formulated to introduce Portuguese-specific conditions for the overt realisation of the indefinite article as *um, uns*, etc. Note however that it is *not* the task of the transfer rules to specify the real phonological values of these alternative realisations of the article in Portuguese: in other words, there is no question of rules converting English [ə] or [ɛɪ] to [ʊm] or [ʊnӠ]. As Makkai says (1971: 168): ". . . the transfer rules do not need to tell me the specific phonological shape of the form transferred to. This is derived from the structural description of the language itself." It is not a matter of converting [ə] to [ʊm], but of specifying how a grammatical category of English gets parcelled out as a corresponding category in Portuguese. Rather than refer to the Portuguese variants as *um, uns*, etc., it might be preferable to use subscripts and refer to them as ind. art. Port.$_1$, ind. art. Port.$_2$, etc.

The IA approach eschews the task of producing algorithms for converting a grammatical system of one language into that of another. Instead it states the relationship in the form of a set of equations. Although this approach lacks the dynamism implied by transfer rules, it is preferable for other reasons to be discussed below, and is in fact the approach anticipated by our 'parallel' descriptions of the English and Portuguese data we have been examining. The equational representation of the pertinent contrasts might take the following form:

English
i) a/–(Adj) + N. sing.

Portuguese
:: *um*/–Adj + N. sing. masc.
uma/–Adj + N. sing. fem.
Ø/–N. sing.

ii) Ø article/–(Adj) + N.pl. :: *uns*/–Adj + N. pl. masc.
umas/–Adj + N. pl. fem.
Ø/–N. pl.

There are three things to notice about such equations. The first is that, being 'static' accounts, they can be read in either direction: left-to-right or vice-versa. Transfer rules, by contrast, are inherently directional: the rules describing the conversion of English into Portuguese are different from those effecting the conversion in the opposite direction. This issue of *directionality* is one we shall return to in a later chapter. Secondly, the equations deal with concrete phonological realisations of the category of indefinite article in the two languages. While it makes little sense to talk of *converting* English [ə] into Portuguese [ʊm], as we have seen, there is no objection to *equating* these phonological strings in the two languages. And thirdly, the equational statement allows one to see at a glance which language has the 'richer' or more finely differentiated set of realisations (system) of the relevant category. In our example we see that there are no fewer than *five* terms (um, uma, uns, umas, Ø) in the Portuguese system, corresponding to the unique term (ə) in English. This fact of inter-lingual *multivalence* has implications for learning, which we shall turn to again in a later Chapter (6).

At this point, with the explicit statement of interlingual contrast, the CA proper is complete. Further processing involves the pedagogic exploitation of the CA: to be discussed in Chapter 6.

4.3 Phonological CA

4.3.1 *Contrastive Phonetics and Phonology*

In the previous section I said that grammatical analysis concerns itself with *types* rather than with their physical manifestations or *tokens*. In other words, the grammarian studies the functional patterning of classes of linguistic units, not individual words and morphemes as physical entities. A similar distinction can be drawn between the role of the phonetician and that of the phonologist. The phonetician is concerned with three types of physical reality when he studies the sounds of language:

i) "He is interested in the way in which the air is set in motion, in the movement of the speech organs . . .. This whole area of interest is generally known as *articulatory phonetics*" (O'Connor, 1973: 16).

ii) "He is interested in the way in which the air vibrates between the mouth of the speaker and the ear of the listener . . .. This is the domain of *acoustic phonetics*" (*ibid.*).

iii) "He is interested in the hearing process . . . in the sensation of hearing, which is brain activity . . .. This is the domain of *auditory phonetics*." (*ibid.*).

Now speakers of the same language may speak with different accents, these differences being attributable to different regional, social, or even purely idiosyncratic conditions, and it is the phonetician's task to identify and classify these variations and to specify their range. At this point the *phonologist* takes over – although, of course, the phonetician and phonologist may well be one and the same person. The phonologist, however, is concerned not so much with the finer details of phonetic variety as with the functional identity, as tokens of a type, of these variants. As a 'functional phonetician' he is interested in "the way in which sounds function in a particular language, how many or how few of all the sounds of language are utilised in that language and what part they play in manifesting the meaningful distinctions of the language" (O'Connor, *ibid.*).

Such a division of the phonetic sciences into these two main branches immediately poses a problem for the contrastivist: is he to do Contrastive Phonetics or Contrastive Phonology? The former will involve him in making detailed descriptions of the sounds of a pair of languages and then somehow equating certain of these sounds inter-lingually for purposes of comparison. But can such equations be made pre-phonologically, *i.e.* without reference to the differences in function? Indeed they can, by taking as the criterion for comparison the articulatory grid employed in the IPA chart: on this articulatory framework he can compare similar sounds of L1 and L2 and match them as being both *e.g.* 'labio-dental fricatives' or 'half-close unrounded vowels'. The feasibility of this approach is guaranteed by the fact that the world's languages do tend to employ sounds produced by a limited number of combinations of articulatory features. This is not surprising in view of the fact that man's vocal apparatus is physiologically uniform throughout the world: "Perhaps the most interesting fact about the pronunciation of language in general is that there are enormous possibilities in the number and variety of sounds that the human vocal apparatus can produce, and yet only a small fraction of this potential variety is actually put to use in natural languages" (Stockwell and Bowen, 1965: 3). The first approach to phonetics CA, therefore, is in the comparison of L1 and L2 sounds with a shared articulatory basis.

A second approach is physical rather than physiological, and is associated with the *acoustic* properties of speech sounds. If we compare the initial consonants [p] in the French word *pâle* and the English word *pal*, we can establish that the English plosive in this initial position is accompanied by a puff of breath or 'aspiration', which is not true for the French plosive. While the difference can be traced to an articulatory source it is more easily demonstrated and described in physical, acoustic terms. There are even instruments, such as the sound spectrograph, which record the occurrence of such aspiration. Similarly, there are acoustic differences, which can be demonstrated instrumentally, between the 'similar' vowels in English *spleen* [splin] and German *Spiel* [ʃpil] 'game'. An *acoustic* approach to phonetics CA consists therefore in comparing L1 and L2 sounds that have much in common physically and noting the differences accompanying this similarity.

The third type of phonetics is *auditory* phonetics: it is concerned with what 'message' the ear transmits to the brain. To take a simple unilingual example: it can be shown that the first and second consonantal segments in English /pit/ and /spit/ respectively are different: in the former /p/ is aspirated, but not in the latter. Nevertheless, the English ear does not send to the English brain any instruction to register this phonetic difference: auditorily, and mentally, [p] and [pʻ] are perceived as the same phoneme /p/. Notice that we are now speaking of two allophones being *tokens* of the same type, as having equal *functions* in the economy of English. We are no longer concerned with physical or physiological reality, but with *mental* reality. Our domain is now functional phonetics, or phonology. Although we have illustrated this principal intralingually, it applies equally cogently interlingually and is the foundation for phonological CA.

Consider the laterals of English and Russian. Each language has two lateral sounds: the 'clear' [l] and the 'dark' [ɫ] of English are both alveolar laterals but [l] is produced with simultaneous higher raising of the front of the tongue than of the back, while [ɫ] has the opposite configuration. [l] occurs before vowels and [ɫ] elsewhere, *i.e.* before consonants and finally. Russian has two laterals also: [ɫ] and [ļ], the former velarised, the latter palatalised. [ɫ] "is a lateral fricative, usually voiced, with mid-tongue depressed, resulting in a 'dull' 'hollow' sound of low tonality, something like [ɫ] in English *bull*" (Bidwell, 1969: 2). There is ample justification, in Bidwell's account, for equating the Russian and English laterals on both articulatory and acoustic grounds. But what is the functional status of each? For the English speaker [l] and [ɫ] are allophones of the same phoneme, in that each sends the same 'message' to the brain, namely that in either case the /l/ phoneme is being used. This can be tested by intentionally switching the clear and dark variants within a word: to the English speaker, [ɫɪp] is still *lip* and [fɪl] is still *fill*, and when he hears an Irishman say [fɪl maɪ glæs] for RP [fɪɫ maɪ gla:s] the message is clear. For the Russian [ɫ] and [ļ] have different status by signalling differences in meaning: [daɫ] means 'he gave' while [daļ] means 'the distance'. Bryzgunova (1963: 83) gives lists of 'minimal pairs'; to illustrate the phonemic status of the /ɫ/:/ļ/ contrast in Russian. The important point to be made in this context is that objectively similar sounds of two languages can have different functional statuses; in L1 the differences may be disregarded and the two speech sounds viewed as 'the same', while in L2 the same objective difference is upheld as constituting a functional difference. This contingency is the cornerstone of contrastive phonetics and phonology.

4.3.2 *Contrasting Sound Systems*

There are four steps involved in executing a CA of the sound systems of two languages: draw up a phonemic inventory of L1 and L2; equate phonemes interlingually; list the phonemic variants (allophones) for L1 and L2; state the distributional restrictions on the phonemes and allophones of each language. By and large, the literature on phonological CA shows a large measure of agreement on these four steps, as we shall see, although there are differences in terminology, and Stockwell and Bowen (1965: 5–6) like Burgschmidt and Götz (1974: 197) add a fifth step: a statement of the *frequency* of each phonemic contrast within L1 and L2. Stockwell and Bowen point out that there are many minimal pairs, within English, exploiting the phonemic contrast between /p/ and /b/, whereas there are only very few centred on the contrast, between /ʒ/ and /dʒ/: *pleasure/pledger*, *lesion/legion*, etc. The latter contrast has a low functional load. One might object that such intralingual contrasting is excessively time-consuming, since one has to take every possible pairing of the phonemes in the inventory, and that the comparison they make between /p/:/b/ and /ʒ/:/dʒ/ is arbitrary, since while the first pair contrast by the feature of voicelessness vs. voice, the second contrast does not hinge on the same feature: fricative /ʒ/ is compared to an affricate /dʒ/. A more systematic contrast would be the voiced/ voiceless pair /ʒ/:/ʃ/. Indeed, the [ʒ]:[dʒ] contrast may be in English a case of free variation, as in [gæra:ʒ]/[gæra:dʒ] as alternative realisations of 'garage'. Burgschmidt and Götz make a better case for the absolute relative frequencies of L1 and L2 phonemes being stated in the CA. They quote Delattre's (1965: 95) frequency-count of the occurrence of the consonantal phonemes of English and German.[6]

We shall now consider each of the four proposed steps in turn:

STEPS 1 AND 2:   INVENTORISE THE PHONEMES OF L1 AND L2

This first, descriptive, step is not really part of CA. In fact, for most languages a phonemic inventory will already have been made available by the phonologist. The contrastivist's task consists in equating phonological categories across the two languages. I have already suggested that the categories of the IPA chart can be adopted for this purpose. The consonants of L1 and L2 can conveniently be classified according to place and manner of articulation and placed in the appropriate cell of the chart, with voiceless/voiced pairs (*e.g.* /p/:/b/) appearing in this order consistently. IPA symbols can be used to represent the sounds. For the vowels, the conventional vowel-diagram can be used, which allows a specification of any vowel according to the tongue position during articulation. Rounded or unrounded variants can be inserted in brackets, and there are diacritics available to indicate any special extra features, such as nasality (~) or length (:). It has been my own practice to use unusually large charts and diagrams to cater for double entries (of L1 and L2), and I use different coloured pens to write in the sounds of L1 and L2. A further possibility, suitable for classroom demonstration of contrasts, is to use two transparencies, one being superimposed on the other for overhead projection. Two vowel diagrams may be used, one for monophthongs the other for diphthongs. The following two figures illustrate how a class of Portuguese teachers handled the inventories of the consonants and the pure, nonnasal vowels of Portuguese, using an adaptation of the IPA charts:

Manner Place	Plosive VCL	Plosive VCD	Nasal VCL	Nasal VCD	Fricative VCL	Fricative VCD	Affricate VCL	Affricate VCD	Lateral VCL	Lateral VCD	Vibrant VCL	Vibrant VCD
Bilabial	p	b		m								
Labio-dental					f	v						
Denti-alveolar	t	d		n	s	z				l		
Palato-alveolar				ɲ	ʃ	ʒ		tʃ				
Palatal	c	ɟ								ʎ		
Velar	k	g		ŋ						t		
Uvular												R
Apical												r

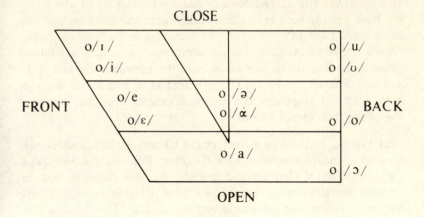

/ɪ/	as in	⌈mɪl⌉ 'thousand'	/a/	as in	⌈ʃa⌉ 'tea'
/i/	as in	⌊fitu⌋ 'goal'	/u/	as in	⌊uvə⌋ 'grape'
/e/	as in	⌈sed⌉ 'thirst'	/ʊ/	as in	⌈fɑbʊlə⌉ 'fable'
/ɛ/	as in	⌈sɛd⌉ 'headquarters'	/o/	as in	⌊ə'vo⌋ 'grandfather'
			/ə/	as in	⌊ə'v ə⌋ 'grandmother'

/ɑ/ and /ə/ as in ⌈'kɑdə⌉ 'each'

I do not pretend that these 'analyses' of Portuguese are either complete or uncontroversial (Strevens, 1954). They are merely illustrative of what students with a bare minimum of linguistic training can produce in the framework I am proposing. Moreover, Portuguese happens to be a phonologically highly complex language, unlike, for example, Spanish, the vowel system of which is "the essence of simplicity and elegance" consisting of only five pure vowels (Stockwell and Bowen, op. cit.: 73).

The question immediately arises as to whether the segments entered into these charts are of allophonic or phonemic status in the language. In practice we rely heavily on the criterion of minimal pairs: we mentally search the lexicon for pairs of words that are differentiated by a single phonological segment. This is what the Portuguese students did: in establishing the status of ⌊b⌋ for example, in /batɑ/, /beŋtu/ and /bɛlɑ/, the following contrasting lexical items were cited: /patɑ/, /veŋtu/, /gɛlɑ/ etc. Likewise for the vowels, minimal pairs like /sed/:/sɛd/ and /ə'vo/:/ə'v ə/ were cited. The allophonic status of ⌊l⌋ and ⌊ɬ⌋ was established by noting that ⌊l⌋ occurred word-initially and medially, but not finally, where ⌊ɬ⌋ occurred. This brings us to the next step in the CA.

STEP 3: STATE THE ALLOPHONES OF EACH PHONEME OF L1 AND L2

We have already seen examples of this procedure: the aspirated and unaspirated pairs [p', p; t', t; k', k] occurring in English, but not in French. Another example was the allophonic variants of the lateral phoneme in English, as contracted with the phonemes /ł/ and /ļ/ in Russian. Politzer (1972: 129) has identified a number of ways in which pairs of languages can exhibit contrasts over the respective statuses of their speech sounds:

a) For two equated phonemes, one of L1 and one of L2, allophonic variants occur for one but not for the other. For example, we equate the laterals /l/ of German and English. We now discover that the German lateral is always realised by a 'clear' [l] while in English there are two allophones in complementary distribution. The German thus says [liŋks] for *links* 'left' and [fɔl] for *voll* 'full', while the Englishman says [liŋks] for *links* and [fʊł] for *full*.

b) What is an allophone in L1 is a phoneme in L2, where the sounds concerned are physically very similar. Our example of this type of contrast was the 'clear' [l] of English, equated with the palatal /ļ/ of Russian: the former has allophonic status, the latter phonemic status.

In Portuguese the phoneme /d/ has two allophones: it is realised as [d] word-initially [daliɑ] *dália*, 'dahlia', after a consonant [aldɑ] *Alda* 'girl's name', and before a consonant [adriɑnu] *Adriano* 'Hadrian'. In intervocalic position, however, it is realised as a dental voiced continuant [ð]. This sound is physically like the English /ð/ in [ðen] 'then', and so we equate them. However, [ð] has phonemic status in English but allophonic status in Portuguese.

In fact, category b) could be conflated with category a): instead of saying that the fricative is phonemic in English but allophonic in Portuguese (or Spanish) we could have said that English /d/ and /ð/ have no allophonic variants, while Portuguese /d/ has.

c) This category of contrast applies to pairs of L1 and L2 sounds that stand in a one-to-one relationship, not the one-to-many relationship characteristic of category b). Here, the two equated segments have different absolute statuses in their respective phonological systems.

There are good reasons for assigning phonemic status to the German palated fricative [ç] in words like [iç] *ich* 'I' and [ʃprɛçən] *sprechen* 'to speak'.[7] This sound occurs in English for some speakers, but only in word-initial position: [çju:dʒ] 'huge' and [çju:] 'Hugh', where it is obviously an allophone of /h/. It is not, however, a positionally conditioned allophone of /h/, since [hju:] and [hju:dʒ] are possible, indeed predominant pronunciations. [ç] and [h] are in free variation in this position. They are optional variants, the selection of one or the other not being determined by the phonological rules of English. I consider this type of interlingual contrast in the status of speech sound to be important: unless a rigorous phonetic CA is carried out, there is the danger of overlooking the fact that a learner of an L2 may have available in his L1 serviceable sounds of such peripheral status.

STEP 4:   STATE THE DISTRIBUTIONAL RESTRICTIONS ON THE ALLO-
PHONES AND PHONEMES OF L1 AND L2

We already embarked on this operation, when we identified the allophonic variants in the two languages. What is called for now is a detailed and fully explicit account of the environments in which typical allophones occur. It is possible for the two languages to have corresponding phonemes with phonetically very similar allophones, but where the environments for these allophones are *not* identical. Both Spanish and English for instance have the two sounds [n] and [ŋ]. The former, [n], occurs before vowels and dental or alveolar consonants as well as word-finally in both languages. But the environments determining the occurrence of [ŋ] are different in Spanish and English, according to Stockwell and Bowen (*op. cit.*: 62). In English [ŋ] occurs as an allophone of /n/ before velars, as in [sɪŋk], [lɒŋgɪst]. In Spanish it occurs before segments which Stockwell and Bowen designate as /h/ and /w/: [estraŋ'hero] *estranjero* 'foreigner', [na'raŋha], *na'ranja* 'orange'; [saŋwiʃ] 'sandwich' and [uŋ'weßo] *un huevo* 'an egg'. This phenomenon, the contrastive distribution of phonetically similar allophones, is probably the most formidable one that faces both the contrastivist and the foreign-language learner.

The relative absolute distribution of equated *phonemes* of L1 and L2 is a less complex analytical problem. Although Brière (1968) suggested the syllable to be the proper unit within which to conduct distributional investigations for CA, most contrastivists have continued to take the word as the relevant unit: so we speak of sounds occurring in word-initial, medial, or final positions. A phonemic-distributional restriction familiar to most British teachers of French concerns /ʒ/ in the two languages. In French it can occupy all three positions within the word: compare [ʒon] 'yellow' [leʒe] 'light' and [gɔʀʒ] 'throat'. In English /ʒ/ occurs *only* medially and finally as in [meʒə] 'measure' and [ru:ʒ] 'rouge'. Consequently the English learner of French will have difficulty with the pronunciation of French words having /ʒ/ initially. For similar reasons, he will experience difficulty with German words having /ç/ in medial and final positions, even though he has initial [ç] as an allophone of English /h/ in a few native words.

We have just discussed what I called 'absolute' distribution of sounds. Another type of distribution contrast concerns the *combination* of sounds: one language may permit certain sequences of sounds at one or another position in the word. This is what is called the *phonotactics* of the language. Contrastive phonotactics is an important part of phonological CA. In Polish the combination /ʃtʃ/ occurs in all three word positions, as in *Szczeczin* 'Stettin' (a town), *jeszcze* 'still' and *barszcz* 'beetroot soup'. This phonotactic sequence is impossible in English, although it is possible to find it distributed across a word boundary as in [freʃ 'tʃi:z] 'fresh cheese'. Oft-quoted is the absence, in Spanish, of English consonant sequences or clusters like /s + $\left\{ \begin{matrix} p \\ t \\ k \end{matrix} \right\}$ + r/ in words like *spray*, *stray* and *scream*; while the word-final clusters / $\left\{ \begin{matrix} n \\ l \end{matrix} \right\}$ + d/ as in *world* or *sound* of English are alien to Spanish.

So far we have restricted our observations to the *segmental* phonologies of the two languages under CA. Of equal or greater importance is CA of the *suprasegmental* phenomena: the features of stress/rhythm and intonation in particular. Space will not permit us to enter into any details of suprasegmental CA. Suffice it to mention the interesting work of Schubiger (1965), who establishes the functional parallelism between English intonation and the German modal particles, and Zimmermann's (1972) account of the relationships between topicalisation, word order and intonation in the same two languages.

4.3.3 *Phonological Models*

A final word in the context of phonological CA harks back to what we said in Chapter 3 about *models* for linguistic analysis. The range of models available for syntactic analysis is large. For phonological analysis we have a two-way choice between *taxonomic phonology* (the model which we have been using throughout this section) and *generative phonology*. The question inevitably arises of the relative merits of these two models. The taxonomic approach, as we have seen, has the aim of "setting out phoneme systems, combinatorial possibilities of phonemes (phonotactics) and non-distinctive variations of these units in different languages" (Kohler, 1971: 84). Kohler goes on to say: "It can be said that on the whole this theoretical assumption works pretty well" (*ibid.*). The main value of the phoneme-and-allophone approach is that it identifies two categories of pronunciation problem which L2 learners face: errors resulting from phonemic asymmetries between the two languages, and those resulting from allophonic differences. The assumption, normally upheld by observation of learners' speech, is that the first category will be the source of more fundamental distortions, often leading to unintelligibility while the second category merely leads to 'foreign accent' without much impairment of communication. In fact, it is on the basis of the difference between phonemic and allophonic contrasts between English and Spanish that Stockwell and Bowen (*op. cit.*: 16) draw up an eight-point scale of pronunciation difficulty. Seeing language performance as a series of segmental 'decisions' on the part of the speaker (and learner), they distinguish *optional* choices from *obligatory* choices: optional or free choice exists where the speaker selects a phoneme, *i.e.* decides whether to say /pin/ or /bin/; obligatory choice or non-choice is when, having selected the phoneme /p/, he is constrained by the environment it occurs in to select one of its allophones. Thus the taxonomic model does provide an interesting and plausible hypothesis about relative difficulties of pronunciation. Admittedly, as Kohler points out, the predicted relativities of difficulty are not always upheld in practice: although English differs from German in lacking initial consonant clusters such as /ʃm-, ʃt-, ʃl-/ the Englishman seems to have little or no difficulty in pronouncing such clusters.

A second failing of taxonomic phonology in CA is its inability to differentiate productive from receptive difficulty: it is assumed that what is difficult to perceive by the learner will *ipso facto* be difficult for him to produce. Such is not the case. Examples are legion of an asymmetry between the learner's receptive and productive control of phonological segments. The English speaker may hear the /k/:/x/ contrast between German /lɔkə/ 'loose' and /lɔx/ 'hole' but be unable to produce the /x/. Kohler claims that "[6] is extremely troublesome to produce for most speakers, but very easy to detect" (*op. cit.*: 85). We shall be returning to this problem of the *directionality* of CAs in Chapter 7, where we consider issues of theoretical contention in CA.

Generative phonology stems from America (Chomsky and Halle, 1968) but is rooted in European phonological theory of the 1940s. Like generative syntax, generative phonology assumes that surface-structure phonology is derived from the deep-structure phonology by means of transformations: "The phonological rules ... mediate between the *systematic phonemic level* (at which all distinctive feature information is specified) and the *systematic phonetic level* (at which all phonetic information is specified)" (Southworth and Daswani, 1974: 77).

This is the first weakness of the model, for purposes of CA: the phonological deep structure is assumed to contain forms which are deleted from the surface representation – 'king' for example is given the deep structure [kiŋg] from which the [g] is deleted. As Kohler (*op. cit.*: 87) rightly stresses "the motor commands are the ones for [kiŋ] not for [kiŋg] with the subsequent deletion of [g]". The phonological deep structure not only lacks psychological reality, but seems to contradict it, with its postulation of these "quasi-mystical underlying forms". Given the choice between taxonomic and generative phonology, while accepting that the latter is probably more powerful for 'pure' linguistic purposes, we should, as Burgschmidt and Götz (*op. cit.*: 199) do, opt for the former and weaker, for the simple reason that it is more practical and concrete.

There is however one element of generative phonology, the element it inherited from Prague School phonology, which has proved useful in phonological CA: the concept of *distinctive features*. Distinctive feature phonology operates on the assumption that the phoneme is not the most convenient unit for phonological analysis, since it can be analysed into a set of phonological 'components' or features, which are more fundamental than the phoneme itself. Thus the English phoneme /t/ is a composite of the features [+ voiceless], [+ apical], [+ stop], which distinguish it from /d/, from the labials /p, b/, from the palatals /tʃ, ʒ, ʃ/ and from the velars /k, g/ and so on. There are two obvious advantages in this approach. The first is the gain in economy: whereas a language may use from 30 to 40 phonemes, it is possible exhaustively to characterise such a language using no more than a dozen distinctive features. Further economy is gained by the binarity of distinctive feature specifications: the presence (+) and absence (−) of one and the same feature can be used as a classificatory index, sparing the analyst the multiplication of categories. The second advantage, of particular interest to the contrastivist, is the *universality* of distinctive features: phonemes, in contradistinction to features are certainly not universal, as we have seen. The universal set of features can thus serve as a *tertium comparationis* for phonological CA. In using it we would be given "a much better chance of making fair comparisons between the systems of one language and those of another" (O'Connor, *op. cit.*: 210).

4.4 Contrastive Lexicology

The layman's misconception of second-language learning is that it is purely a matter of the learner learning the lexical equivalents of L2 corresponding to his L1 words. The structuralist movement in linguistics, and the allied Audio-Lingual Method, with their emphasis on the priority of grammatical patterns, tended, in contrast to the layman's view, to *neglect* the role which vocabulary undoubtedly plays in the process of communication. Recent research on language acquisition – of the L1 as well as the L2 – has redressed the balance, in pointing out how reliant infants, as well as adults learning an L2 in the natural setting, are, upon lexis for communication. It is these insights, together with a renewal of interest among linguists in problems of semantics (including lexical semantics) that promise a heightening of activity in Contrastive Lexicology, which has been relatively neglected as one of the three branches of microlinguistic CA (Roos, 1976; Dagut, 1977). While explicit Contrastive Lexicology has suffered from this neglect, one should bear in mind that many of the problems to which it will ultimately have to address itself have been the concern of scholars in related disciplines throughout this century. In the 1920's and '30s Edward Sapir, and B. L. Whorf, concerned themselves with the problem of linguistic determinism, a hypothesis claiming that, since language determines our perception of reality, and since languages are structured differently, different language communities have different views of what is, objectively, the 'same' reality: "Languages have a tendency to 'impose structure on the real world' by treating some distinctions as crucial, and ignoring others" (Leech, 1974: 30). The Sapir–Whorf hypothesis, then, views language as the determinant of perceived reality. This view of determinism can, and has been, reversed, into a claim that culture is reflected in language: "the language of a particular society is an integral part of its culture, and ... the lexical distinctions drawn by each language will tend to reflect the culturally important features of objects, institutions and activities in the society in which the language operates" (Lyons, 1968: 432). Here we have a two-stage view of determinism: *first* culture determines language, and *then* the language determines our view of reality.

The Sapir–Whorf hypothesis seems to have been a particular source of stimulation for anthropologists. It is they who have investigated cultural relativity, and in so doing have shed much light on matters of semantico-lexical relativity. The two best-known areas of endeavour on the part of anthropologists are the studies of colour categories (Berlin and Kay, 1969)[8] and of kinship terms (Lounsbury, 1956; Goodenough, 1956). It is in this tradition that Kalisz (1976) produced his CA of Polish and English kinship terms.

A second area in which contrastive lexicology has been kept alive is that of translation. Here again cultural barriers to effective translation have been in the forefront, notably among the Bible translators (Nida, 1964; Wonderly, 1968). Wonderly's book, *Bible Translations for Popular Use* has a chapter devoted to lexical problems, of which very many are illuminating. Spanish *cimiento* is an acceptable translation of 'foundation' in some countries, and more familiar than *fundamento*: it must, however, be avoided in Peru, since its use there would lead to confusion with *cemento* 'cement'. Similarly, in some Spanish-speaking countries 'mature/ripe' (from Greek *teleios*) can only be applied to grain and fruit, not to people. Wonderly suggests the need for providing expansions in translation in certain cases: "the meaning of 'to serve' (*douleuein*) is delimited contextually as to the quality of service . . . by introducing words for 'slavery' and 'master' into the context":

Romans 6:6	'so that we may no more serve'	que no estuvieramos ya en esclavitud, sirviendo al pecado como a un patrón.

(Wonderly, 1968: 110)

Wilss (1977), in his work on translation theory, discusses problems of cultural and linguistic relativity attendant on the rendering into an L2 of "einzelner für die jeweilige Sprachgemeinschaft charakteristischer Wörter" (individual words that are characteristic of a certain speech-community). He lists such words as: esprit, patrie, charme, gentleman, fairness, Sehnsucht, Ostpolitik, Tüchtigkeit (p. 44).

And of course, where there are L2 learners and translators, there are bilingual dictionaries. This, bilingual lexicography, is the third area in which a practical concern for, if not a theoretical commitment to contrastive lexicology has been maintained. Any reasonably good bilingual dictionary bears witness to this. Consider the entry under *hawk* in *Cassell's New German Dictionary* (1957). Three key-words appear:

hawk$_1$ – die Falke, Habicht (bird of prey)
hawk$_2$ – verhökern, feilbieten (offer for sale)
hawk$_3$ – sich räuspern (clear one's throat)

We have here, then, a 1:3 correspondence in equating the English and the German lexical items; *hawk$_4$* in the sense of a 'plasterer's tool' is not included. Derivatives of *hawk$_1$* such as *hawk-eyed, hawk moth, hawk's beard*, though at least as rare as *hawk$_4$* are included. We are already in a position to criticise *Cassell's*, on the strength of this one entry. This raises the question of what the ideal bilingual dictionary should offer its users, a question which will be one of our concerns in the rest of this section on lexical CA.

We must not, however, equate lexicology with lexicography: the latter is one of several practical applications of the former. Likewise, the *lexicon* of a language is not the same as a (monolingual) *dictionary* of that language. Both Nowakowsky (1977) and Leech (1974) emphasise the distinction between a dictionary and the lexicon. Leech (*ibid.*: 202) draws a distinction between the practical dictionary or "reference-book on the living-room or library shelf" and the theoretical or 'inbuilt' dictionary "which every one of us carries around as part of his mental equipment as a speaker of a language" and constitutes his "semantic competence". This definition is in line with our general conviction, expressed elsewhere in this book that a CA is a differential account of the monolingual's L1 Competence and the L2 Competence which, as a learner, he aspires to. It is the task of contrastive lexicology, therefore, to compare linguistic accounts, stated within the same lexicological framework, of the lexical competence necessarily possessed by speakers of the two languages concerned. This is a large-scale and arduous undertaking, as we shall presently discover, and not to be confused with such exercises as the writing of bilingual dictionaries, not even if they are conceived contrastively, as is the case on the Romanian-English CA Project, which has, among other things, set itself the task of producing a contrastive bilingual dictionary of the 20,000 most frequent words in Romanian and English.

As on the other linguistic levels, the contrastive analysis proper presupposes the prior analysis of the lexicons of L1 and L2. To quote Leech (*op. cit.*) again: "The lexicon will be considered as an unordered list or set of lexical entries. A lexical entry, in turn, will be considered as a combination of three specifications: a morphological specification, ... a syntactic specification, ... and a semantic specification." For several reasons, not the least of which is the enormity of the task required, I shall not adopt this approach to lexicology for the conduct of lexical CA. Instead of producing an 'unordered list or set' I shall advocate the preselection of various semantic domains (or fields) for the purpose of delimiting the scope of the CA; and I suggest further that the lexical entries identified as belonging to the particular fields selected should be studied and specified according to their strictly *semantic* properties: the only syntactic information pertinent will be in the form of statements of the co-occurrence restrictions imposed on particular lexical items. In fact, while not denying that the lexicon constitutes a highly complex and ultimately monolithic system (how else could one use it?), for our present purposes it will be an advantage to view it as a system of subsystems: these subsystems are the lexical fields we have mentioned. The view we take of lexis is, therefore, a polysystemic one.

Opting for this approach is not to deny the relevance to our enquiries of the general principles of lexical design, which we further assume to be true for all human languages. Although each field will have its idiosyncrasies, in terms of the number and natures of its constituent lexemes, as well as of the ways in which they interrelate, these relationships will be of recurrent types; we are thus in a position to view language diversity, and contrast, in the lexicon, against a background of universal formal constraints. Another task we set ourselves, therefore, in this section is to characterise the kinds of relationships into which lexical items enter with each other, within the same field.

4.4.1 *Word Fields*

The concept of word field, which has received much attention in diachronic work from the German linguists Trier and Weisgerber, was introduced for the purpose of delimiting the lexicon into cohesive subsystems. It has affinities with the thesaurus (*cf. Roget's*), and contrasts with the conventional dictionary in identifying within the lexicon a number of semantic, cognitive, attitudinal or notional areas of concern; the dictionary by contrast, is organised on the simple alphabetical principle. Hartmann (1975) lists word fields that have been studied; these include: OFFENCE, JOY, VISUAL PERCEPTION, SOUNDS, FACIAL EXPRESSION, COLOURS, EATING, VERBA DICENDI, PARTS OF THE BODY, VEHICLES, COOK-

ING, ARTIFACTS FOR SITTING, PIPE JOINTS, to name but a few.

An interesting recent CA of *verba dicendi* in English and German is Lehmann (1977). The *verba dicendi* constitute a notional class of verbs, and moreover an intuitively plausible class. Their function is to refer to speech acts, the basic semantic conditions for which are uniformly: A says x to B. More precise specification determines the selection of one member from the class: *say, speak, talk, tell.* In other words, the selection of any one of these four lexical realisations depends on the values selected for the variables A, x, B in the formula. Such *verba dicendi* as *answer, deny,* etc., are not analysable by this formula, but would call for a more complex one containing such further variables as antecedent speech act and speaker's presuppositions. Lehmann (*op. cit.*) identifies a number of contrasts between the four English verbs and their German 'equivalents' *sagen, sprechen, erzählen, reden.*

  i) SAY can have as its grammatical subject a person, 'text' or institution:

My mother
The brochure   }   says . . .
Scotland Yard

SAGEN prefers a human subject and rejects 'text':
*Ihre Broschüre sagt . . .

  ii) SPEAK refers to the faculty and quality of oral communication:
He speaks six languages: He's a French speaker.
He speaks well: He's a good speaker.

TALK, however, refers to *quantity*:
He's a great talker.

REDEN carries both the qualities of SPEAK and TALK:
Er ist ein guter Redner.
Er redet zu viel.

  iii) TELL conveys the fact that the addressee was given information, was commanded, or was entertained:
The smoke told us a new Pope had been found.
He told the kids to make less noise.
He told her a dirty joke.

SAGEN corresponds with TELL in its informative and imperative functions:
Sein Gesicht sagte uns, daß er ärgerlich war.
Er sagte den Kindern, ruhig zu bleiben.

whereas the 'entertain' function is carried by ERZÄHLEN:
Erzähl 'uns mal eine Geschichte'.

Another recent word-field CA of interest is that by Bančila (1974) on terms for physical pain in English and Romanian: *pain, ache, headache, stitch, sting, cramp, heartburn, twinge, sore, smart, earache, sore throat* would be the list of English nouns. The addition of adjectives and participles would extend the list, of course, but limitation by grammatical class in this way is one legitimate way of narrowing the field. Since German is better known than Romanian, I shall use German to exemplify the interlingual correspondences.

  i) *pain, ache, smart, headache,* and *sore throat,* are all realised by German *Schmerz* or *Schmerzen,* with appropriate modifications. So *headache* and *sore throat* are compounded with *Kopf-* and *Hals-* to give *Kopfschmerzen* and *Halsschmerzen* respectively, in both cases with the plural morpheme added. For *smart, Schmerz* is adjectivally modified to give *heftiger Schmerz,* in the singular.

  ii) *stitch, twinge, sting, prick* are all realised by *Stich,* with occasional noun modification, *stitch* is frequently *Seitenstich, sting* by a noun for the insect agent: *Wespenstich.*

  iii) *Cramp* is *Krampf(en)* while *heartburn* is *Sodbrennen,* a compound consisting of morphemes indicating *boiling* and *burning.*

The first impression we gain of this style of CA is that its delimitation is somewhat arbitrary. On what objective basis does one select a word field? We have suggested that it is identified on the basis of some sphere of human behaviour or human conceptualisation. Even if we accept that this is feasible, and find that our intuitions about what constitutes a 'sphere of human endeavour' are inter-subjectively endorsed, *i.e.* other people's intuitions agree with ours, we have still to solve the problem of what to exclude and include. We might agree that *depression* does not belong to the field of physical pain, but what shall we do with *lumbago, neuralgia, piles, constipation*? Are these not pains but discomforts? Are they not pains *per se* but causes of pain?

These questions become philosophical in nature, and Linguistics at least is in no position to give clear answers to them. The apparatus that is available within linguistic semantics is the COMPONENT, to which we now turn.

4.4.2 *Semantic Components*

In the previous section we showed how phonemes may be analysed into phonological features. Similarly, lexemes can be shown to be composed of semantic features or 'components'. We stated above that a language using 25–40 phonemes can be economically analysed at the phonological level by reference to about a dozen phonological features. Now a typical native speaker has a vocabulary of some 20,000 words. Compare this figure with that for phonological units and it would seem that the number of semantic components needed to specify a speaker's vocabulary will be in the region of 10,000. Such is, however, not the case; it has been calculated that: "The surprisingly low number of 17 features (Log 100,000) would suffice to characterise the lexical units of a language (or dialect) with a lexical inventory of 100,000 units" (Nemser and Vincenz; 1972: 288).

A clear account of components and how they are identified is given in Lyons (*op. cit.*: 470). He asks us to consider the following sets of words in English:

man	woman	child
bull	cow	calf
ram	ewe	lamb, etc.

We feel that these triads of words represent a common pattern horizontally, so that we could set up proportions like:

man : woman : child = bull : cow : calf

Both 'man' and 'bull' are (+ male), 'woman' and 'cow' (+ female), and 'child' and 'calf' (+ immature). Vertically we see further contrasts: all the first set are (+ human), all the second (+ bovine), all the third (+ ovine). The features we have isolated are semantic components. Each lexeme is a complex of such components: 'lamb' for example is specifiable as (+ ovine, + young) corresponding to the dictionary definition of this item as 'young sheep' or 'young gregarious ruminant of the species *ovis*'.

Components, like phonological features, may be universals:

> "It has frequently been suggested that the vocabularies of all human languages can be analysed, either totally or partially, in terms of a finite set of semantic components which are themselves independent of the particular semantic structure of any given language" (Lyons, *op. cit.*: 472).

He goes on, however, to criticise the arbitrariness of component-assignment: why for example, should we differentiate man:woman, bull:cow, cock:hen according to the criterion of sex, *i.e.* (+ male) or (+ female)? In everyday reality, perhaps we differentiate man:woman by the clothes they wear or by the length of their hair. To what extent these attributes, however, are reflections of a more basic sex difference is another philosophical quandary. Leech (*op. cit.*: 232) gives some further depth to this question of the universality of components. He first distinguishes *formal* and *substantive* universals: claims for such universals, on the semantic level, would be:

i) "All lexical definitions in all languages are analysable as a set of components." (formal)
ii) "All languages have the contrast between (animate) and (inanimate)." (substantive)

Leech argues that belief in i) is usually taken for granted by any theoretical linguist – linguistics is all about formal universals. Most of the disagreement in linguistics surrounds the postulation of ii), the substantive universals: one need not, as a linguist, claim that all languages operate the same contrasts. There are in fact two versions of the substantive universals hypothesis. The strong version is that all languages have this or that semantic category: and this strong version is manifestly untrue. The weaker version takes the form: "There exists a universal set of semantic features, of which every language possesses a subset" (Leech: 233). Although this formula could be vacuous, Berlin and Kay (1969) have shown it to be interestingly true. They calculated that there are 2,048 possible combinations of 11 basic colour categories, whereas, on the basis of their study of 100 languages, they found only 22 combinations occurring: this suggests very powerful constraints being imposed by languages on the way in which their vocabularies in the field of colour terminology are organised. So there is some evidence for the existence of substantive semantic universals of language, evidence which is highly attractive to the contrastivist of course, for two reasons. First, the set of universals provides him with the *tertium comparationis*, a vital ingredient for any comparative-contrastive enterprise. Second, it defines for him that background of likeness against which the idiosyncrasies of L1 and L2 stand out, and which sets the process of interference in motion.

Componential analysis provides the contrastivist with a third vital instrument for his work. This is the *semantic feature complex*. The English word *hand* is polysemous, in having at least four senses:

   i) part of the arm, with fingers
   ii) on a watch or clock
   iii) a person who helps with work
   iv) a round of applause

To do a CA at this stage would involve merely providing the L2 lexical correspondences, as:

   $hand_1 =$ die Hand $hand_3 =$ der Hilfsarbeiter
   $hand_2 =$ der Zeiger $hand_4 =$ der Beifall

Likewise, a word-for-word CA of German *Fleisch* with its English equivalents would merely register the $1:2$ relationship, the fact that *Fleisch* is at times translated *meat*, at other times *flesh*: "lexeme-to-lexeme comparison of languages would not be very fruitful" (Di Pietro, 1971: 121). What we must do is specify the conditions governing 'at times'.

Componential analysis allows us to do this by identifying an intermediate level of semantic organisation between the components themselves and the lexical item: this level is that occupied by the *semantic feature complex*. Each such complex specifies one of the *senses* of a lexeme, as in the diagram:

COMPONENTS   SENSES   LEXEME

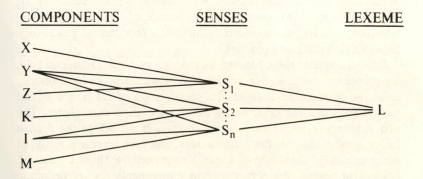

If L = English *hand* and $S_1 \ldots S_4$ are its four senses, we now specify each sense in terms of its components, these being drawn from a set $x - m$. I suggest the following assignments of components:

$hand_1$: (part of body), (end of arm), (for holding), etc.
$hand_2$: (part of clock), (on dial), (moving) . . .
$hand_3$: (human), (working), (wage-earning) . . .
$hand_4$: (human agent), (public appreciation), (movement), . . .

Note that some components are shared by more than one sense of the lexeme *hand*: $hand_1$, $hand_3$, $hand_4$, are all (human), while $hand_2$ shares with $hand_4$ the component (movement).

This approach to lexical CA involves the contrasting of all the identifiable senses of equated lexemes from L1 and L2. We have discovered that English *hand* serves for German *Hand* as well as for *Zeiger*, *Hilfsarbeiter* and *Beifall*. Such interlingual asymmetry or 'divergent polysemy' is a very common source of errors among L2 learners: the English student of German is prone to use *die Hand* to refer to *der Zeiger* of a clock. However, there is an alternative approach based on a different *tertium comparationis* than the chance formal identity of German *Hand* and English *hand*: this is the approach based on the semantic field. Notice that the polysemous *hand* intersects four semantic fields, those of PARTS OF THE BODY, PARTS OF A CLOCK, EMPLOYMENT, and EX-PRESSION OF PUBLIC EVALUATION. Now, it is *within*, rather than across, such semantic fields where semantic homogeneity, and maximum commonality of semantic components are to be found. It is for this reason that Bančila (*op. cit.*) is able to specify fully the English and Romanian terms for physical pain by reference to a mere half-dozen components: (diffuse), (continuous), (sudden), (profound), (localised) and (physical agent). With similar elegant economy Di Pietro (*op. cit.*: 118) specifies eleven senses of *meat* and *flesh* by reference to six components: (human), (concrete), (localised), (animal), (internal), and (edible).

Having specified the L1 lexemes defining a particular semantic field, we proceed to the CA. We are faced now with a procedural option: either we produce an independent specification of L2 lexemes (and senses) for the same field, or we utilise translation equivalence. The two approaches are in fact mirror-images. If we adopt the first, a native speaker supplies the L2 inventory, and each lexeme is analysed componentially. Then follows a matching procedure: those L1 and L2 lexemes or senses receiving the same components are by definition

translation equivalents. The second approach *starts* with tentative
translations and the subsequent componential analysis is a check on
their 'fit'. Let us illustrate the approach by reference to the field of
COOKING in English and German: the field for English has been
analysed by Lehrer (1969). She regards *cook* as having three senses.
Its most general sense ($cook_1$) means 'to prepare a meal' and this
belongs to the field of household tasks with *clean, wash, repair*, etc.
$Cook_2$ is less general and contrasts only with *bake*, *i.e.* it refers to the
preparation of all foods other than those sold in bakeries. $Cook_3$ is the
most marked sense, and the one on which our CA will focus: it
involves the application of heat in some way to food. Lehrer says:
"The lexical field covered by $cook_3$ can be divided into four main
categories headed by the lexemes *boil, fry, broil*, and $bake_2$ (the
specific sense) . . . These four lexemes, then, are hyponyms of $cook_3$."
$Cook_3$ is the hyperonym or archi-lexeme of the field. *Broil* is an
American English usage meaning 'to cook directly under a heating
unit or directly over an open fire' (Lehrer, *ibid.*: 44). It is matched in
British English by *grill* and *toast*.

Let us take a subset of lexemes from the *cook* field in English and
German. First we assign to them their semantic components, and then
we shall be in a position to do the CA.

	C1: with water	C2: with fat	C3: in oven	C4: contact with flame	C5: Gentle
cook	O	O	O	O	O
boil	+	−	−	+	−
simmer	+	−	−	+	+
fry	−	+	−	+	O
roast	−	−	+	−	O
toast	−	−	−	+	O
bake	−	−	+	−	O
$kochen_1$	O	O	O	O	O
$kochen_2$	+	−	−	+	−
$kochen_3$	+	−	−	+	+
braten	−	O	O	O	O
rösten	−	−	−	+	O
backen	O	O	+	−	O

C_1–C_5 refer to the five components whereby these sets of lexemes can
be specified and differentiated. By convention + signifies that the
lexeme is marked by having the relevant component, − that it is

marked by lacking it, and O that it does not apply distinctively one way or the other.

Note what equations and nonequations (contrasts) this analysis reveals:

cook = *kochen*$_1$: both mean to prepare food in any of the ways specified by C_1–C_5.
boil = *kochen*$_2$: *i.e.* in water, on-flame, rapidly.
simmer = *kochen*$_3$: *i.e.* in water, on flame, gently.

braten is specified positively only by the absence of water in the cooking process, all the other components being non-distinctive (marked by O). Now *braten* can be with fat or without, *i.e.* dry; one can also *braten* in the oven or on the flame. In fact *Bratkartoffeln* are cooked in a pan, on the flame, with fat, *i.e.* they are *fried*; while *ein Rindbraten* is prepared in the oven, without fat: it is *roast beef*. In other words *braten* is a more general term, occupying the semantic space of both *fry* and *roast*. This is a case of interlingual divergent generality. To differentiate the senses of *braten* we could establish two terms *braten*$_1$ (= *fry*) and *braten*$_2$ (= *roast*). Such a division could be motivated from within German – avoiding a 'dependent analysis' – if we introduced more components. The most obvious candidates for these components would be *selectional features*. We would say that *braten*$_1$ selects objects like *Schinken* 'bacon', *Spiegeleier* 'fried eggs' while *braten*$_2$ selects as objects such nouns as *Rind* 'beef', *Schweine-* 'pork' and *Kalbs–* 'veal'.

toast selects the same components as *rösten*, giving us *Röstbrot* for *toast* (n). However, the relationship is not always so clear-cut: we have *Röstkartoffeln* 'baked potatoes', *Röstpfanne* 'frying pan', and *Röstofen* 'kiln'.

C_1–C_5 fail to distinguish *roast* from *bake*, as Lehrer (*op. cit.* 45) discovered: her compromise solution is in "making *roast* only a partial hyponym of *bake*". Once again we can distinguish this pair if we resort to further specification by selectional features: *bake/backen* select objects composed of flour (*cake/Kuchen/Gebäck*) while *roast/braten* select animal substances, *i.e.* meats, as we have seen above.

We have so far made use of three notions from semantics: *boil*, *fry*, *roast*, etc. were called COHYPONYMS of the archilexeme *cook*; *hand* and *die Hand* stand in a relationship of DIVERGENT POLYSEMY; and *braten*, in covering the semantic space of *fry* and *roast*, shows DIVERGENT GENERALITY. A fourth notion of value is SYNONYMY. In that they have the same sense, translationally equivalent lexemes of two languages may be said to be synonymous. This may appear somewhat trivial, but no longer so if we consider that "It is of course possible to extend the application of the term 'synonymy' so that it also covers *groups* of lexical items" (Lyons, *ibid.*: 451). On these grounds it is possible to equate, intralingually, *female fox* with *vixen*, even *mature bovine quadruped* with *cow*. One might have reservations about such equations, since native speakers have to have special definitional reasons for using the complex forms; however, in American police jargon it seems that 'juvenile Caucasian male' freely substitutes for 'White boy'.

Such reservations do not hold, however, for interlingual equations of simple and complex lexical items. It is characteristic of any inter-lingual lexical confrontation, whether in the bilingual, the proficient translator, or the L2 learner, that such simple-to-complex corres-pondences are set up: they ought, therefore, to be accounted for in a lexical CA. Kirkwood (1966: 177), in a discussion of German/English lexical contrasts, mentions that while German has a set of simple lexemes for 'brush' like *Bürste, Pinsel, Besen*, English has the complex equivalents *hair/clothes brush, painting brush, sweeping brush*. Lipińska (1974: 168) phrases the generalisation thus: "a certain meaning x which is expressed in L1 by means of one lexical item is expressed in L2 by means of more than one lexical items which stand in a well-defined syntagmatic relation to one another". Examples are Russian *zavtrakat'*: *to have breakfast*, Polish *swąd: a smell of burning*. It is this possibility of interlingual paraphrasability which guarantees the feasibility of translation, even in cases where one of the languages has a 'lexical gap'.

Another feature of this simple-to-complex lexical relationship connects it with another of our lexical CA categories: divergent generality. Where a lexical item of one language, *e.g. hand* or *smell* or *kochen* is more general than a simple lexeme in the other language, it can be 'narrowed' by the addition of words, so producing a complex lexeme: *hand* (of a *clock*), *smell* (*of burning*), (*langsam*) *kochen*. The resultant complexes then correspond 1:1 with corres-ponding simplexes in the other language: *Zeiger, swąd, simmer*, respectively. This amounts to a claim that *all* lexical correspondences are of a 1:1 nature, for example that *leicht kochen* or *langsam kochen* correspond to English *simmer*. The objection to this is that while *kochen₃* (in the sense of *simmer*) may be used in combination with adverbs like *leicht/langsam*, native speakers of German do not usually use the adverbs: they seldom feel the need to be explicit about the slow rate of boiling. It seems to be a general feature of the use of lexemes in languages that speakers use minimally specific words and phrases: only just specific enough to avoid misunderstanding. The contexts of utterance usually convey these ancillary features, so that in:

   i) Schmutzige Wäsche muss man *kochen.*
   ii) Die Milch *kochte,* bis sie sahnig wurde.

We have a case of *kochen₂* ('boil') in i) and a case of *kochen₃* ('simmer') in ii) without any adverbs occurring: one knows that dirty linen gets boiled but milk simmered.

The study of such conditions for the co-occurrence of lexical items, which determine "the selection of some senses and the exclusion of others" (Katz, 1966: 205) belongs to the study of *selectional restrictions.* These are regulations for what kinds of lexemes can occur in certain grammatical contexts, and explain for instance the possibility of *John snores* and the unacceptability of **The symphony snores* by the fact that the verb *snore* requires an animate subject. Selectional restrictions are of an all-or-none nature, which distinguishes them from Firth's *collocations,* which is a statistical notion. The lexicologist can identify classes of 'habitual' collocations such as *take pictures, take a walk, sit an exam.* The contrastivist will study their counterparts in other languages, discovering contrastive collocations for the same senses, as in *Bilder machen, einen Spaziergang machen, passer un examen,* and the like.

In this short account of contrastive lexicology many aspects of lexical contrast have necessarily been unmentioned: in the context of SYNONYMY, for instance, we might have discussed the distinction drawn between *cognitive* and *connotative* synonymy: in languages there are pairs of lexemes that are cognitive, but not connotative, synonyms: *freedom/liberty; hide/conceal; Angst/Furcht.* I hope, nevertheless, to have suggested what seem to me to be the most fruitful areas and procedures for this rather neglected level of CA.

NOTES

1 For example, Stockwell, Bowen and Martin: *The Grammatical Structures of English and Spanish* (1965).
2 These projects are listed in Appendix A.
3 As we have already stressed, CA, being a branch of Linguistics and not of Psycholinguistics, is not *per se* concerned with *how* language is learnt, merely with *what* must be learnt.
4 *Third*-order applications involve "organisation and presentation" of the target language to learners: that is, the *teaching* stage of applied linguistics.

5 F. de Saussure's division is in some ways similar to Chomsky's Competence: Performance dichotomy (*cf.* Derwing, 1973).

6 Frequencies for English, in descending order: /t n r l s d z m ð k w b h v f p ŋ j g θ ʃ dʒ tʃ ʒ/. For German: /n t r d s l x m f v g z b k ts ʃ h p ŋ j pf/.

7 I am aware of the arguments for viewing [ç] as an allophone of /X/.

8 Berlin and Kay in fact strive to demonstrate, beneath the superficial variety of colour term systems of different languages, a certain universality of basic distinctions: so they are anti-Whorfian.

5

Macrolinguistics and Contrastive Analysis

The previous chapter presented a traditional view of linguistics and of CA: the view, which has been sustained since classical times, that language is a self-contained calculus, a mechanism for the production of sentences. It is this view of language which has given to linguistics the appearance of a discipline closely akin to mathematics or formal logic, which are likewise concerned with abstract formal systems. The formal system of any language which linguists set out to describe has been called different things by different people: Saussure talked of *langue*, Chomsky of *Competence*, while another term is *code*. I have referred to this kind of approach as 'microlinguistics', but 'code-linguistics' would do as well.

To gain access to the code 'underlying' a language it is necessary, linguists claim, to disregard much that goes into language. This purging of aspects which are seen either as irrelevant or as complicating factors has been called by Lyons (1972) the 'idealisation of data'. He identifies three ways in which data is idealised in linguistics:

a) REGULARISATION: Spontaneous speech, even that produced by rational native speakers of a language, is full of false starts, hesitations, backtracking, mixed constructions and the like. Chomsky (1965: 3) attributes these to "such grammatically irrelevant conditions as memory limitations, distractions, shifts of attention and interest". They should be regularised out of the data for linguistic analysis.

b) STANDARDISATION: There are two senses in which linguists may be said to standardise their data. The first and literal sense means the selection of the Standard dialect for description. This practice has a long history into pre-structuralist times (*cf.* Quirk, 1962) and is associated with such factors as: linguistic conservativism, classically determined and logic-determined views of correctness, and the selection of a pedagogic norm of the language for foreign learners. The second sense of standardisation has to do with the homogeneity of the data: since the task of linguistic description would be complicated by having to cope with data taken from speakers with a mixture of regional or social backgrounds, informants are selected who speak the same, Standard, variety. Most recently, the Transformational-Generativists, in response to Chomsky's claim that "Linguistic theory is concerned with an ideal speaker-listener" have achieved Standardisation by limiting their attention to the data from one single individual – usually the linguist himself, who serves as his own informant.

c) DECONTEXTUALISATION: The traditional 'universe of discourse' or field of enquiry for linguistics has been the single isolated sentence of the language under description. This held true for the Structuralists as well as it does for the T-G grammarians who followed, in whose grammars $\sum$ (for 'Sentence') is the recurrent symbol. A sentence can be decontextualised in two ways, either by being removed from the company of the sentences that precede or follow it in a text (its *context*), or by being separated off from the real-world situation in which it is used (its *context* of situation).

The arguments for this sort of idealisation of linguistic data are not to be dismissed out-of-hand. There are, I think, two ways of justifying the practice. In the first place, one can argue that initial idealisation is a sensible step in the context of a long-term strategy for linguistics. Let us first find our way to the code, the very heart of the labyrinth of language, even at the expense of missing some of the forces which determine its nature – these can be attended to later, as 'variables', once we have identified the constant (*i.e.* the code). A germane argument in applied linguistics might seek to justify teaching L2 learners first the code, and later providing them with opportunities to build onto this code situational and stylistic flexibility: after all, the code *is* generative, that is, capable of producing an infinite number of sentences appropriate for a wide range of situations. The second argument for code linguistics is that in the processes of idealisation, the various psychological, socio-situational and cultural variables are not merely being jettisoned, but they are being systematically identified, and once identified, they can be placed at the disposal of other disciplines, or of other sorts of linguist, for careful study: What in essence is being proposed then, is a division of labour. But it is not a plausible proposal, for the simple reason that the study of these 'contexts' in which language is used is no longer a linguistic study, but the province of the psychologist and sociologist. Those who take this stance argue that the 'division of labour' approach is as infeasible as the code-linguistics approach is unrealistic, and that it is not the contexts *of* language that need to be studied, but language *in* those contexts. I refer to linguists of this persuasion as *macrolinguists*: they see their task as the study of 'situated speech' as Coulthard (1977: 3) calls it.

5.1 Macrolinguistics

Macrolinguistics is what Yngve (1975) calls 'broad' or 'human' linguistics, the goal of which he defines as "to achieve a scientific understanding of how people communicate". Compare this with the goal of code linguistics, which is to specify the universal and particular properties of human languages. Attention has shifted from the code to a process: the process of communication. In antithesis to Chomsky's Competence, Hymes (1972) proposes that a speaker's *communicative competence* should be the object of linguistic enquiry. This raises the whole question of how people communicate. Obviously they do so predominantly by means of language. To a lesser degree other signalling devices such as gestures, facial expression, and other such paralinguistic devices also play a part – but we shall overlook them here. Since people communicate through language, code linguistics has a major say in any account of the process. Nevertheless, it is not language itself which communicates, and knowledge of the code is not a sufficient condition for the achievement of communication. But such knowledge is a necessary condition, since there can be no verbal communication without the code. So we need to ask ourselves what else is required for communication besides knowledge of the code (Competence). One word to embrace all these non-codal aspects is *sensitivity*: the communicating individual must be able to identify the situational constraints to which speech-events are subject and produce utterances that conform to them. These constraints are socio-cultural variables that in part determine the form of successful utterances. Hymes (1974) identifies six such variables which he suggests the ethnographer of speaking must refer to in characterising any particular speech event: Setting, Participants, Purpose, Key, Content and Channel.

SETTING: The time and place of speech determine its form: thus questions put to a lecturer in the bar after the plenary session will be formulated differently from those put in the conference hall.

PARTICIPANTS: Hymes identifies four participant roles: addressor, speaker, addressee and audience. Speech to one's boss is different from speech to one's inferiors.

PURPOSE: Every speech act has a purpose: even Malinowski's "phatic communion", as Laver (1975) has shown, is far from purposeless. Much attention is currently focused on the purposes or 'communicative functions' of language, as applied linguists try to produce notional syllabuses (Wilkins, 1976). Some obvious purposes of speech acts are: persuasion, command, advice, greeting etc. Note that a speech act such as persuasion may embrace several sentences: it is still one act however.

KEY: Hymes uses this label for the 'tone, manner or spirit' in which the speech act is performed. Thus advice can be issued in a friendly, flippant key or in a stern, distant key. Compare "I'd get your brakes looked at if I were you" as said by a friendly passenger and by a stern policeman to the motorist.

CONTENT: What one is talking about – the *topic* – codetermines the language forms selected. One speaks for example of the register of science. In some communities certain topics are not spoken about in polite society, they are 'taboo': excrement, sexual matters, personal finance are such categories in British society.

CHANNEL: The two primary channels for verbal communication are speech and writing. Even with the other five variables kept constant, a written message is likely to have a different form from an equivalent spoken one. Some writers, like Alistair Cooke, who delivers a weekly BBC 'Letter from America' are able to narrow the gap, and their message read aloud closely resembles spontaneous speech.

There is a simpler formula to express these six Hymesian variables, sensitivity to which, as I have suggested, determines a speaker's communicative competence: who says *what* to *whom*, *where* and *when*, *how* and *why*.

5.2 Two Areas of Macrolinguistics

From the preceding section, certain points emerge to characterise macrolinguistics:

i) A concern for communicative competence rather than for 'linguistic' competence in Chomsky's sense.

ii) An attempt to describe linguistic events within their extra-linguistic settings.

iii) The search for units of linguistic organisation larger than the single sentence.

In general, a broadening of scope is aimed at, both 'vertically' in terms of larger linguistic units and horizontally, to incorporate socio-cultural settings within linguistics. This broadening of scope has so far been achieved in two ways. The first is on the *formal* level and addresses the question of how sentences are organised into larger, suprasentential units or *texts*. The second direction is the *functional* one, and looks at the ways in which people put language to use: this is the field of *discourse analysis* (Coulthard, 1977).

The two terms *text analysis* and *discourse analysis* have sometimes been confused. Some have suggested that the former refers to the European traditions and the latter to Anglo-American traditions for doing the same thing. Another approach is to see them as complementary, discourse analysis starting with the outer frame of situations and working inwards to find the formal linguistic correlates to the situational variables, while text analysis starts with linguistic forms and asks in which contexts they are appropriate. As indicated above, we shall here view text analysis as concerned with the formal devices used for establishing inter-sentential connections, and units 'above' the sentence, and view discourse analysis as handling considerations of use. This accords with Van Dijk's (1978) position: "As soon as the analysis goes beyond the boundaries of linguistic/grammatical notions we find ourselves in the inter-disciplinary field of discourse studies."

The distinction being made is parallel to that drawn by Widdowson (1978) between *usage* and *use*. The former, he says, has to do with the grammaticality of sentences, and an important part of foreign-language learning "involves acquiring the ability to compose correct sentences". Such ability, though necessary, is not sufficient to equip the learner for communication in the FL, however: he also needs to know which sentences are appropriate to a particular context. Rules of *use* need to be acquired, as well as rules of *usage*. Now, a well-formed sentence can be appropriate to its context in two ways: it can be *formally* appropriate, in not violating the rules of textual organisation, and it can be *functionally* appropriate, in that it communicates what its speaker intends (to do this, as we have seen, it must conform to the extralinguistic constraints imposed on it). Or a sentence can be *formally* as well as *functionally in*appropriate. Formal inappropriacy to linguistic context (*i.e. cotext*) results in incohesive text, while functional inappropriacy will lead to a breakdown in communication, that is, to incoherence. Consider the following crass example, which will clarify the two notions of cohesion and coherence.

> A   Who switched off the lights?
> { B1   What Mary did was switch off the lights.
> { B2   There are fairies at the bottom of our garden.

Seen as responses to A's question, B1 and B2 are incohesive and incoherent respectively. B1 approximates a reply to A, in that A can, if he makes the effort, derive from it the information he seeks: but B1 does not 'package' the information in a form expected by A. B1 is really a reply to the question *What did Mary do*? rather than to A. B1 infringes cotextual constraints operative in English, and is incohesive to A. B2, on the other hand, seems either irrelevant or simply facetious: its speaker has made a logical nonsequitur, and if A is convinced that B is neither irrational nor prone to facetiousness, he must try to reconstrue the missing link: perhaps B is an armchair philosopher wishing to remind A that when something happens, like lights going off, one need not necessarily look for a human culprit – supernatural or just natural forces sometimes can be the source of such everyday events.

Our example is one involving dialogue, that is, two speakers. Here is another distinction between text analysis and discourse analysis, as they have been pursued in recent years. Text analysis has studied written, and therefore monologic (one-'speaker') texts, while discourse analysis has focused its attention on unscripted (literally) spoken interaction. There is no reason why this should be so, since written texts have to be coherent as well as cohesive, and there is ample evidence that dialogic interactions conform to the rules of cohesion as well as being coherently negotiated.

We are now ready to take a closer look at these two macro-linguistic areas of text analysis and discourse analysis.

5.3 Text Analysis

A text, then, is not just a random sequence of content-related sentences: the sentences appear in a fixed order, and, over and above this, there are formal devices which signal the exact nature of the relationships holding between successive sentences. These devices may be grammatical, lexical, or, in speech, intonational. For CA we need to identify constants and variables, and I suggest that it is the formal *devices* which differ from language to language, while the *relationships* that can obtain between sentences are very probably universals: intersentential relationship-types, therefore, will serve as the *tertium comparationis*.

First, we shall demonstrate the existence of cohesion in text. To do so, we only have to face the reader with a scrambled text, that is, a succession of sentences which once constituted a coherent text, but which have been randomised: for example.

    i) He will give you the name of one or two suitable doctors.
   ii) Should there be any hitch, ask to speak to the physician-in-chief.
  iii) If you need a doctor for your child in a strange town, find the name of the best hospital.
  iv) The physician-in-chief will in all probability not be a children's specialist.
   v) Telephone and ask for the name of a pediatrician on the staff.

                      (Dr B. Spock: *Baby and Child Care*)

A scrambled text is, of course, incoherent, since the 'ideas' appear in an order not corresponding to the natural real-world order of events. And it is to his knowledge of the real world that the reader will first appeal in order to unscramble this text. So, iii) must precede v) since you can't telephone an institution until you have had it identified. To this extent, then, the sentences of our text are time-ordered, and the same order is very likely to be upheld in any version of this text (*i.e.* a translation) in another language. In addition to these pragmatic clues to the right order of the five sentences – which is iii), v), ii), iv), i) – there are formal linguistic cues, both to order and to the relationships between the sentences. Let us consider these:

5.3.1 *Lexical Devices*

Foremost among the lexical cohesive devices are the relations of synonymy and hyponymy into which lexical items in the various sentences enter. The Dr Spock text has instances of both. The three expressions 'pediatrician' v), 'children's specialist' iv) and 'doctor for your child' iii) are near-synonyms. This does not mean that they are freely substitutable for one another in all contexts, but that their referents *in this text* are capable of being seen as the same. Their use in these three sentences weaves a thread to bind them together, even where, as in the case of v) and iv), they are not even continuous in the text, since ii) separates these two sentences physically. We should attribute this thread to Hymes' category of Content. We also have examples of a hyperonym or superordinate term being linked to its hyponyms, and these as co-hyponyms to one another: the hyperonym is 'doctor' iii) and the hyponyms are 'physician', 'specialist' and 'pediatrician'. Since one of these lexical items occurs in each of the five sentences, the whole passage achieves a "continuity of lexical meaning" as Halliday and Hasan (1976: 320) put it. The question arises of the relative textual *status* of sentences containing hyperonyms and hyponyms. The hyperonym is the most general term, and is likely to occur in the sentence which is overall the most general. Since texts have a high probability of opening with a general proposition, or of closing with a generalisation which has been derived from the specifics of the text, the sentence containing the hyperonym is likely to be the first or the last: in the Spock text, iii), containing 'doctor', is the opening sentence.

One-to-one lexical correspondence of the kind we have seen is not the sole means of achieving cohesion lexically. We have already seen how the semi-technical simplex (one word) lexeme 'pediatrician' corresponds to the complex (many-word) lexeme and synonym 'doctor for your child'. An extended form of simplex-to-complex lexical correspondence serving cohesion can occur: there are, for example, lexical items which summarise complete propositions expressed elsewhere in the text. Note how 'bias' and 'precautions' in the second sentences of the following two-sentence texts refer back to the whole previous sentence:

> One hundred hours a week were devoted to study and 45 minutes to football. This *bias* was not wholly popular.

> The management have installed closed-circuit television, hired store detectives, and attached padlocks to all portable goods. These *precautions* have reduced shoplifting at Harrod's.

Note two things about these two 'summative lexemes'. First, *bias* performs an extra function besides summarising the antecedent sentence: it evaluates the content of that sentence, that is, expresses a judgement about the imbalance between work and play in the school. And second, bear in mind that such summative-evaluative words figure prominently also in dialogue: a second speaker can use them to signal, lexically, that he sees the implication of the first speaker's remark, or to express a reaction which was not expected by the first speaker. For example

A I don't mind selling a few raffle-tickets.
B Your *cooperation* is most welcome.

5.3.2 *Grammatical Devices*

Halliday and Hasan (*op. cit.*), in a lengthy discussion of textual cohesion in English, identify four major grammatical means to this end: reference, substitution, ellipsis and conjunction. Let us look at two of these.

a) REFERENCE

Language can refer – or make reference – in two ways. When I say 'my car' or 'your son', I refer to some entity in the real world: real-world reference is called *exophoric* reference, and plays a secondary role in textual organisation. But it is also possible to refer, by language, to another bit of language: this, reference-in-text, is called *endophoric* reference. Consider the following sentence:

i) *George* didn't like *work*. *He* avoided *it* whenever possible.

'George' and 'work' are two nouns with exophoric reference, while *he* and *it* have endophoric reference: they refer to 'George' and 'work' in the cotext, and not directly to real-world entities. This is why they are traditionally classified as *pro*nouns.

Compare the pronouns 'he' and 'it' in the previous sentence with 'he' in:

ii) When *he* visited ladies, *Peter* wore his white suit.

Here, 'Peter' has exophoric reference and 'he' endophoric. There is a second difference between the ways in which the pronouns in these two sentences refer to reality via full nouns: in i) the pronouns refer back to nouns which have already appeared in the text, while in ii) the pronoun anticipates the full noun 'Peter': back-referring reference is called anaphoric, while anticipatory reference is known as cataphoric reference.

A third way to categorise types of reference is according to the size and nature of the segment referred to. Quirk et al. (1972: 701) highlight two main types: in the first, the proform refers to a sentence (or clause), in the second to a noun phrase. Consider this text:

i) High rise living will raise tension among urban dwellers to disastrous proportions. ii) Such is the prediction of the authors of a report out today. iii) In it, they offer figures to show that ...

'Such' in ii) refers anaphorically to the whole of the first sentence while 'it' in iii) refers to the NP 'a report out today'. Notice also an example of a summative lexeme 'prediction' which encapsulates the whole communicative import of sentence i).

On close inspection we find that pro-forms can refer to a whole range of full forms used elsewhere in the text, not just sentences and NPs. Pro-forms, which are abbreviations of the full forms, can stand for adverbs and predicates (*i.e.* parts of sentences) as in the following:

Look *under the carpet*. You'll find the key *there*.
John will be here *at 7 p.m.* I'll meet him *then*.

Here the pro-adverbs 'there' and 'then' recycle the explicit adverbs used in the previous clauses. In the following the auxiliaries 'did' and 'may' encode the whole of the predicates in the preceding sentence, and so carry forward the meanings of those predicates:

May I *have a cigarette*? You certainly *may*. (have a cigarette)
Who killed Cock Robin? I *did*. (killed Cock Robin)

b) ELLIPSIS

It will be clear to the reader that when pro-forms are used they represent fuller forms occurring elsewhere in the cotext. A degree of reduction is achieved by their use. Ellipsis takes this process one step further and brings about the total elimination of a segment of text. Its effect is "to create cohesion by leaving out ... what can be taken over from preceding discourse" (Halliday and Hasan, *op. cit.*: 196). As these authors suggest, ellipsis is usually anaphoric in English, but may also be cataphoric – compare i) and ii), where the ellipted segments appear in brackets.

i) A Have you been to Moscow?
   B (I have) never (been to Moscow).
ii) Because Alice won't (dust the furniture), Mary has to dust the furniture.

It may at first sight seem paradoxical that the elimination of part of the message should serve to achieve textual cohesion: indeed, one expects the opposite to happen, and the speaker or reader to lose the thread. We might explain its positive effect in terms of the work that the reader or interlocutor has to do. If, in a conversation, I ellipt in my contributions segments of text which you, my interlocutor, have made explicit, I thereby show a willingness to accept your explicit contributions as 'given', and my not repeating them shows you that I value your contribution as taken for granted. We shall return to this concept of 'given-ness' presently. First, let us mention two other syntactical devices for achieving cohesion. These are: comparative constructions and parallel structure.

c) COMPARISON

Comparison is not invariably located in one sentence, although this is probably the most economical and most explicit way of stating comparison, as in:

> John is more intelligent than his sister.

Comparison can equally be achieved across sentence-boundaries, as in:

> i) My father is over 70. My mother is only 60.
> ii) There are ten boys in his class. John is the most intelligent.

These two sentence-pairs are not related in the same way. In i) there is no statement of comparison, no use of a comparative morpheme: the comparison is implied, and the reader must 'work' to relate the two sentences in his mind. In ii) there is a marker of comparison – 'most', yet here also the reader must work to recover ellipted segments, that is, to understand the second sentence of ii) as ". . . the most intelligent (of the ten boys in the class)".

d) PARALLEL STRUCTURE

Sentences in sequence normally exhibit a variety of different structures: indeed, in training the young to write compositions, teachers stress the need to vary the successive sentence-patterns. Yet the experienced writer sometimes reverses the maxim of variety and strings together two or three sentences with parallel structure: the effect of this is to tie the sentences together conceptually, so that they are read as one cohesive entity of text. Some mediaeval poets cultivated this practice into a poetic convention. Quirk et al. (*op. cit.*: 716) illustrate parallel structure by the following sentences:

> i) Have you ever seen a pig fly? Have you ever seen a fish walk?
> ii) My paintings the visitors admired. My sculptures they disliked.

In i) we have a sequence of two 'rhetorical questions' – they are not normal questions expecting answers, but challenges expressed by interrogative structures. The fact that the speaker or writer produces two such sentences does not mean that he is issuing two challenges: it is *one* challenge, and the two structures are to be read as functionally reiterative: their identity of form reinforces their functional unity. In ii) the two sentences show the same departure from 'normal' word order in English: they are both Object-Subject-Verb sequences. Now, it is not unusual for a writer to use *one* O-S-V pattern occasionally in his text, but the sequence of two or more serves a special function: to indicate that the two sentences are to be read as contrastive. We could in fact, supply a contrastive conjunction *but* or *however* to link the two sentences, but this linking is achieved just as successfully by the parallelism of the two sentence structures itself.

5.3.3. *Functional Sentence Perspective*

Successive sentences in text must do two things: they must be informative, and, at the same time be relevant. Being informative involves presenting 'new' information to the reader, while being relevant involves associating that 'new' information with information which is already known to the reader, 'given' either by preceding cotext or by the situational context. This subtle organisation of the information content of the sentences of texts in terms of 'given' and 'new' determines their 'communicative dynamism'. Its specification is an approach to text analysis that was developed by a group of Czech linguists, notably Mathesius and Firbas, in the 1950s (*cf.* Deyes, 1978). The approach has come to be called the Functional Sentence Perspective (FSP) approach, this label being derived from the assumption that sentences-in-text not only need to convey facts, but have to convey them in the *perspective* of the surrounding sentences and in conformity with information so far presented in the text or inferrable from context.

In FSP terms, 'given' items of information are ascribed to the function *Theme*, and 'new' information to the function *Rheme*. English is an SVO language, as noted earlier, and normally Subject is Theme, Object is Rheme, and Verb is what is referred to as the Transition between these two. It follows that a sentence like *Englishmen drink beer* (SVO) is Theme-Transition-Rheme: the 'new' information introduced by this sentence is *beer*. When we say that SVO is the 'normal' order of elements in the English clause, we imply the possibility of departures from that normality: such departures from normal order are traditionally referred to as inversions. Halliday, in his account of what he calls the *Textual Function* of language (Halliday, 1970), talks of 'marked theme': markedness is a concept used by linguists to refer to departure from the norm. One obvious way of achieving theme is by transposing Object, Verb, or even Adverb to sentence-initial position:

    i) Beer/he'll drink for hours on end
    ii) Sing/I can't very well
    iii) Three times/she's rung me this morning

Each of these three sentences would only be used where the thematic elements had already been established in context. Possible antecedents to each would be:

    ia) Why not offer him beer if he gets drunk on gin.
    iia) John, you'll sing at the concert, won't you?
    iiia) She'll ring at least three times before she gives up.

A second way of reversing the normal sequence of theme-rheme in the English sentence is by displacement of tonic stress. Normally this falls on the last lexical item of the clause, *i.e.* the rhematic element. Muir (1972: 99) points out that in *John read the book* "*John* is already known and *book* is the 'new' information and takes the tonic syllable." By transposing the tonic to *John* in this sentence we mark *John* as the 'new' or rhematic element. Such suprasegmental devices for marking FSP apply of course only to spoken texts.

The principles of FSP were elaborated on the basis of a study of Czech, which is a Slavonic language with a 'free' word order. This means that the major constituents of the clause – Subject, Verb, Objects, Adjuncts – are grammatically free to occur in almost any order, to satisfy the demands of communication and cohesion. These units may be only one word in size, but may just as well be whole phrases: 'element order' would be a better label than word order. Firbas (1959: 42) recognised that for Czech "word order creates what we call the basic distribution of communicative dynamism". English, more limited than Czech in its permissible word order permutations, uses other means, some not available to Czech, to achieve the same ends. One of these is the use of the Substitute-Subject *It*, as in:

    It was John who read the lesson.
    It was the red car that John bought.

Compare these 'predicated' variants, as Halliday (1970) calls them, with their unpredicated partners:

John read the lesson.

John bought the red car.

and it is obvious that the syntactic device of *it*-predication performs the same function in written texts as tonic shift does in spoken ones.

What we have been calling *it* — predication is handled in a T-G grammar under the label of 'Cleft-Sentence'. Such optional transformations operating in English provide the language with a repertoire of referentially identical but textually different variants for the writer or speaker to select from and ensure that the communicative dynamism is effectively and economically maintained in his text. It is therefore with justification that these optional transformations have often been referred to as 'stylistic' transformations: we shall mention just a few of these transformations in English.

a) CLEFTING: Compare the following pair of sentences: the first is a SVO 'kernel' sentence, while the second is its clefted variant.

   i) We want Watneys

   ii) It is Watneys that we want

In each sentence the object ('Watneys') has a different textual value. In i) there is a gradual build-up of dynamism along the sentence, 'Watneys' being the climax, while in ii) the climax is reached earlier and loses some force by being followed by the relative *that we want*. For ii) to occur there must have been prior mention of 'Watneys'. The probable sequence is:

   A) Sorry, Sir, but the only beer we have is Watneys.

   B) It is Watneys that we want. (Don't apologise)

An alternative to ii), in the same context, would be

   iii) Watneys is what we want

Its use would be more categorical but less dramatic than the use of ii).

b) PSEUDO-CLEFTING: A pseudo-cleft form of i) would be *What we want is Watneys*, which was actually used by Watneys Breweries as an advertising jingle. Here, the 'new-ness' of the rheme is further heightened by being postponed, after being announced by the first word of the sentence: *what*. A probable context for iii) is the following:

   We don't want Carlsberg. Oh no: What we want is Watneys.

c) PASSIVISATION: The basic function of the passive transformation is to reorder, relative to one another, the two semantic categories Agent and Goal. *cf.*:

i) John has picked these strawberries

Agent	V active	Goal
Theme	Transition	Rheme

ii) These strawberries were picked by John

Goal	V passive	Agent
Theme	Transition	Rheme

The same effects can be achieved by a relocation of the tonic, as noted above. The passive transformation opens up the possibility of making the (original) Transition into the rheme, if the Agent ('by John') is deleted:

iii) These strawberries were picked (not bought)

The point is that each of these three variants has a probability of occurrence in different contexts: i) would be selected if John were known from previous cotext or from the context, and the important 'new' information was that it was *'strawberries'* that he picked. ii) would be a mirror-image, in terms of contextual probability, of i); and iii) would be selected if the origin or procurement of the strawberries was the issue in question.

d) DEFINITENESS-MARKING: We noted above that FSP was closely allied to word order as a result of having been elaborated on Czech. Now the Slavonic languages, while they enjoy a greater freedom of word-order than English, have no *article system*, unlike English. In English, theme:rheme allocation can be marked by the co-occurrence of the respective Subject or Object NP with a definite or indefinite article, compare:

i)	A girl	came out of	the room
	A girl	baked	the pie
	Rheme	Transition	Theme
ii)	The girl	came out of	a room
	The girl	baked	a pie
	Theme	Transition	Rheme

In other words, an invariant SVO (or SVA) element order is neutral as regards theme/rheme allocation in English – hence the ambiguity of *Girls like pies*, in the absence of any indication of tonic-placement. In Russian, another Slavonic language, translations of i) and ii) would be

iii) and iv) respectively:

iii) Iz 'komnati 'vishla 'devushka
      (*Lit.*: Out-of room out-came girl)

iv) 'Devushka 'vishla iz 'komnati
     (*Lit.*: Girl out-came out-of room)

Now we see why the Czech investigators of FSP felt justified in viewing word order as basic: 'lacking' such a surface-structure category as articles to mark definiteness or indefiniteness of NPs, Czech naturally exploits word order as the carrier of FSP. English, having only limited potential for the manipulation of word order, has, as we have seen, a whole range of 'stylistic' transformations available for organising information flow in text.

5.4 Towards Contrastive Text Analysis

Our consideration of 'free' and 'fixed' word order languages and their achievement of FSP has already taken us into areas of textual CA. Let us now consider how textual CA might be approached. I would like to suggest three possible approaches, which I shall label: textual characterisation, text type, and translated texts.

5.4.1 *Textual Characterisation*

This label really refers to the collection of data on the preferences shown by each of a pair of languages for the use of certain devices for achieving textual cohesion. In the first half of this chapter we have seen a sample of the textual devices which English employs. Had this book been written in Russian, the concept of cohesion would have been illustrated through Russian and it is likely that I would have mentioned some devices that I have not mentioned here, or I would have given them more emphasis. The point is, that while every language has at its disposal a set of devices for maintaining textual cohesion, different languages have preferences for certain of these devices and neglect certain others. The Bible translators are certainly aware of these kinds of idiosyncrasy of languages. For example, Wonderly (1968: 189), points out that while ellipsis is a mark of "good style" for English, there are languages, including the Mayan languages of Central America, for which the exact opposite holds: repetition is a sign of good style. Consequently, a Mayan translation of Luke's Gospel 15: 22 would require a repetition of the verb 'put':

'Put a ring on his hand and (put) shoes on his feet.'

Similarly, these languages contrast strikingly with English when it comes to the marking of logical connections between sentences: instead of conjunctions, one finds constructions like the following: *When they got to town they went to the store. Having gone to the store, they bought some candy. After they bought the candy . . ..* Cohesion is maintained by repetition of part of each preceding sentence, in a grammatically different form. As Wonderly (*ibid*.: 192) correctly observes: "This is almost the opposite of the use of anaphora (in English), in which the omission of an item and the use of an anaphoric substitute not only avoids repetition but is used as a device to show connectedness."

This type of textual work involves scrutinising large stretches of text in each of the two languages, indexing what types of cohesive device are used, with what relative frequencies, and in what contexts. At this stage, the information about frequency as well as environment will have to be impressionistic. In order to illustrate, we shall look at a short German text:

i) Heute geht ja alles so schnell.
ii) Die kleine Geschichte mit dem Berliner, der sich über einen Amerikaner ärgert, weil der behauptet, in Amerika würde viel schneller gebaut als bei uns, und die damit endet, daß der Amerikaner auf ein Hochhaus deutet und nach der Bauzeit fragt, worauf der Berliner scheinbar erstaunt antwortet:
iii) Nanu-det stand jestern noch nicht da![1]

(*Ein Skizzenbuch von Berlin*. G. Neumann, p. 29)

LEXICAL DEVICES: There are three lexical threads permeating this text. First we have 'Amerikaner' (twice) and 'Amerika'; second, two occurrences of 'Berliner'; and third 'gebaut' linking to 'Bauzeit'. The three recurrent themes in this text are thus: an American, a Berliner and building, in fact the speed of building. There are two overt occurrences of 'schnell' and one covert, implied by the Berliner's witty punch-line.

REFERENCE: We see several instances of anaphoric pronouns: 'der' in the second clause of ii) refers to 'Berliner', 'die' in the fifth clause of ii) back to 'die kleine Geschichte', 'der' in clause three of ii) to 'Amerikaner', while the dialectal form 'det' in iii) refers to 'Hochhaus'. Of particular interest is the second occurrence of 'der' in ii): Its referent is 'Amerikaner' and not 'Berliner', and in a more formal text the pronoun used would have been 'dieser' (in contrast with 'jener': *cf.* English 'the former/the latter'). This second 'der' would be phonologically different from the first 'der', always attracting a greater degree of stress in pronunciation. A second interesting pro-form here is the adverb 'bei uns' in ii). Note that I have translated it into English with 'over here'. The point is that *bei uns* means 'in Germany' and *over here* means 'in Britain' simply because the texts are in German or English respectively.

ELLIPSIS: There are two interesting incidences of this in our text. The first involves an elliptical 'gebaut würde' in clause four of ii). The second seems to be permissible in a German text but not in an English one: the elliptical introductory element right at the beginning of ii), realised in English by such phrases as 'there's (the story)', 'did you hear . . .?', 'as illustrated by . . .' and their German equivalents.

FUNCTIONAL SENTENCE PERSPECTIVE: Text comes into being when a succession of sentences becomes an integrated whole. How this integration is achieved may well vary from language to language. Newsham (1977) has shown that this is the case for English and French, the paragraph structure of these two languages being a reflection of different organisations of theme and rheme in successive sentences.

Newsham selected at random twenty-four paragraphs in French and twenty-four in English from textbooks used in freshman classes in various disciplines at Montreal University. Her two assumptions were that the theme of each sentence would be linked to the theme or rheme of some other sentence, and that each paragraph, by definition, centres around one original theme. She found that four types of patterning were recurrent in her data:

a) Relationship of subsequent themes to first theme:

T1-R1	Cats eat rats
T1-R2	Cats sleep a lot
T1-R3	Cats chase their tails

b) Relationship of subsequent themes to the first rheme:

T1-R1	Cats eat rats
TR1-R2	Rats live in holes
TR1-R3	Rats are bigger than mice
TR1-R4	Rats are hard to catch

c) Relationship of subsequent themes to first (or subsequent) rhemes:

T1-R1	Cats eat rats
T2-R1	Dogs eat rats
T3-R1	Snakes eat rats

d) Relationship of subsequent themes to immediately preceding theme:

T1-R1	Cats eat rats
TR1-R2	Rats live in holes
TR2-R3	Their holes are usually in old buildings
TR4-R4	These old buildings are deserted

The findings are very interesting to the contrastivist. It was more common to find patterning of Type a) in the French than the English paragraphs. Moreover, most themes in French were nominals, and the most common reference forms in French were pronouns and synonyms, so that French seems to prefer a 'nominal style' of writing, a feature noted by several students of French stylistics.

Types b) and d) were more common in English. In both types, the rheme is the more important part of the sentence. Rhemes are mainly verbals, so that this style could be characterised as being 'verbal'.

Type c) was found only in French. Here, the rheme is a constant, and new themes are introduced in succession. Since the theme is the focal point of the sentence, the exclusive incidence of Type c) in French suggests French allows multi-topic paragraphs. This finding, however, is highly tentative.

5.4.2 *Text Typology*

Although the cultures carried by different languages may be highly distinctive, we shall usually be able to point to types of text in different languages which perform approximately the same function. In a sense the ethnographers of speaking have, through their concentration on ritualistic text-types or what Scherzer (1977: 50) calls "ritual, ceremonial, verbally artistic, and other marked and special uses of speech", tended to select for analysis the exotic and the culture-specific. They have correspondingly neglected more 'banal' and more universal text-types like hints, suggestions, reports, advising and the like; and it is exactly these that are of greatest interest to the contrastivist.

Reiss (1971), following Bühler, suggests that there are basically three types of text, according to whether they place emphasis on *content, form* or *appeal*. Similarly Nida (1975) distinguishes between the *expressive, informative* and *imperative* functions of text, adding that the reader will often be totally reliant on context to determine how to interpret any particular text. Apart from being potentially ambiguous, texts are seldom 'pure' in the sense of carrying just one of the three functions we have mentioned. In a paragraph we may well find equal numbers of sentences performing each of the three functions, although it is probably true that any text will be *predominantly* informative, expressive or appellative. One inroad to a textological CA, therefore, would be the description of, say, 'expressive' texts in L1 and L2. This will lead to an enquiry into how each of these two languages generate texts, which native speakers respond to as being 'expressive'.

Appeal to native speakers' typical response presupposes the existence of *institutionalised* text-types. By 'institutionalised' I mean that they perform certain conventional functions in the daily life of a society. Examples of these text-types are to be found in newspapers and magazines; in the commercial and governmental literature that the postman brings more and more of; in the form of the assembly, maintenance and operating instructions accompanying most mechanical things we buy; and on the radio and television. Some cultures lack text-types cultivated in others, as is well-known in the case of literary text-types. Thus Hartmann (1978) points out that the short descriptive poem of Japan, the *haiku* "has no stylistic equivalent in the West", and Kaplan (1972) comments on the uniqueness of the Chinese 'Eight-Legged Essay'. *Ehewünsche*, a text-type so common in German newspapers, the function of which is to advertise one's wish to meet a marriage-partner, appears hardly ever in British newspapers.

5.4.3 *Translated Texts*

Translated texts are an obvious basis for textual CAs. Their main limitation is their potential for translation-distortion, that is, the target-language text can show signs of interference from the source-language. Since the translator must be given access to the original, there is no way of preventing him from transferring features of its texture onto his TL rendering. If he does this, the TL version will be inauthentic, *i.e.* not what an originally composed text in that language would look like. But at the same time you cannot forbid the translator the use of certain grammatical or lexical features in the TL version just because they are present in the SL text: they may be equally authentic in both.

In bilingual societies one often sees paired texts, in the form of road signs, official circulars, press announcements and so on. They should ideally be equated texts, that is, independently produced texts of La and Lb which are functionally equated. Normally, however, there is evidence of the translation process, as, for example in the following Welsh/English pair of texts advertising a job. The Welsh version seems to have been produced by translation from the English, as seems to be borne out by the inauthenticity of the Welsh in places: for example *ddim hwyrach na* is a word-for-word translation of *not later than*:

LLANERCHYMEDD COMMUNITY SCHOOL

―

PART-TIME WARDEN

―

Applications are invited for the post of part-time Warden at the above Community School. Weekly hours of work – 6 hours, mainly evenings. Salary £650 per annum.

Applications by letter giving the names of two referees to be sent to the Chief Recreation Officer, Plas Arthur Sports Centre, Llangefni, not later than Monday, 16th April, 1979.

10D5B1

YSGOL GYMUNED LLANERCHYMEDD

―

WARDEN RHAN AMSER

―

Gwahoddir ceisiadau am swydd Warden rhan amser yn yr Ysgol Gymuned uchod. Gweithio 6 awr yr wythnos, gyda'r nos yn bennaf, am gyflog o £650 y flwyddyn.

Ceisiadau trwy lythyr yn rhoddi enw dau ganolwr i'w hanfon i'r Prif Swyddog Adloniant, Plas Arthur, Llangefni, ddim hwyrach na dydd Llun 16 Ebrill, 1979.

5.5 Discourse Analysis

To approach the study of language as discourse is to emphasise its functionality. This means that the question to be asked about any particular segment of language is not one about its form but about its *uses*: what is the speaker (or writer) hoping to achieve, and what does he in fact achieve, with this particular bit of language? The educated layman probably recognises three things that we can do through language: make statements, issue commands and ask questions. Traditionally writers of foreign-language teaching materials have seen these three functions as basic, and of these three, as Wilkins (1976: 42) observes, statements (or 'reports') have been given special attention at the expense of the other two.

When we do things through language we perform what Austin (1962) called *Speech Acts*. The number of speech acts performed by the average individual in the course of any ordinary day when his work and leisure bring him into contact with others probably runs into the thousands. To test this contention, make a recording of say fifteen minutes of real or broadcast conversation and count the speech acts performed in that short space of time. Some speech acts are more general and more frequent in a given culture than others: common ones will include *ask, refuse, praise, describe, excuse, explain* while rarer ones are *commiserate, condemn, blaspheme*, fortunately! And how many speech acts are there in all? Austin suggested that there are about 10,000 without however specifying them or claiming that the average speaker controls them all. Searle (1969) more optimistically suggests there is a nucleus of "basic illocutionary acts to which all or most of the others are reducible". In fact this section will be concerned with the basic problem of how it is that speakers signal which speech act they are performing and how hearers identify this speech act for what it is.

Whereas textual cohesion, as Widdowson[2] observes, is always overtly marked in some way, the functions of speech acts can either be marked or just implicit. So, if I perform the speech act of *advising* in English I may choose between the following realisations:

i) I *advise* you to see a doctor.
ii) I'd see a doctor if I were you.

In i) the speech act is lexically marked. Austin raises the question of whether potential lexical marking of this kind is a defining characteristic of a particular category of speech act called *performative*: "any utterance which is in fact performative should be reducible or expandable or analysable into a form with a verb in the first person singular present indicative active" (Austin, 1962). Two questions immediately arise: Is Austin's prediction about performatives true of *all* languages? and Do we have marking of other than performatives? I shall leave the reader to ponder the first question, and, to the second, point out that English makes use of a rather large class of words called *discourse markers* to indicate the function of, and the logical relationships between sentences.

Discourse markers are optional; compare:

i) He huffed and he puffed and he blew the house down.
ii) He huffed and he puffed, and consequently he blew the house down.

i) and ii) refer to the same objectivity. They are different in ii) being explicit about the three actions performed by the Big Bad Wolf: his blowing down of the house is stated in ii) to result from his huffing and puffing. Whether or not we are explicit depends on how precise we need to be, which depends on the setting of the communication: a legal contract or an international treaty have to be unambiguous, and will therefore be maximally explicit. It seems to be the case that the process of education involves learning how to use these discourse markers effectively. And, something which concerns the contrastivist, it is probable that some language communities set a higher premium than others on discourse marking.

There have been numerous attempts to classify the discourse markers of English. One tradition in which there have been studies is that of 'Freshman English' or 'College Rhetoric' courses in the USA, so well represented in Harbrace (1977) for example. Another impetus has come more recently from the 'English for Special Purposes' vogue. It is from this movement that Winter's (1971) categorisation of what he calls 'connectives' originates. He identifies the five most frequent categories in scientific texts: these account for 89% of all the connectives in the texts analysed. The five categories are:

i) *Logical sequence*: thus, therefore, then, thence, consequently, so . . .
ii) *Contrast*: however, in fact, conversely . . .
iii) *Doubt and Certainty*: probably, possibly, indubitably . . .
iv) *Non-contrast*: moreover, likewise, similarly . . .
v) *Expansion*: for example, in particular . . .

The function of these connectives is to indicate to the reader (or hearer) the kinds of logical relationship which the writer (or speaker) feels should hold between successive utterances or blocks of utterances in a text. In the absence of such markers the reader would have to work harder to 'see' the logical relationships the writer has in mind. Compare the following two sentences, the first of which contains a marker which is lacking in the second:

i) Medicines can kill and therefore should be kept out of the reach of children.

ii) Medicines can kill: they should be kept out of the reach of children.

The question is: why and how do speakers of English give ii) the same interpretation as i)? Kaplan (1972) offers a simple but cogent answer: because this is how speakers of English organise their thoughts. The conventions for the organisation of thought and argument (*i.e.* rhetorical devices), are, in Kaplan's view, language or culture-specific. As he says: "My original conception was merely that rhetoric had to be viewed in a relativistic way; that is, that rhetoric constituted a linguistic area influenced by the Whorf-Sapir hypothesis" (Kaplan, *ibid.*: ix). He further claims that English speakers demonstrate particular skill with six rhetorical functions: definition, classification, comparison, contrast, analysis and synthesis. These would appear to be those most frequently used in scientific discourse, perhaps even constituting the basis of scientific method, suggesting perhaps that it is no historical accident, but a linguistically determined necessity that English is the international language of science. Kaplan attempts to characterise the rhetorical structure of a number of language types: English, perhaps ethocentrically, he views as 'direct', while he considers much Oriental writing to be indirect or circumlocutionary. About Romance he claims: "Much greater freedom to digress or to introduce extraneous matter is available in French, or in Spanish, than in English" (p. 61). Semitic languages make use of "a complex series of parallel constructions", and Kaplan demonstrates that speakers of Arabic tend to transfer to L2 English this preferred rhetorical structure. We also find many instances of it in the King James version of the Old Testament, which was of course translated from the Hebrew.

Kaplan's explanations rely on his claim that speakers of a language are users of a distinctive set of rhetorical devices. An alternative and broader explanation of why speakers of the same language process discourse in ways that ensure intelligibility is that they have shared conventions for linking language events with context. The investigation of how language and context are related to achieve interpretation is known as Pragmatics, or, more recently, Pragmalinguistics. Stalnaker puts Pragmatics on an equal footing with other branches of linguistics: "Syntax studies sentences, semantics studies propositions. Pragmatics is the study of linguistic acts and the contexts in which they are performed" (Stalnaker, 1972: 383). What he means by 'context' is something very broad, for example ". . . the intentions of the speaker, the knowledge, beliefs, expectations, or interests of the speaker and his audience, other speech acts that have been performed in the same context, the time of utterance, the truth value of the propositions expressed . . ." and so on.

Both Kaplan and Stalnaker, to explain how communication is achieved, invoke the notion of speaker(s) and hearer(s) possessing shared knowledge and shared conventions. Communication stands the best chances of success when the individuals involved belong to the same group. This group Yngve (1975: 56) calls a *colingual community*, which he defines as "a group of individuals who can communicate with each other in certain ways characteristic of the group".

The problem that faces the foreign-language learner is of how to become a member of a colingual community whose business is conducted in the foreign language. Of course, knowledge of the linguistic code is a *sine qua non*, but just as important a qualification for colingual group membership is shared knowledge of the non-linguistic dimensions of experience. Where the latter is thoroughly mastered, knowledge of the code need not be elaborate: this is why foreign scientists can quite easily communicate about science in a lingua franca like English, and this is why they find it comparatively difficult to discuss non-scientific matters in the bar at night. They are not members of the colingual community when it comes to politics, sport and other general topics.

Labov (1972) shows clearly to what extent speakers' interpretations of utterances can depend on presumed sharedness of knowledge. He distinguishes three types of events to which speech refers:

> *A-events* These are those primarily concerning the present speaker[3] S.
>
> *B-events* are those concerning H.
>
> *AB-events* are those presumed to be the common concern of S and H.

Labov points out that different interpretations are assigned to an utterance according to whether it is viewed (by H) as referring to an A, B, or AB event. Thus, if S makes a statement about a B-event, H hears it as a request for confirmation, implying something, like 'I think I'm right in believing that:

> S: You live in Bradford.
> H: Yes/No/That's right, etc.

Note that S expects an affirmative response from H, and H knows this. Therefore, if H does have to correct S he will tend to do so in an authoritative way. There is a sociolinguistic convention at work here: B assumes that statements made by A in B's presence must be appeals to B's authority.

This two-way division of events into A and B events is based on the observation that one of the participants in an encounter has privilege of access to some item of experience or knowledge. This principle of assumed access to knowledge is a pervasive one: much of what we say is said in the way it is simply because we *presuppose* that our interlocutor shares knowledge with us. We could say that utterances contain two sorts of information: that which is new to H, and that which S assumes he already knows. Thus, in uttering

> My car won't start and Joe's on holiday

S tells H two things, and assumes that he knows who Joe is: someone with mechanical expertise, who, if he were here, would be able to start the car. If in fact S overestimates H, and H does not know who Joe is, the communication can fail and S is guilty of false presupposition. This is exactly what happens very often when native speakers, as members of a colingual community, talk to foreign learner newcomers.

Presupposition plays a crucial role in the rhetorical organisation of discourse, as Selinker et al. (1974) have shown. They point out that certain grammatical options in English are to be differentiated according to whether or not they presuppose the fact they refer to. For example, the verb *report* may be followed by an accusative with infinitive, by a that-clause, or by a gerundive; compare:

i) It was Rutherford who first reported the dodo to have become extinct.

ii) It was Rutherford who first reported that the dodo had become extinct.

iii) It was Rutherford who first reported the dodo's having become extinct.

Now iii), unlike i) or ii) contains the presupposition that the dodo *is* in fact extinct.

As Selinker et al. point out, this is an important difference, one which would preclude iii) from being used to introduce a core generalisation, since it would be unnecessary to go on and adduce evidence for something already presupposed. The significance of this for CA should be obvious: given that L1 and L2 seem to correspond formally in having these three clause types, the question remains as to whether they carry the same presuppositions. Of course the scope of such CA transcends clause complements of this sort: we need initially to identify, for each language, which grammatical categories are carriers of presuppositions.

Related to presuppositions are the rules of interpretation (and their symmetrical rules of production) which Hs apply to utterances in order to identify the speech acts they carry. The following is such a rule:

"If A requests B to perform an action X at a time T, A's utterance will be heard as a valid command only if the following preconditions hold: B believes that A believes that

1) X needs to be done for purpose Y
2) B has the ability to do X
3) B has the obligation to do X
4) A has the right to tell B to do X

These preconditions appear in almost every rule of interpretation and production which concerns making and responding to commands" (Labov, 1972: 255).

A number of points can be made about these conditions. The first is that they are almost certainly universals, *i.e.* every S/H of every language refers to them when performing the act of *command*: they therefore provide us with a very convenient 'tertium comparationis' for CA. The second point relates these conditions to context and pragmatics, in that S will select different realisations of the act in different settings. The usual strategy he adopts is to select that realisation which adds information to what is made available to H by context. For example, if the setting confirms any three out of these four conditions, S will refer explicitly only to the fourth, the one not obvious from the setting. So the parent who says to a child 'Your ears are filthy' is allowing context to specify conditions 2), 3) and 4) and himself invoking verbally only condition 1). The child will infer from this conjuction of contextual and verbal information that he should go and wash: he will interpret the utterance as a *command*. In a different setting, perhaps the actor's dressing-room in a theatre, where the actor has been blackening his ears to play the role of Eliza's father in 'My Fair Lady', the make-up artist's 'Your ears are filthy' will be received as a statement.

Widdowson (1975) exploits Labov's framework in two ways that are extremely interesting to the contrastivist. He lists no fewer than seventeen ways in which commands are issued in English.

a) S can refer to any one of the four conditions *directly* by a declarative sentence.

    1) These windows need cleaning.
    2) You can clean windows John.
    3) You are in charge of windows.
    4) It's my duty to make sure the windows get cleaned.

b) S can refer *indirectly* to the four conditions. He performs an 'indirect speech act', which Searle (1975: 60) defines as "cases in which one illocutionary act is performed indirectly by way of performing another". Searle gives as an example B's reply to A's proposal in:

    A: Let's go to the movies tonight.
    B: I have to study for an exam.

He adds that indirect acts of this sort are used for "hints, insinuations, irony and metaphor". Possible hints for getting B to clean the windows include:

    5) I can't see through these windows
    6) *I'm* too ill to clean these windows
    7) Somebody's forgotten to clean the windows
    8) I hate having to tell people to clean the windows

c) S can draw H's attention to the four conditions by using an interrogative that refers directly to each:

    9) Are those windows clean?
    10) Have you been too ill to clean windows?
    11) Aren't you in charge of the window-cleaning?
    12) Did I forget to tell you to clean the windows?

d) S refers *indirectly* to the conditions by means of interrogatives. None of these makes explicit reference to the conditions. H has to do the work of making the necessary connections:

    13) Do you like living in a dark room?
    14) Have you run out of 'windowlene' then?
    15) Have I met the new chap in charge of window-cleaning?
    16) Do you think I like going round giving people orders all day?

And finally, there is the imperative for issuing commands:

    17) Clean those windows

An imperative – at least in English – is the least marked of all the ways of issuing command, since it singles out no one of the conditions for particular mention. It is the form for commands, which "might be thought of as the standard or explicit form of a command in which the nature of the act is signalled by the form the proposition takes" (Widdowson, *ibid.*: 20). The force of an imperative is direct, and it contains very little politeness, since H is not allowed to work things out for himself.

A word of caution here. When we say that the imperative is the 'standard' form of command we do not mean that it is the most normal or frequent. The point has often been made that since speech is situated in context, it rarely needs to be maximally explicit.

Widdowson's second point is that this approach to speech act specification in terms of sets of conditions can be extended to encompass whole *sets* of related speech acts. First, there is that family of speech acts which, in English at least, share with *command* the feature of conventional realisation by the imperative:

> *Instruction*: Report to General H.Q. at 0:600 hours.
> *Direction:* Turn left at the supermarket.
> *Advice*: See a doctor about that cough.
> *Appeal*: Be a blood donor.
> *Prayer*: Forgive us our trespasses.
> *Warning*: Watch out for falling rock.

Now, if we add a further six conditions to the four needed to specify the act of *command*, we are able to distinctively specify these six related acts also. The six extra conditions are:

> 5) S refers to an action necessary for the achievement of a particular goal.
> 6) S refers to an action necessary if H is to avoid unpleasant consequences.
> 7) S refers to an action which benefits H.
> 8) S refers to an action which benefits S.
> 9) S possesses knowledge which H lacks.
> 10) S cannot carry out the action which S refers to.

On page 127, we can specify each act according to conditions it obeys. Notice how *advice* differs from *appeal* for example: *advice* conforms to condition 7, *appeal* to 8, that is, the beneficiary will be hearer in the case of *advice* but speaker (or those he speaks for) in the event of *appeal*.

	1	2	3	4	5	6	7	8	9	10
Command:	/	/	/	/						
Instruction/Direction:		/		/	/			/		
Advice:		/		/			/	/		
Appeal:		/		/				/		/
Prayer:		/						/		/
Warning:		/				/			/	

Now it is likely that all cultures and their representative languages make use of roughly the same range of speech acts. Some may lack distinctions maintained by others: thus, an atheistic culture may lack the notion of, and therefore have no use for the speech act of *prayer*. We return again to a version of the Sapir-Whorf hypothesis of linguistic relativity.

A more practical application of this approach to the specification of speech acts by sets of conditions involves the assessment of the pragmatic equivalence of acts the labels for which are conventionally viewed as being translationally equivalent. Thus, German *Befehl* as a lexical item is equated with English *command*: but is it a pragmatic equivalent also? In other words, is *Befehl* specified by the same four conditions as specify *command*? Secondly, does it hold true for *Befehl* that it can be executed by a S in the same 17 ways as *command* is? Or does the former have a smaller (or larger) range of realisations? And, finally, of the 17 or so possible realisations of this act in German and English, which are preferred by speakers of each? These are the kinds of question that contrastivists must begin to answer. The reader, it is hoped, might feel encouraged to attempt to answer them with reference to the pair of languages that interest him contrastively.

5.6 Conversational Interaction

So far we have assumed that communication is unilateral, in the sense that there is one S, one H, and one direction for information to flow. But communication is just as often two-way and dyadic: this is what characterises conversation. Riley (1979) in fact characterises discourse as involving not one but two simultaneous act-sequences: the sequence of illocutionary acts and the sequence of 'interactive' acts. The former, as we have seen, is typically comprised of such acts as *inviting*, *accepting*, *thanking*, *apologising* etc., while the latter type of sequence is made up of such acts as *opening, closing, side-sequencing, nominating next speaker,* and so on: We turn to these later (p. 131). Riley emphasises that while these two activities on the part of conversation partners are simultaneous, they do not stand in a one-to-one relationship: that is, they are parallel without necessarily being in phase. Thus an exchange may consist of a sequence of six illocutionary acts but only four interactive ones.

Ability to sustain a conversation in the foreign-language is one of the main goals of L2 teaching. Therefore it would seem sensible to enquire what is involved in holding a conversation in *any* language, and then to consider the question of what differences there are between conversations in the L1 and in the L2: this is the contrastive dimension, of course.

One might expect the study of dyadic communication to be a much more complex undertaking than the analysis of single, unilateral speech acts. Fortunately, recent work in conversation analysis has succeeded in identifying two pervasive principles according to which conversations are organised. These are: Grice's Principle of Cooperation and Lakoff's Rules of Politeness. We shall briefly present these, then consider their implications for CA.

Grice (1975) proposed that conversations conform to four maxims. These are the maxims of:

1) *Quantity*: Be as informative as is required but no more than that – avoid redundancy.
2) *Quality*: Say only what you believe to be true or what you have evidence for.
3) *Relevance*: Be to the point.
4) *Manner*: Be clear and succinct: avoid obscurity.

The striking thing about these maxims, differentiating them from rules of grammar for example, is that speakers flout them much of the time: indeed, a conversation that observed them consistently would be a very dull affair! When hearers notice these infringements they continue to assume that the speaker is making infringements for a good reason: S intends H to notice faults and draw conclusions. These conclusions Grice refers to as *conversational implicatures*. We have met these already, under the slightly different guise of *indirect speech acts*. The difference is that there are very many ways of being indirect, but only four avenues for the uptake of an implicature. Kempson (1975: 143) gives two examples of implicature:

i) The police came in and everyone swallowed their cigarettes.
ii) You're the cream in my coffee.

i) is informative by flouting the maxim of *relevance*, while ii) is so by flouting the maxim of *quality*.

Now, to take i), why should people swallow cigarettes just because the police came? One reason for swallowing something is to conceal it, and one reason for concealing something (from the police) is that it is illegal. What kinds of cigarettes are illegal in our society? Those containing marijuana. The implicature contained in i), retrievable by a British or American hearer, is that the cigarettes did contain pot. Of ii) Kempson says: "In order to interpret ... [ii)] ... as not breaking the maxim of quality, the hearer must assume that the speaker is trying to convey something other than the literal meaning of the sentence. Since cream is something which is not only a natural accompaniment to coffee, but a perfect accompaniment, the speaker is perhaps saying that the hearer possesses similar attributes. He is therefore paying the hearer a great compliment" (Kempson, *ibid.*).

Notice that for H to interpret the implicature intended, he must share the cultural assumptions of S: in our example, each must agree that coffee is delicious with cream. In a coffee-less culture, the equivalent of ii) might well be 'You are the lemon in my tea'.

Lakoff (1973) reduces Grice's maxims to two: *Be clear* and *Be polite*. For her these two rules are sufficient to guarantee "Pragmatic Competence". The clarity requirement is accounted for by Grice's four maxims, and so Lakoff concentrates on the Rules of Politeness, of which there are three:[4]

    i) Don't impose on your H.
    ii) Give H options.
    iii) Make H feel good: be friendly.

The first rule has to do with minding one's own business, that is, not intruding on H's privacy or embarrassing H with the citation of 'unmentionables': for private affairs and unmentionables are 'non-free goods'. If one must intrude, one seeks permission while so doing:

    May I ask what this car cost you?
    What did you pay for it, *if I may ask*?

Asking permission is unnecessary and downright odd in the context of public knowledge, or 'free' goods:

    *May I ask how much 12 + 74 make?

English has two ways of referring to unmentionables without giving offence: either the technical term or a euphemism is used:

Prisoners *defecated* on the floor of the cell.

Prisoners *did their toilet* on the floor of the cell.

while Prisoners *shit* on the floor of the cell is taboo.

There is obvious contrastive analytical scope in this area. We need to know what different cultures consider unmentionables, since this is a relativistic notion. Then it would be useful to know whether other cultures have available means for referring to unmentionables other than technical terms and euphemisms; and in what circumstances these avoidance lexemes are used. Sex and defecation are the most obvious taboo areas that spring to mind. Money matters are another area. I have the impression that in middle strata of American and West German Society enquiry about the cost of some item, or enquiry about the state of H's finances is not considered as impolite as it is in the corresponding stratum of British society. It seems also that to mention in complimentary terms some possession of H will be interpreted by Arabs as a request for that object: and since nobody likes to give his trousers away, such mention must be construed as impolite.

The second rule, calling for the giving of options to H, is related to the rule of non-imposition, since if you let the other person make his own decisions he can't complain that you are imposing your will on him. Although Lakoff sees the essence of this rule as "let the addressee make his own decisions" I feel it is often applied more subtly: S leads H to *think* he is making his own decisions, if he is consoled by that thought. We have already seen this rule in operation when *commands* are issued. If a master says to his servant 'It's chilly in this room', the latter will act to remedy his employer's discomfort by closing a window or providing some form of heating. Yet, even though he is a servant, he is not made to feel servile; after all, the master has not directly or conventionally issued an order: he has, on the face of it, merely made a rather prosaic observation. The servant, for his part, has drawn conclusions which have the attractiveness, to him, of being *his* conclusions; and it is a fortunate bonus that these conclusions benefit the master. Here's one way to beat the 'them' v 'us' syndrome of British society.

The contrastive dimension of this rule for leaving the addressee's options open involves initially statement of which kinds of implicature different languages exploit. Some languages, like some individuals, will doubtless tend to be more direct than others. The reader might care to consider at this point whether in his L1 (if it is not English) commands can be issued by means of the indirect interrogatives which we described on p. 125.

The third rule of politeness involves establishing rapport, cameraderie, a sense of equality *or* respect, distance and a recognition of inequality between S and H. This rule has converse realisations according to the real relative statuses of S and H. If S is of higher or equal status to his addressee, the use of 'familiar' or 'solidary' forms of address on his part will put the addressee at ease. But if the speaker's status is lower than that of his addressee he must not use these familiar forms, lest he be seen as 'taking liberties': he will have to use forms which are deferential or polite.

The contrastive dimension of this rule will involve initially some documentation of what the linguistic markers of 'power and solidarity' (Brown and Gilman, 1960) are in L1 and L2. Some languages, like Thai and Japanese, reflect a very status-conscious social order, it seems, and offer several grades of deference marking. Most European languages except English have at least a two-term 2nd person pronoun system differentiating 'polite' and 'familiar' address. But, of course, the fact that English lacks this dualism in the pronouns does not mean that it never makes such distinctions: it does, by other means. After all, English has forms of address like *Your Grace*, *Your Honour*, *Your Excellency* which are clearly status-marking. At the other end of the scale English freely generates familiar forms of address such as *Billy*, *Teddy*, *mate*, *my friend*, *old boy* etc. What would be informative would be a CA of the process of familiarisation in two languages. When two people first meet, they are *Mr X*, *Herr X* and the pronouns polite. The *Mr* gives way to plain *Roberts*, and perhaps eventually there is a move to first-naming (*duzen/tutoyer*), and finally even nicknaming. This CA would study the stages involved, their linguistic marking, and the speed of familiarisation.

5.7 Components of Conversation

So far we have looked at two conversation tasks: making sense and maintaining rapport. We now turn to the management of conversations, by which we mean the ways in which they are opened, maintained, and eventually terminated. Conversations, like so many other things, have beginnings, middles, and ends.

OPENINGS: There is the joke about the English businessman and the beautiful girl who spent a year together shipwrecked on a desert island. On being rescued they were asked how they had got along together: they replied that they had not even spoken, since they had not been introduced! Most people, even without introductions, are able to 'break the ice' and strike up a conversation with people they meet by chance. According to Goffmann (1976: 266) we open (and close) conversation by means of a fixed repertoire of *ritual exchanges* which "are patently dependent on cultural definition and can be expected to vary quite markedly from society to society". If this is so, there would seem to be ample scope for CA in this area.

The suggestion that openings and closing are negotiated by 'ritual' exchanges is reminiscent of how some early sociologists of language identified a class of verbal formulae which they called *phatic communion*. This consists of "choices from a limited set of stereotyped phrases of greeting, parting, commonplace remarks about the weather, and small talk" (Laver, 1975: 218). From this description one gains the impression that *phatic communion* is something trivial, and perhaps not worth study; this is a misunderstanding, however: although trivia are the subject-matter of phatic communion, the function it performs is a vital one indeed. And what exactly constitutes trivia? The English are notorious for their ability to sustain conversations about the weather (which is what their phatic communions appear to be), perhaps because their weather is so fickle, but more probably because their climate is so temperate. If British weather were seen as a matter of life or death, it would not figure in phatic communion. One of the questions to be answered by CA, therefore, is: what serves as the subject-matter for phatic communion in different linguistic communities?

According to Laver, phatic communion is *indexical* and *deictic*. By 'indexical' is meant that its function is to transmit to H information about the speaker's personality and social status. Saying that phatic communion is 'deictic' means that it refers to "factors narrowly specific to the time and place of the utterance" (Laver, *ibid.*: 222): it can therefore involve either time or place deixis. Time reference is divisible into present, past and future, and so are phatic expressions with time deixis:

Nasty storm last night.	(Past)
What a beautiful time of year it is!	(Present)
D'you think we'll get rain tonight?	(Future)

Place-deixis is two-termed, according to whether the place referred to is 'here' or 'there'; but of course, 'there' will in any case be viewed from the perspective of 'here':

Nice hotel this.
What a boring play.
They served afternoon tea at the other hotel.

The two dimensions exploited in *indexical* communion are determined by whether one refers to oneself or to one's addressee: self-oriented or other-oriented indexical expressions are the two available. (Note the parallelism between these categories and those of A-events and B-events proposed by Labov: *cf.* p. 122). To summarise so far:

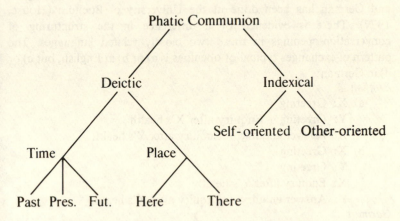

Here are some examples of indexical expressions:

> *Self-oriented*: Hard work, this. My feet are killing me.
> *Other-oriented*: That looks a bit tricky. Do you come here often?

As these examples show, the distinction between deictic and indexical expression is sometimes blurred. If I say *Hard work, this* I am of course referring to *my* work (self-oriented) but 'my' work is also *this* work (deictic). Other-oriented expressions tend, in English, to be interrogative, while self-oriented ones tend to be declarative: but this is no more than a tendency, and not a rule. Compare:

> Do you come here often?
> This is my first time ever.

Now, the selection of self-oriented or other-oriented expressions by the speaker seems to be determined by his view of his own status relative to that of his addressee. In fact:

> a) Inferior S uses self-oriented tokens to a superior H.
>   and
> b) Superior S uses other-oriented tokens to an inferior H.

Compare:

    a) I've been waiting here for the bus 15 minutes now.
    b) You were here before me.
       Have you been here long?

Some exploratory CA work on conversation openings in English and German has been done at the University of Bochum (House, 1977). There is evidence of a difference in the structuring of conversation-openings in these two closely related languages. The pattern of exchanges typical of openings is a) or b) in English, but c) or d) in German:

English

    a) X: Greeting
       Y: Greeting + Enquiry after X's health
       X: Answer enquiry + Enquiry after Y's health
    b) X: Greeting
       Y: Greeting
       X: Enquiry after Y's health
       Y: Answer enquiry + Enquiry after X's health

German

    c) X: Greeting
       Y: Greeting + Enquiry after X's health
       X: Answer Enquiry
    d) X: Greeting + Enquiry after Y's health
       Y: Greeting + Answer enquiry

The reader might like to do his own CA of the structures of these exchange-types in English and German. The major contrasts are: i) Opening is an exchange typically consisting of 3–4 turns in English and of 2–3 in German, and ii) Germans may dispense with the reciprocation of an enquiry about health: neither c) nor d) has this reciprocation. Why should this be so? It may be explained in terms of the German viewing this health-enquiry as nothing more than a formula, a bit of etiquette which need only be observed once by one speaker.

CLOSINGS: Phatic communion, as defined above, is used also to terminate conversations amicably. Of course one can intend to, or by accident dispense with the etiquette, whereupon one will be viewed as socially gauche or one's partner will be led to believe he has upset one. One thing is sure: conversations terminated without phatic communion will not be easy to resume on some future occasion. The function of polite closing is to ensure easy resumption. Laver (*ibid.*) identifies six strategies employed in closings:

1) Giving one's reasons for terminating the encounter. These, if indexical, may be either self-oriented or other-oriented.

> Well, I'll really have to get on my way.
> Now, I mustn't keep you any longer.

Note that the second expression here invokes quite clearly Lakoff's maxim of non-imposition.

2) Assess the quality of the encounter. Presumably one can make a favourable or a critical assessment:

> It's been nice talking to you.
> Well, I don't think all this has got us far.

3) Express concern for the other person's welfare when you will no longer be with him:

> Take care now.
> Mind how you go.

4) Reference to future resumption of encounter. Some languages have fixed forms of *farewell* that refer to future encounters: *auf Wiedersehen, au revoir, do svidaniya* etc. These are, however, not so much signals that one wishes to terminate, but symbols that termination has been agreed and even accomplished. English is more literal in this respect, using such forms as *See you next week then* or *Can we fix a date for next time*? and people may flick through their diaries to reinforce the signal.

5) Reference to a mutual acquaintance, where that acquaintance is closer to H than to S: *i.e.* the expression is other-oriented. Thus one says such things as:

> Give my regards to Mary. (H's wife)
> Say hello to the kids.

These correspond to the German *Schönen Gruss zu Hause*, but I have no knowledge of whether this device is used in non-European cultures.

6) Increased use of terms of direct address: this has the effect of reassuring one's addressee, lest he should interpret one's desire to close the conversation as a rejection. In a sense, it is compensatory. It also tells him that, although business is necessarily impersonal, one has not lost sight of him on a personal level.

These six devices were identified by Laver in English speech communities. The question must arise as to their universality: specifically, do some societies make use of other devices for closing? A second question is that of their relative frequencies of use in different colingual communities. And finally, since there is no suggestion that these six devices are mutually exclusive, one would like to know in what combinations they typically occur. These are the kinds of questions which many of my readers may well be in a position to provide answers to.

5.7.1 *Maintaining Conversations*

Conversations can fail in two basic ways. The participants can realise that they are not achieving their communicative goals, and so they abandon the conversation. Or one of the participants can cease to contribute, in which case either a monologue results or there is complete abandonment. To have 'communicative competence' is to be able to activate strategies for avoiding such failures, and while such breakdown may even occur among native speakers, it is more likely to occur when one of the conversationalists is a learner. Let us consider these two types of failure:

5.7.1.1 FAILURE TO ACHIEVE COMMUNICATIVE GOALS

An Englishman visiting a German restaurant (perhaps the busy, impolite Bahnhofsgaststätte), or a German an English one will want to place an order. Two ways available to the German for performing this speech act are exemplified in:

a) Herr Ober, wir hätten gern zwei Bier bitte.
b) Bringen Sie uns zwei Bier bitte.

These realisations of *order* are declarative and imperative respectively. Both would be unlikely in this setting in English:

? Waiter, we'd like two beers please.
? Bring us two beers please.

In English an interrogative would be used:

Could we have two beers please?
Would you bring us two beers please?

The English *order* is less direct than the German, and, since it leaves open the waiter's options, is more 'polite'. To transfer the German realisations to an English setting, and vice-versa, would lead to pragmatic infelicity. Communication would fail, since the German would be ignored by the English waiter to chastise his arrogance, while the German waiter would ignore the English customer because the latter's signals cannot compete with those of the Germans present.

That L1 discourse conventions are transferred to L2 performance, often leading to breakdown in communication, now seems to be beyond question. Kasper (1977) analysed the pragmatic errors committed in 48 recordings of face-to-face dialogues between a German first-year student of English and an English native. One recurrent deficit was the speaker failing to perform the speech act intended. In the following exchange, for example, X is a German student in English whose landlady Y has given her sandwiches for a journey:

> Y: I hope it'll be enough.
> X: Yes, of course it will be enough.

X's utterance is no doubt intended to reassure Y and at the same time express gratitude. Instead of that, it rings dismissive, and even censorious, probably being heard by Y as: 'Anybody can see there's plenty there, you old fool!' X should have said something like: 'Yes, that'll be just fine, thank you'.

5.7.1.2 ABANDONMENT OF CONVERSATION

The essence of conversation, at least in Anglo-Saxon culture, is that "at least and not more than one party talks at a time". The person talking is said to have the TURN, and conversations are organised round the alternation of turns. These are organised into MOVES, defined by Goffmann (1976: 272) as "any full stretch of talk or its substitutes which has a distinctive unitary bearing on some set or other of the circumstances in which participants find themselves". This definition is far from lucid, but the important thing is that a MOVE is a talk-task that S and H are co-operating over, having reached some tacit agreement on the goal of their talk. Talk is goal-directed work. MOVES are organised into EXCHANGES, and these into CONVERSATIONS; so we have the following scale of units of discourse:

Conversation

↑

Exchange

↑

Move

↑

Turn

Now, since each participant contributes his turn to a move, moves consist of pairs of turns, which are known as *adjacency pairs*. The first part of each pair is said to have 'transition-relevance' to the second, and it is participants' skill in recognising first-parts to respond to, and having second-parts to respond with, that keeps conversations moving. Obvious adjacency-pairs are: Question + Answer, Statement + Agreement, and so on.

Scope for CA is provided in the form of the types of adjacency-pairing which different languages (or cultures) show preference for. Earlier (*cf.* p. 130) we touched upon this area in the context of pragmatics: the English, compared with the Arab response, in action, to admiration. Adjacency pairing has to do with talk-response rather than with response-in-action. Consider, as an example, what a colingual community sees as a second-part to the first-part compliment. Pomerantz (1978) points out that Americans conventionally respond to a compliment in a fixed number of ways. One simple way is:

A Compliment: That's a beautiful job
B Thanks: Thanks

But a widespread strategy in that culture is to invoke machinery to demonstrate one's modesty: "Recipients of praise are subject to self-praise avoidance or modesty constraints" (Pomerantz, *ibid.*: 96). There are three ways of doing this:

a) *Scaled-down agreement*

A: I've been given a scholarship to Oxford.
B: That's absolutely bloomin' fantastic!
A: It's quite pleasing.

A: My, you've lost a hell of a lot of weight.
B: Just an ounce or two.

b) *Reassignment of merit to a third party*

A: You're the best pastry-cook in town, Vera.
B: It's that new Kenwood mixer.

c) *Return the compliment: tit for tat*

A: That was a fantastic party.
B: You were the life and soul of it.

Once again, we have some data from English, but to my knowledge little or none from other languages. The non-English reader may be inspired to provide this from observation of responses to compliments, and other kinds of adjacency-pairings in his language.

One way, therefore, in which conversation is kept moving is by participants' continually making valid contributions, that is, contributions seen as valid by the culture involved. In addition, there are certain conventions (of a linguistic type) which Edmundson (1976), following Strevens (1972), calls *gambits*, which are "used to lubricate discourse already initiated". He labels six of these as:

The Pick-Up; The Cajoler; The Uptaker; The Downtoner; The Undercover; and The Aside. Let us consider two of these:

The Pick-Up occurs when H repeats part of what has been said to him, as:

> X: I wonder whether you've finished servicing my Ford Escort.
> Y: Ford Escort, Sir: Well, let's just see.

This gambit serves a number of functions: first, it is a time-gaining device, used by someone short of a ready answer. If he is a clerk, he can be looking up the information he needs in a timetable or similar while uttering his pick-up. It is used not only to save one's own face[4], but at the same time to show respect: the question must not be ignored, even if I have no ready answer. My pseudo-contribution does at least signal that I don't find his question outlandish — in fact, it can look as if I was expecting this question. For this reason Edmundson refers to the Pick-Up as a *theme — rheme* device.

The Downtoner is the classic case of Lakoff's first maxim of politeness: *don't impose*. As the name suggests, its force is to attenuate the force of the speech act it happens to accompany, so as to make it less blunt and abrasive, *i.e.* more acceptable to the hearer. It may, in English, either precede or follow the central speech act, but normally precedes:

> {I think I'm right in saying that X = Y.
> {Correct me if I'm mistaken but X = Y.

> {X = Y unless I'm mistaken.
> {X = Y or I'm imagining things.

The frequency with which The Downtoner is used in British English might in part explain the stereotype of the Englishman as being diplomatic, tactful, even polite. The question of interest to the contrastivist is whether the learner of English employs a related gambit in his L1 which might transfer happily to English. And, more generally, does the learner's L1 make use of these six major gambits as identified for English, and, if not, which does he lack and which does he use that would not be 'happy' in an English discourse?

5.8 Scope for Research

It must be clear to the reader that macrolinguistic CA is a new field of enquiry, awaiting exploration. It is certainly true that there is little published data on textual and discourse CA. And it is here where the reader who knows two languages well – and this I expect of my reader – has a contribution to make. Informal observation of language behaviour in these two domains would in many cases lead to supervised research and its publication and dissemination. And yet, there is a sense in which all of this is not really *new*, but has rather been neglected. Sapir and Whorf, and Lado – who thought in terms of linguistics across cultures – surely pointed in this direction. Only now are we beginning to see that they were to be taken literally.

NOTES

1 i) Today everything happens so quickly. ii) There's the story about the Berliner getting annoyed with a certain American who boasts that things get built faster over there than they do over here. Well, this American happens to point to a tower block and asks when it was built, to which the Berliner, apparently surprised, answers iii) "Now, come off it: that building wasn't there yesterday!"
2 "Cohesion, then, is the overt relationship between propositions expressed through sentences" (H. G. Widdowson, 1978: 28).
3 Henceforth we shall abbreviate: S = speaker/writer; H = hearer/reader.
4 Brown & Levinson (1978) explain politeness phenomena in terms of strategies designed to avoid acts which would threaten the 'face' of one's conversational partner: "it will be to the mutual interest of two [persons] to maintain each other's face" (ibid: 65). Note that B. & L. rebut, as anthropologists, what they call "the old-fashioned doctrine of cultural relativity in the field of interaction" (ibid: 61). They set out to demonstrate that "superficial diversities can emerge from underlying universal principles" (ibid). Their concern with the deep and surface structure dichotomy is reminiscent of the linguists': we return to it in the context of CA in Chapter 7.1. Compare also B. & L. with Goffmann, quoted on p. 132.

6

Pedagogical Exploitation
of
Contrastive Analysis

6.1 Applied CA

In the previous chapter we suggested some ways of executing CAs. Here we shall ask what we are to do with the finished product: has it any practical use? To answer this question I shall need to make a number of distinctions, the first of which involves the notion of 'pedagogical exploitation'.

Wilkins (1972: 217 ff.) considers in general the relevance of linguistics for language teaching, raising the whole question of what is meant by 'applied linguistics'. He suggests that while most teachers look for direct *applications* of linguistics, that is, "... cases where notions and information drawn from linguistics act directly upon the process of language teaching", it must be borne in mind that besides these, linguistics provides *insights* and carries *implications* for teaching. These are less direct: by 'insights' Wilkins means "linguistic notions that increase one's understanding of the notion of language and consequently of the nature of language learning", while 'implications' are guidelines for materials production based on general observations of how language is learned. While Wilkins' point is a valid one, it has its dangers, increasingly so in these days when society clamours for demonstrations of 'relevance' from its educational system. Ambitious teachers of foreign languages enrol in applied linguistics courses expecting to be helped as teachers by the experience. All too often they discover that linguistics seems to have little to offer for the solution of their practical problems. Wilkins' statement that linguistics may have only indirect, intangible or long-term relevance can all too easily be used by academics to dodge the issue and to parry the teacher's anxious enquiries. My view is that unless those who offer MA courses in applied linguistics are prepared to live up to expectations and make committal statements about the *applications* of their discipline, they should drop their pretence, or face a Consumer Council! In this chapter I shall attempt to suggest some direct applications of CA, even at the risk of being controversial.

141

It has been suggested that there are two kinds of CA: theoretical and applied. They are diagrammed in Figs. a) and b) below. As Fisiak et al. (1978: 10) put it, theoretical CAs "do not investigate how a given category present in language A is represented in language B. Instead they look for the realisation of a universal category X in both A and B". Applied CAs on the other hand, "are preoccupied with the problem of how a universal category X, realised in language A as y, is rendered in language B". This means that applied CAs are *unidirectional* (*cf.* p. 171) whereas theoretical CAs are static, since they do not need to reflect any directionality of learning:

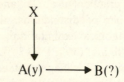

Fig. a): Theoretical CAs   *Fig. b): Applied CAs*

The question must arise as to whether applied CAs can be executed independently of theoretical ones, or whether the former are best derived from the latter: can the 'applied linguist' dispense with theoretical CAs and save his effort? One advantage of exploiting the theoretical CA is that it contains information about *both* directionalities of learning, and so offers a measure of economy: it is precisely because the University of Chicago CA Series (ed. Ferguson) are applied that they contain information only on the English L1 learner's problems with Spanish, German and Italian, but no information on the obverse directionality. A second advantage of using a theoretical CA as a basis is that it makes constant or recurrent reference to the universal *tertium comparationis* X: a direct applied CA is liable to lose sight of the contact between X and (?) – the L2 realisation – since it is mediated by y. Nevertheless, it must be admitted that this question of whether applied CAs should be based upon or independent of a theoretical CA is undecided. My own view is that an applied CA executed independently is liable to lose its objectivity; that is, its predictions will tend to be based on teachers' experience of learners' difficulties rather than derived from linguistic analysis: this is an accusation that has been levelled at the English–Spanish CA of

Stockwell et al. Applied CAs, therefore, are interpretations (of theoretical CAs) rather than independent executions.

The danger of advocating this approach is that contrastivists will be tempted to concentrate on, and to proceed no farther than, the execution of theoretical CAs. The question of their pedagogical exploitation then gets shelved. This has happened, and explains why so little is known about applied CA. Theoretically inclined contrastivists leave the applied contrastivist with a lot of unexploited potential, potential which few methodologists are able to exploit on account of the communication gap (in the form of theoretical apparatus) which separates the two. This is true of the PAKS German–English CA as well as of the Poznan Polish–English CA. The Zagreb Serbo-Croatian–English CA alone has attempted to bridge the gap and produce pedagogical materials. Another disadvantage of theoretical CAs is that they have tended to be done by target-language linguists with little interest in the learner's L1 (although they are usually native speakers of the L1). The inevitable consequence of this L2 bias is of course that the descriptive neutrality between L1 and L2 which is the proclaimed virtue of the theoretical CA is abandoned. One CA Project director (Filipović, 1975) has recently become acutely aware of this kind of bias, and of the need to undertake an English-to-Serbo-Croatian CA to compensate for the directional bias that arose in his earlier Serbo-Croatian-to-English CA.

The result of the kinds of inadequacies I have described is that the pedagogical exploitation of CA has tended to be in the form of Wilkins' (*op. cit.*) 'insights' and 'implications' and has stopped short of classroom *application*. It has been in the form of 'background' reading for teachers rather than pedagogic materials for learners. This is all that the University of Chicago CA Series offers. The Poznan Project has been slightly more explicit, in issuing its *Introductory English-Polish Contrastive Grammar* (Fisiak et al.: 1978) which is a theoretical CA and not a pedagogical grammar. As such it is "entirely neutral towards any type of application" (*ibid.*: 7) and "designed primarily to meet the needs of students of English at Polish universities" (*ibid.*: 5). In short, it is a compendium of 'insights'.

It is in no way surprising that few in recent years have ventured to suggest pedagogical applications of CA. Gone is that confidence with which Fries (1945: 9) could write: "The most efficient materials are those based on a scientific description of the language to be learned, carefully compared with a parallel description of the native language of the learner." In Chapter 7 we shall be explaining the 'issues of contention' surrounding CA which have sapped its confidence, and which explain why the proponents of applied CA have been forced on to the defensive, trying either to vindicate CA (James, 1971) or to modify the claims that are made on its behalf (Marton, 1974).

The critics of CA have in particular been encouraged by the putative demise of Behaviourism in learning psychology and with it the Theory of Transfer upon which classical CA is predicated. As we saw in Chapter 2, the emergence of Cognitive psychology has been seen as having removed the very foundations of CA, so Interference has been dubbed a vacuous and outdated concept, and the Ignorance Hypothesis proposed as a stronger alternative: "the cure for interference is simply the cure for ignorance: learning" (Newmark, 1970: 225). There have since been indications, however, that Behaviourist and Cognitivist accounts of learning may not be irreconcilable. Hok (1972) invoked Koestler's (1964) notion of *bisociation* as a link: "all learning – whether it be sensori, motor or cognitive – is at some stage habit learning in the sense that once performed it can more easily be performed again . . .. Thus, ready-made at our disposal for *cognitive* teaching-learning is subject matter organised in such a way that the elements to be learned and the system of their relationships are presented as such in the format we receive from the descriptive-contrastive linguists" (Hok, *ibid.*: 266). More recently, in his account of 'psychologically respectable' applied linguistics (which for him means consonant with cognitivism) Sharwood Smith (1978) cites as ". . . one of the two basic principles that are broadly accepted by cognitivists of whatever persuasion . . . that *new* knowledge is to a greater or lesser degree acquired via *old* knowledge". Corder, whose reservations concerning CA we have mentioned elsewhere in this book, seems now to be prepared to accommodate the notion of L2 learners having recourse to their L1. In his recent paper (Corder,1978a) he proposes as a weak version of his hypothesis of the built-in syllabus "that the developmental sequence [of L2 acquisition] is conditioned by the nature of the mother tongue". Yet he still rejects the notion of L1-interference, claiming that "'failure to facilitate' is not equivalent to 'interfere' or 'inhibit'". Instead of the usual opposition between positive transfer (facilitation) and negative transfer (interference) he prefers a dichotomy between facilitation on the one hand and *zero effect* of L1 on the other: "It is perfectly logical to propose that the nature of the L1 may make passage along the built-in syllabus faster when it bears a similarity to the L2, but simply has no effect when it is different" (Corder, *ibid.*). Recall that Osgood's

Paradigm C ($S_1 - R_1$: $S_2 - R_2$: p. 15) also allows for the possibility of *zero transfer*, but under different conditions than those Corder has in mind. One must also concede that with experience of error-making learners come to evade negative transfer, but again Corder seems not to find it necessary to hypostacise such a feedback mechanism. Kellerman (1977) does lend support to Corder, in demonstrating that learners have aprioristic intuitions about what L1 lexical items are likely to be transferable or not to L2 usage. But it is still difficult to see why only positive transfer should be amenable to Behaviourist explanation, and zero transfer has to be accommodated by Cognitive psychology: Corder claims this is so in saying that where L1 and L2 forms are different the learner has to figure out the nature of the L2 rules "with his own unaided cognitive capacities". Of course he must, ultimately, if he is to learn the L2 rules, but these are not grounds for denying that the learner's *initial* tendency is to transfer from L1.

6.2 Traditional Applications of CA

We shall mention briefly what have traditionally been viewed as *the* pedagogical applications of CA. There are three of these, all prepedagogical, by which I mean that they do not influence classroom procedures. The reader should bear in mind that these are *claims* made for CA, claims which in certain quarters have been veiled in scepticism. CA has applications in *predicting* and *diagnosing* a proportion of the L2 errors committed by learners with a common L1, and in the design of *testing instruments* for such learners.

6.2.1 *Prediction*

In his *Preface*, Lado (1957) states that: "The plan of the book rests on the assumption that we can predict and describe the patterns [of L2] that will cause difficulty in learning and those that will not cause difficulty". Oller (1971: 79) again speaks of CA as ". . . a device for predicting points of difficulty and some of the errors that learners will make". There seems then to be three things that a CA can predict: it can predict – in the sense of 'pre-identify' – what aspects will *cause problems*; or it can predict *difficulty*; or it can predict *errors*. I would suggest a fourth possibility: of CA predicting the *tenacity* of certain errors, that is, their strong resistance to extinction through time and teaching.

I would like to make a distinction at this point concerning the 'prediction of error'. In fact this phrase is ambiguous: it can mean either prediction *that* there will be error or prediction of the *form* of that error. Obviously, to claim that CAs have predictive capacity of the second kind would, given the present 'state of the art', be quite presumptuous. So, rather than risk making wrong predictions about the form of errors, contrastivists have more cautiously made predictions of an either/or type: learners with a certain L1 learning this L2 will produce either x or y types of errors. Wilkins (1968) refers to a clear case of such "unpredictable alternation between two potential substitutions" namely, French speakers' propensity to use *either* French /s/, /z/ *or* /t/, /d/ for L2 English /θ/, /ð/. So much, then, for *what* CAs predict, and for the confidence with which such predictions are made.

There are, of course, purely quantitative limitations on the numbers of learner errors that CAs can predict, limitations stemming from the fact that not all errors are the result of L1 interference, *i.e.* interlingual errors. Other major sources of errors have been recognised (Selinker, 1972; Richards, 1974) which are of a 'non-contrastive' origin. These include: the effects of target-language asymmetries (intralingual errors); transfer of training; strategies of L2 learning; and L2 communication strategies. Several attempts have been made to determine the proportion of interlingual errors among all errors. Tran-Thi-Chau (1975) found 51% to be interlingual (L1-induced) and 29% intralingual, strikingly confirming Richards (1971) who suggested 53% interlingual and 31% intralingual. Mukattash (1977: 5) found 23% of the syntactic errors in English of his Jordanian students to be cases of L1 (Arabic) interference. Grauberg (1971: 261) found that for his advanced L1 English learners of German "interference from English . . . can be observed in 71 errors out of 193", *i.e.* in 36% of cases. H. V. George estimated that about a third of errors are traceable to the L1 (George, 1972). It seems then that between a third and half of learner errors may be caused by the L1:L2 misfit. Given that a CA predicts "behavior that is likely to occur with greater than random frequency" (Lado, 1968: 125) about 60% of the third to half of all errors, it will not try or claim to predict the other 70% to 80%. One must be careful not to exaggerate the claims made on behalf of CA.

There are further arguments surrounding the gross predictive capacity of CAs, to which we shall return in Chapter 7. There is a further aspect of their predictive capacity that is rather less assured, but which is of great pedagogical relevance: this is their alleged capacity to predict a *scale of incremental difficulty*. If this scale can be validated, it will have powerful implications for pedagogic Grading and for Evaluation (Testing).

6.2.2   Scales of Difficulty

The most well-known hierarchy of FL learning difficulty is that proposed by Stockwell & Bowen (1965) for phonology, and again, with certain elaborations by Stockwell, Bowen & Martin (1965) Attempts to design scales for the level of vocabulary are those of Higa (1966) and Rodgers (1969). The Stockwell et al. scales are based on the notions of positive and negative transfer potential, and the conditions for such transfers are assumed to be statable in terms of the relations holding between matched rules of L1 and L2 (*cf.* p. 172). There are three possible interlingual rule relationships:

a) L1 has a rule and L2 an equivalent one.
b) L1 has a rule but L2 has no equivalent.
c) L2 has a rule but L1 has no equivalent.

The second step is to identify the types of *choices* that either language makes available, and relating these choices. There are three types of choice: optional, obligatory and zero (∅). An optional phonological choice "refers to the possible selection among pho-nemes": one is free, in English and German, to choose either /s/ or /ʃ/, etc. in word-initial position, to say (English) *show/so*, (German) *Schau/Sau*. Russian allows the 'free' choice of either *on budit pisat'* or *on napishet* to express future reference. An obligatory phonological choice involves little freedom, since phonetic context determines which of a set of allophones is required to represent a freely selected phoneme: thus /ɫ/ and /l/ are optional choices in Russian while [ɫ] and [l] as realisations of /l/ are each obligatory choices in English. In French, the choice of auxiliary (*avoir/être*) for Perfect Tense form is obligatory, since determined by the lexical verb involved. Zero choice reflects the absence of a category in one of the languages while it is available in the other: for example, English is unlike Spanish in lacking 'erre' and 'jota' and unlike Arabic in lacking pharyngeals. Russian has no grammatical category such as the English articles.

These different availabilities of choice in L1 and L2 allow eight kinds of relationship between the two languages: the result is an eight-point · hierarchy of difficulty, which is simplified to a scale of three orders of difficulty by coalescing 123(I), 456(II) and 78(III):

| | Order of Difficulty | Comparison of Choice Type | |
		L1	L2
Most ↑	I 1	Ø	Ob
	2	Ø	Op
	3	Op	Ob
	II 4	Ob	Op
	5	Ob	Ø
	6	Op	Ø
	III 7	Op	Op
Least ↓	8	Ob	Ob

The details of this scale are not uncontroversial, as its authors were the first to admit. Tran-Thi-Chau (*op. cit.*: 130–134) points to several shortcomings: *e.g.* placing verb form (concord) on the same level of difficulty as the Perfective/Imperfective contrast in Spanish when the former "requires only memorisation" whereas the latter calls for knowledge of the contextual determinants of either category. Space forbids further assessment of the proposed hierarchy. It is sufficient, I think, to applaud the author's attempt to set up such a scale on the basis of L1 and L2 rule relatedness. The scale is, of course, subject to empirical validation, though when one attempts this a whole array of other complicating factors – motivation, aptitude, teaching or learning style, etc. – enters the picture.

6.2.3 *Diagnosis of Error*

A good teacher cannot indulge in the luxury of the 'ours not to reason why' attitude. An important ingredient of the teacher's role as monitor and assessor of the learner's performance is to know *why* certain errors are committed. It is on the basis of such diagnostic knowledge that the teacher organises feedback to the learner and remedial work. Even the learner should know why he has committed errors if he is to self-monitor and avoid these same errors in the future.

Wardhaugh (1970) suggested that the CA hypothesis is only tenable in its 'weak' or diagnostic function, and not tenable as a predictor of error: "The weak version requires of the linguist only that he use the best linguistic knowledge available to him in order to account for observed difficulties in second language learning" (Wardhaugh, *op. cit.*: 126) and "reference is made to the two systems [L1 and L2] only in order to explain actually observed interference phenomena" (*ibid.*: 127). Since there are very few published CAs of very few language-pairs to refer to, it will normally be necessary to do such on-the-spot *ad-hoc* mini CAs anyway. The purpose of doing them is to see if a particular attested error is explicable in terms of L1 interference. If no L1 structure can be found that the structure of the errors seems to be a reflection of, then we have to start the long job of finding some cause other than L1 transfer. One is certainly given an illuminated short-cut when the L1 suggests the obvious source of the error. For example, in a composition written by a Singaporean learner of English describing a naughty pupil, I found the passage: "My class has naughty boy name call Seng Haut . . .. He everyday in class likes scold people bad words and fighting". A non-contrastive diagnosis of these underlined errors turns out to be difficult, longwinded, and not plausible. A diagnosis in terms of the learner's L1 (Chinese) is simple and plausible: *name call = [mɪŋt'iau], and *scold people bad words and fighting = [ma:'rantʃɔ:wa]. Simple explanations are always the best.

6.2.4 Testing

One of the requirements of a good language test is that it should have *validity*: it should be a true measure of the student's command of the language he has been taught. The most valid test therefore would be one that was comprehensive, *i.e.* it would test *everything* that has been taught. For obvious reasons such a test would be impracticable to administer to students after their first week or two of instruction. Therefore we must attempt to achieve test validity by testing a representative sample of the student's repertoire. This is where CA has a part to play, and Lado (1961) based his theory of testing to a considerable extent on CA. Testing experts since Lado have endorsed his approach: "If a test is constructed for a single group of students with identical language background and identical exposure to the target language then contrastive analysis is essential" (Davies, 1968: 12).

CA will have two roles to play in testing. First, since sampling is required, it will carry suggestions about *what* to test, and to what degree to test different L2 items. If items isomorphic in L1 and L2 are assumed to be easy for the learner, they can be bypassed in the test. It will be more informative for the tester to test only the learning problems predicted by the CA. As for the *degree* to which to test, it depends on the level of the learner, but a test for the intermediate student that is CA-based should contain more items of, say, difficulty levels 4, 5 and 6 on the Stockwell & Bowen Scale (*q.v.*) than items of difficulty levels 1 and 2.

Turning to the matter of *how* to test, if a multiple-choice type of objective test is being constructed, a CA of L1 and L2 will suggest the types of distractors to use: as Harris says: "The most effective distractors in a test item will be those which evoke first-language responses from those subjects who have not fully mastered the very different patterns of the target language" (Harris, 1968: 39). For example, since Polish has no modal corresponding to English *needn't*, expressing 'Lack of Compulsion' (Fisiak et al., *op. cit.*: 129) but uses the modal *musieć* in such cases, Poles will tend to say the erroneous:

> *You mustn't be back by 10 o'clock
>   for the intended
> You needn't be back by 10 o'clock
>   corresponding to Polish
> Nie musisz być z powrotem przed dziesiątą.

Therefore a discrete-point test of the English modals for Polish learners ought to contain at least one distractor evoking *You mustn't* . . .. It is less obvious how CA predictions might inform the writer of the 'integrative' tests that are in vogue today: cloze tests and noise tests for example (*cf.* Stig Johansson, 1975); but it is not inconceivable that a cloze test could be designed in which only those elements of the L2 test are deleted which are predictably difficult for learners of a given L1 to operate: for instance, deleting the articles in an English test for learners whose L1 is Russian or Polish (*cf.* Oller and Redding, 1971).

It has been suggested (Davies, *op. cit.*: 13; Harris, *op. cit.*: 39) that although CA predictions may in theory be applicable to test construction "practical considerations generally prevent much reliance on contrastive analysis" (Harris). These practical considerations centre on the fact that tests must be produced for world-wide use, by students with a heterogeneity of L1s. This, Davies points out, is why even Lado was forced to abandon his attachment to CA in testing in devising his own proficiency tests: "the task of preparing separate language tests for all language backgrounds is so enormous that we may never hope to have such tests except for a limited few languages" (Lado, 1950). These reservations are not wholly justified, for a number of reasons. First, it is questionable that FL tests should be and need to be 'universal': why should a foreign student from a developing country lacking educational resources be evaluated by the same instrument as one from a prosperous, technologically advanced country? Should learners of English as a *Foreign* Language be expected to reach the same proficiency levels as learners of English as a *Second* Language?

Should learners for whom the L2 is highly exotic (difficult) be expected to reach the same level as learners whose L1 is cognate with English? I think not. Secondly, English, as an international auxiliary language, is a special case: arguments true for the testing of English do not apply to the testing of other languages. Thirdly, CA does not require the *whole* test to be based on its findings, but perhaps between a quarter and a third of the items should be contrastively motivated: we saw in the previous section that CA does not even aspire to account for *all* errors. And fourthly, there is a possible compromise somewhere between a 'universal' test and a multitude of L1-oriented tests: tests devised on the basis of typological groups sharing contrastivity with English: promising information along this dimension is emanating from current work on Multiple Contact Analysis (F. A. Johansson, 1973). It should not exceed the capacities of modern technology to create a universal bank of test items, each marked for specific utility in testing learners with a given language or language-family background, which can be assembled into instruments that do justice to the CA hypothesis.

6.3 Course Design

Having considered some traditional pedagogical applications of CA, we shall now proceed to substantiate our suggestions. In this section we shall be concerned with the two pedagogical principles of Selection (WHAT to teach) and Grading (WHEN to teach) of target-language items. These, to use Corder's (1974) industrial analogy, are aspects of *Product Design*. In 6.4 we shall consider the CA implications for Method, that is HOW to teach: for Corder this phase is that of *Process Design*.

6.3.1 *Selection*

A CA specifies those features of L2 which are different from the corresponding features of the L1, and, by implication, those which are identical. Our assumption is that the L1:L2 identities will not have to be learned by the L2 learner, since he knows them already by virtue of his L1 knowledge. Thus, though I have never attempted to learn Icelandic, some aspects of this language are nevertheless known to me in advance: on the one hand, I 'know' those features of Icelandic that are universal, and those that are shared by it and my native language. This is not an absurd claim, certainly no less plausible than Chomsky's (1965: 51) claim that ". . . the procedures and mechanisms for the acquisition of knowledge [and language] constitute an innate property of the mind".

The learner must be allowed, indeed encouraged, to transfer this 'suitable' L1 knowledge to L2 usage. This means that those L2 structures that match L1 structures must constitute part of the materials, since materials do not only teach what is 'new' and unknown, but provide confirmation of interlingual identities. This point has been missed by the opponents of CA, of whom the following is representative: "it seems unsound to say that the linguistic content of a foreign-language course should be based on the apparent *differences* between the learner's native language and the language to be learned, as if the apparent identities and similarities could be ignored" (Lee, 1972: 61). Certainly the learner needs to be given opportunities to discover for himself that transfer from L1 in cases of isomorphism will result in acceptable L2 utterances. There is a further, non-contrastive, reason why we must not select *by exclusion*: this is that the terms in any linguistic SYSTEM (*cf.* Chapter 3) are mutually defining and their values co-determined: in Saussure's words, a language is "un système où tout se tient". In English, it is impossible to fully grasp the value of *mustn't*, without seeing in what relation it stands to *needn't*, and so the Polish learner must be given access to the former if he is to grasp the latter. We therefore reject the notion of selection in the sense of inclusion/exclusion, and prefer to use the term *Intensity Selection*. By this we mean that while the learner is exposed to *all* parts of the L2, he must be given opportunities to confirm his positive transfers on the one hand and to learn what he does not know on the other. If the latter are denied him he will negatively transfer. This suggests that we recognise two basic types of teaching materials (Corder (1973: 337) identifies four types, but does not cater for the contrastive dimension): those for confirming, and those for learning. Confirming will obviously be less time-consuming than learning: hence our term Intensity Selection. The obvious candidate for L1:L2 isomorphic constructions is the now much-maligned translation exercise: "The strongest charge yet against the use of translation . . . is the claim that it enforces the expectation of isomorphism . . . in the students' minds" (Kirstein, 1972: 74) . Transfer is exactly what we want in those cases where it will be positive, or facilitative. For contrasting structures we need a different kind of exercise, one which will suppress L1 transfer: audiolingual structure drills would seem to be suitable here, insofar as they develop automatisation without mediation by the L1.

6.3.2 *Grading*

The classical CA statement pertinent to grading is: "the student who comes in contact with a foreign language will find some features of it quite easy and others extremely difficult. Those elements that are similar to his native language will be simple for him and those elements that are different will be difficult" (Lado, 1957: 2). We see here an assumption that learning difficulty is a function of interlingual distance, an assumption that has been questioned (*cf.* Chapter 7). Since it is a universal principle of education that learning should proceed from the simple to the difficult, it seems to follow that isomorphic L2 elements should be taught first. There are a number of objections that can immediately be raised, however. The first is the one we mentioned in the previous section concerning the *integrity* of linguistic systems: if we postpone just one term of a system in the syllabus, the student's grasp of the terms he has learnt must be not only partial, but distorted. Yet is is undeniable that learning takes time, and so must be linearly organised: one must be prepared to compromise and to produce pedagogic grammars that distort as little as possible. Additional optimism about necessary distortion comes in the form of evidence, from natural (*i.e.* non-classroom) L1 and L2 acquisition processes, that learners are capable of revising, with continued exposure, their hypotheses about the target language.

A second objection to Grading by contrastivity is that as a criterion it may clash with other equally important criteria: for example, since the English articles are contrastively difficult for Slavonic L1 learners, they should be delayed; but they have such high frequency and utility (functional load) that they must be taught early. But this clash of Grading criteria is in no way peculiar to the contrastive dimension: it usually happens that the noncontrastive criteria themselves are contradictory. Once again, informed compromise is the only solution – find the optimum denominator.

A third objection to following the precept of 'easiest first' is a psychological one: extended early experience of positive transfer (+T) sets up expectations of continuing +T. So the learner will inevitably be disappointed when he comes to learn contrasting L2 structures: ". . . interference and confusion resulting from the pupil's native language habits can . . . be aggravated by using parallel constructions first" (Politzer, 1968). To test this hypothesis, Politzer conducted a number of experiments to investigate which alternative approach to grading resulted in more successful learning: teaching contrasting patterns before parallel ones (C-P) or vice-versa (P-C). For example,

French L2 Learning Problem:
(Position of indirect object pronoun in Imperatives)

| P | Donne-moi le livre! |
| C | Ne me donne pas le livre |

Spanish L2 Learning Problem:
(Subject of 2nd verb)

| P | Quiero hablar |
| C | Quiero que hable |

In four out of five experiments with first-year learners of French or Spanish, the C-P ordering resulted in better learning than the P-C order. However, very low significance levels were registered, and the overriding determinant was the 'recency effect', *i.e.* for both orders of teaching, that which was known best was what had been learnt most recently. As I said, Politzer's experiment casts some doubt on the assumption that parallel constructions should invariably be taught before contrasting ones.

6.3.3 *Contrastive Teaching*

An alternative to sequencing, and an attractive one where it seems impossible to defend the superiority of one sequencing option over another is to abandon it in favour of *simultaneous* presentation. In the previous section we proposed intralingual reasons for preserving system-integrity; here we are proposing additional interlingual reasons. 'Contrastive teaching' involves presenting to the learner at the same time all the terms in a linguistic system of L2 which, as a system, contrasts with the corresponding L1 system. Some individual terms of the two systems may be noncontrasting, of course. The systems concerned may be grammatical, phonological, or lexical: for examples of each, consider

Grammatical

| *L1 English* | *L2 French* |
| He has V past-part. | Il $\begin{cases} a + V^1 \\ est + V^2 \end{cases}$ past-part. |

In English the Perfect is formed with auxiliary *have* for all lexical verbs, while French forms the Perfect either with *avoir* or with *être*, according to the class of lexical verb selected (V^1 or V^2). By transfer, the English learner will produce such errors as **Il a arrivé.*

Phonological

| *L1 German* | *L2 English* |
| $/l/ \rightarrow [l]$ | $/l/ \begin{cases} [ɫ] \\ [l] \end{cases}$ |

As we saw above the two systems of allophonic variation for the laterals of German and English are contrastive: the German learner of English will underdifferentiate and say [fɪl] for nativelike [fɪɫ].

Lexical

	L1 English	L2
a)	know	kennen/wissen (German)
b)	leave	salir/dejar (Spanish)

In each case, L2 exhibits finer lexical differentiation than L1. The English learner will produce such errors as in:

*Er weiss Fritz. *Dejé la cuidad.

On each level of language CA can identify such 'problem-pairs', although the asymmetry may be even greater than a 1:2 relationship. Lado (1957) identifies English *work*(s) with no fewer than five Spanish lexemes: *trabajo, obras, movimiento, usina, fabrica.* Contrastive teaching involves presenting the learner with selected, especially transparent instances of such 'pairs', each term being suitably contextualised, for instance:

Ich *weiss*, dass er berühmt ist, aber ich *kenne* ihn nicht:

'I know₁ that he is famous, but I don't know₂ him'

From such instances the learner may infer that *wissen* refers to 'factual knowledge of' and *kennen* to 'being acquainted' (*cf.* Carton (1971) for a discussion of INFERENCING by learners). Either the learner is given the opportunity to infer from instances, or he may be given a certain amount of prescriptive assistance, in the form of explicit formulations: in either case, it is contrastive teaching.

Although such an approach is not beyond criticism, as we shall presently see, it would nevertheless seem to be harmonious with current tendencies to emphasise the cognitive aspect of L2 learning. Carroll's (1965) cognitive code learning theory stresses the need for foreign-language learners to base their behaviour on *knowledge* rather than on habit: contrastive teaching indubitably imparts packaged information, in a form easily assimilated as knowledge, about the intricacies of L2 systems. Finocchiaro (1966: 3) speaks of the need "to make students aware of the contrasts so that they will understand the reasons for their errors and avoid committing them". Nickel & Wagner (1968: 253) suggest that ". . . there may be instances where a contrastive comparison is useful to explain certain aspects of the language to be taught". Hammerly (1973: 108) defends the use of contrastive drills for pronunciation on the grounds that they "allow the student to compare his right with his wrong". Lewis (1974: 103) explains the relatively high success of foreign-language teaching in the Soviet Union in terms of the policy of making use of *conscious* learning: "Schcherba had offered a theoretical justification for the use of the native language", while Ushinsky had insisted on "the intellectual origin of habits". And such ideas about the efficacy of cognitive involvement on the part of the learner are gaining wide currency here now. Sharwood Smith (1978) cites work by Landa on the use of *algorithms* in L2 learning, an algorithm being a procedure for making choices on the basis of information. The learner is taught how most efficiently to solve a problem – such as whether to use *kennen* or *wissen* – by following a set of instructions in controlled steps. I would submit that a CA has a significant role to play in all this, not only in pre-identifying the learning problems, but also in specifying the 'controlled steps' whereby the learner can most efficiently solve his learning problem. A learner whose L1 system is isomorphic with the L2 system has no learning problem, and where the L1 and L2 systems do contrast, the algorithm will have to be specified at least in part in conformity with the kind of contrast involved.

Objections have been raised to contrastive teaching: *cf.* Wolfe (1967); Hadlich (1968) and Richards (1974). They are unanimous in their claim that so-called 'problem-pairs' are only rendered problematical by contrastivists, and that contrastive teaching, rather than preventing errors, actually precipitates them: "The point is that 'problem-pairs' are non-native" and "Awareness of the possibility of erroneous substitution fosters in itself the substitution it is designed to forestall and so defeats its own purpose" (Hadlich, *op. cit.*: 427). Confirmation of this comes from Richards (*op. cit.*: 178) who claims that confusions between *too/so/very* or between *come/go* can be ". . . traced to . . . presentation which is based on contrastive analysis".

Hadlich's argument is that such problem-pairs as *salir/dejar* are non-native: Spaniards do not find this pair difficult to separate, just as no English native speaker stumbles over *do* and *make*. I somehow doubt this: there are times when the English do hesitate over *do/make*: *He's done/made a good job* (*of it*), and many adults are unhappy over *left/right* and *port/starboard* – that is why we develop mnemonics, such as 'The '*port*' is passed to the *left*' (each has four letters). Dyslectics are native speakers who fail to distinguish 'd'/'b' or 'p'/'q', etc. (Miles, 1970). Moreover, the learner of *salir/dejar* is doubly disadvantaged, both in being extraneous to Spanish, and in having the undifferentiating *leave* in his L1. Even if the teaching syllabus were to ignore CA suggestions and present *salir* and *dejar* separately at different times, it is highly likely that the English learner will invest considerable effort in reassociating them, as soon as he has had contact with the second term. Hadlich seems to favour the explanation for such difficulties in terms of Cross-Association (*cf.* Chapter 2. 5.1). As I argued there, it is impossible to exclude contrastive considerations from even this sort of explanation: the German learner of French is familiar with the 'redundancy' of having two words for 'know' in his L1 (*wissen/kennen*) and so will be unperturbed by the identical redundancy of L2 French *savoir/connaître*: indeed, it would bother him if French did not have it.

One area in which contrastive teaching was advocated was in the Dialect Expansion movement in the USA in the late 1960s (Alatis, 1969). The aim was to bring about bidialectism in disadvantaged Blacks, by teaching them when to use their Negro Nonstandard and when to use Standard American English. Feigenbaum (1969) advocated a series of adaptations of Audiolingual Second Language teaching techniques for Dialect Expansion. One suggestion was for minimal-pair recognition drills in which Standard and Non-standard equivalents are contrasted: the student must respond 'same' or 'different' upon hearing such pairs as

He work hard/He works hard.
She is working/She be workin'.

Such 'drilling' involves the learner in making specific comparisons between the two dialects rather than aiming at the mechanical conditioning of responses. In this way the CA is enacted, or rather re-enacted in class under the teacher's guidance. This approach involves overt contrasting, unlike the practice adopted in conventional L2 teaching, where the contrasts detected by the CA are covert.

6.4 'Method' and Contrastive Analysis

6.4.1 *What is 'Method'?*

We saw in Section 6.3 how difficult it was to keep separate the considerations of Grading and Presentation, in that questions of *when* to teach imply questions of *how* to teach. In this section I wish to consider Presentation is greater detail. By Presentation I intend Method, but not Technique: this latter term has to do with 'tricks of the trade' (but see Brooks (1975) for a different interpretation) and is the concern of Institutes of Education, not applied linguists. For Method one could substitute the more explicit term "instructional strategy" used by Bosco and Di Pietro (1970). Method is motivated by theories of the nature of human language, how it is acquired, and how it is put to use.[1]

The last century has witnessed three major Methods in L2 teaching: Grammar-Translation, Direct, and Audiolingual. Among these the first and third might be called 'artificial' and the second 'natural'. The 'natural' Method is based on the premise that an L2 should be learnt in the same way as infants acquire the L1: "The term 'nature method' (developed by A. M. Jensen in the late thirties) evoked the partly false idea that the second language could be learnt in the same way as the mother tongue was in early childhood" (Malmberg, 1971: 7). At the opposite extreme the Audiolingualists adopt highly artificial instructional strategies, such as substitution drills, with the justification that L2 learning by adults can never proceed in the same way as L1 acquisition did, on a 'tabula rasa', and that the 'naturalist' pretence that it can is futile. Notice that these two 'Methods' are polarised over what instructional strategies should be utilised, but, paradoxically, are in agreement about what it is that to a large extent determines success in L2 learning: the L1. One is justified, therefore, in saying that the CA hypothesis is Methods-neutral: whatever Method one subscribes to, one will always view the learner's possession of the L1 as a powerful factor to be reckoned with.

6.4.2 Simplification and Simplicity

I suggested before (cf. footnote 1) that Linguistics, like Psychology has three concerns: structure, function and growth. Traditionally the role of the L2 materials writer and teacher has been seen as one aimed at mediating between the learner and the L2 by a process of simplification. Such simplification has been interpreted only in terms of *structural* simplification. I would like to suggest that it would be profitable to contemplate two other forms of simplification: functional and developmental simplification.

By 'functional simplification' I mean providing the learner with a language which does not make fine functional distinctions. It is relatively insensitive to variations in situation, style, register, and nuances of meaning. There is evidence that language learners spontaneously resort to functional simplification. Littlewood (1977) lists examples from 'Gastarbeiterdeutsch', including "Reduction of semantic distinctions, for example by overgeneralising the use of *nicht* in place of *kein*: *du nix Urlaub*?; use of analytical paraphrases: *nix gut* for *schlecht* ...". Richards (1975) has found similar forces at work among learners of Indonesian: he notes that the affixes *ber/me* are dropped by learners, this dropping being also done by natives "as a sign of informal register". Corder (1977a) also has discussed the kind of language variation that I have in mind: he terms it *lectal* variation. He suggests that such variability is not on a scale of (structural) complexity, the variants being "of equal linguistic complexity and equal functional power" (*ibid.*: 15). This does not mean however that they are functionally synonymous: while they do get the message across, they transmit very different sorts of 'social' information about the speaker, in labelling him as a foreigner.

'Developmental simplification' is a process that has been more widely studied than lectal simplification. Selinker (1969, 1972) introduced the term *interlanguage* for this phenomenon. He defines interlanguage as "a separate linguistic system whose existence we are compelled to hypothesise, based on the observed output which results from the [L2] learner's attempted production of a target language norm". Other terms introduced for the same process were *transitional competence* (Corder, 1967), *transitional dialect* (Corder, 1971) and *approximative system* (Nemser, 1971a). A major feature of interlanguage (IL) is that it is *simple* in comparison with L2 norms. Corder (1975) prefers to call ILs *simple* than to use the process noun *simplification*, insisting that "... to characterise them as less complex does not entail that they have been *simplified*". His is a valid objection: it would be misleading to suggest that learners take target L2 forms and then simplify them, since if they could 'take' these forms in the first place they would have no need to modify them – they could assimilate them in their full form. Learners, either of the L1 or L2 seem to have an inborn capacity to take recourse to a simple code, which is lexically and phonologically oriented to the target, but is grammatically and semantically simple. In fact, child language, interlanguage, pidgin, and foreigner talk manifest universal features of simplicity.

Now, what relevance has all of this for Method? It has been suggested more recently than the Direct Method movement that L2 instructional strategies should replicate "... that case where the most successful language learning takes place – namely, in the child"

(Reibel, 1969), but the concrete proposal – "the powerful tool of dialogue memorisation" – is not very convincing. Widdowson (1975) grasps the nettle: rather than "remedial teaching through which errors are eradicated" he proposes that we recognise the learner's propensity to simplification and "devise syllabuses which actually presented the erroneous forms which particular groups of learners were prone to produce, gradually bringing 'correct' standard forms into focus as the course progresses". I wish to endorse this proposal, in particular as it applies to *functional* simplification. The means to this end involve cultivating in learners what I have elsewhere called an INTER-LINGUA (James, 1969, 1972, 1979).

6.4.3 *The Interlingua*

'Reduction', then, is functional contraction, while 'simplification' is a term to be reserved for structural contraction. An interlingua is a functionally reduced *dialect* of the target language. Now reduction, as Widdowson saw, "can involve either an increase or a decrease in complexity" (Widdowson, 1975). This is where the CA re-enters the scene. An L2 form may have high *inherent* complexity, but, if it is isomorphic with a certain equivalent L1 form, it may well be easier to learn than some other inherently simple form which is exotic to the L1. For example, Russian *on budit pisat'* 'he will write' is inherently more complex than its paraphrase *on napishet*, but easier for the English learner. Or *From whom did you buy that*?, while more complex than *Who did you buy that from*?, is easier for the German, whose L1 has *Bei wem hast du das gekauft*? but no **Wem hast du das gekauft bei*? There are of course problems about criteria for sentence complexity (*cf.* Kress, 1971).

Notice two things: a) structural simplification can be effected in the direction of the L1, which is quite independent of both inherent relative complexity and of developmental simplification, and b) the price paid by the learner for this L1-directed structural simplification is functional contraction. For a time, until his learning progresses, the learner will have only a limited control of the stylistic and registral options that the native speaker has: he will know only *on budit pisat'* or *From whom ...* and be unprepared to make the nicer functional distinctions carried in the L2 by *on napishet* or *Who ... from*. As Levenston (1971) put it, the learner will tend to 'overindulge' certain patterns and to 'underrepresent' (in fact not represent at all) other options open to the native speaker. This order of priorities corresponds to that selected by children learning their first language. Although they have more or less mastered the structural potential of their language (the 'code') by the age of five or six, it may not be before the age of ten that they have developed some rudimentary sense of stylistic appropriacy.

I must emphasise that I am not advocating the teaching of a learner-pidgin, nor of erroneous forms: every form taught as part of the interlingua must be structurally well-formed. This kind of decision is easy to make. What is a less easy decision is that concerning the stylistic effects of the interlingua. I have suggested for example (James, 1981) that the interlingual approach has a certain implication for teaching a Pole how to ask polarity questions in German. German has two alternative forms (a) (b) for such questions, one of which is isomorphic with the Polish form (c): (b) and (c) each uses a clause-initial question particle, *ob* or *czy*:

a) Kennen Sie ihn?   c) Czy pan go zna?
b) Ob Sie ihn kennen?

The obvious implication is to teach the Pole question form (b) first. The objection is that (c) and (b) are of different stylistic status, (b) being [Familiar/casual] and (a) [Polite]. Undeniably, the exclusive use of (b) will often be infelicitous, and may offend some native speakers of German. The fact remains, however, that it will unmistakably always perform its intended function of question, and is preferable to an erroneous *Sie ihn kennt*?

These proposals are not novel. Politzer (1972: 96) suggests "If there are pseudo-parallel constructions in L1 and L2, these should be utilized frequently at the beginning of the course". Valdman (1972) defines pedagogic facilitation, as I have done, in terms of "reduction of inherent variability", and elaborates this as "redefining as provisionally synonymous constructions and forms that show partial semantic overlap" (Valdman, 1975). His example is for English learners of French "we can avoid the inflectionally complex future tense forms by initially teaching only the periphrastic *aller + Infinitive*" (*ibid.*). His term 'avoid' is significant, since there is some evidence that L2 learners develop a certain skill in avoiding L2 patterns which experience has shown them to be difficult: the so-called 'Avoidance Strategy' (Schachter, 1974; Kleinmann, 1977). My interlingual approach involves making it unnecessary for the learner himself to invoke this strategy in the earlier stages of learning.

There is some psychological support for teaching the interlingua, derived from psychology experiments. Terrace (1963) conditioned (taught) pigeons to peck a red key and ignore a green one. Then stimulus control was shifted *i.e.* they were required to peck a key with vertical lines and ignore one with horizontal lines. The learning that had taken place with coloured keys had no effect on learning which of the lined keys to peck. The shift from colour to line (L1 → L2) had been too abrupt. Terrace found however that when the lines were superimposed over the colours and the colours gradually faded out, learning to respond to the lined keys was facilitated. The explanation for such facilitation lies in the fact that the stimuli now constituted *continua* rather than being discrete. This brings us to the property of a continuum which the interlingua possesses.

6.4.4 *Naturalisation of the Interlingua*

Interlinguas are approximative systems occupying points on a continuum between L1 and L2. We have hitherto concentrated on processes of pedagogical simplification in the direction of the L1, and have also mentioned the plausibility of universal processes of simplification. Continued learning and teaching involves the *elaboration* of the interlingua. Since this elaboration is wholly determined ultimately by the nature of the L2, I shall use the term 'naturalisation' for it, since this word evokes the notion of aliens becoming officially accepted by the community of the indigenous. I must reject Corder's (1975) 'complexification', since naturalisation can equally well involve structural simplification as complexification, just as reduction (*q.v.*) could.

Bearing in mind that earlier interlinguas are progressively truncated functionally, the main task of naturalising them is that of expanding their functional potential. A language user who is able to put the structural resources to use as functionally appropriate is said to have *Communicative Competence* (Hymes, 1972). So naturalising the interlingua essentially involves providing learners with the resources to exploit an L2 communicative competence. Hymes (*ibid.*: 281) recognises four sectors of communicative competence "of which the grammatical is just one", *viz.*:

i) "Whether (and to what degree) something is formally possible." This is the grammaticality sector, and the one which we concentrated on developing in the earliest interlingua.

ii) "Whether (and to what degree) something is feasible." This is the sector of acceptability and concerns 'performance' factors such as memory and cognitive factors (*cf.* Cook, 1977). The language to be learnt by the learner must not exceed his capacities.

iii) "Whether (and to what degree) something is appropriate." This is defined in relation to context, or how the learner's language responds to demands of style and register.

iv) "Whether (and to what degree) something is in fact done." This relates to probability of occurrence and statistical aspects of language use. For example, F. R. Palmer (1965: 63) suggested that *will/shall* are not the commonest forms used for Future Reference in English, though subsequent corpus analysis proved him wrong (Martin and Weltens, 1973). One hopes that not too many EFL materials were based on Palmer's guesswork.

I wish to suggest that while decisions about the forms early interlinguas should take are most receptive to 'formal possibility' and 'feasibility', the naturalisation of the interlingua, while bearing i) and ii) in mind, pays more and more attention to Hymes[2] sectors iii) and iv): 'appropriacy' and probability. This means viewing language teaching, essentially, as a two-stage operation, with early emphasis being on form and later emphasis shifted to function. As Hymes (*op. cit.*) suggests in the context of L1 learning "one should perhaps contrast a 'long' and a 'short' range view of competency, the short range view being interested primarily in understanding innate capacities as unfolded during the first years of life [read 'of L2 instruction'. C.J.], and the long range view in understanding the continuing socialisation and change of competence through life".

These suggestions for long and short range views of L2 teaching are relevant, I feel, to the current debate over Notional/Functional syllabuses and their uses (Wilkins, 1976; Brumfit, 1978). Teachers, while convinced of the value of such a syllabus, are sceptical about how it could be implemented with beginners, and there is a feeling that such a syllabus is more suited to post-initial, remedial and 'special purpose' language teaching. I suggest that the interlingua, subsequently naturalised along the lines I have suggested, would solve the problem: early teaching is structurally based, and later work involves more and more attention being given to the two sectors of appropriacy and probability-of-occurrence (*cf.* Marton, 1974).

During naturalisation, those L2 patterns not paralleled by equivalent ones will be introduced to the learner: the order of their introduction will be dictated by all the sequencing criteria we have mentioned, including L1:L2 isomorphism. That is, postponed items, such as *on napishet, who . . . to?, Kennen Sie ihn?* will now need to be taught. Their presentation will be facilitated by the prior introduction of the isomorphic variants: they can be presented as L2 equivalents, obviating the need for any explanation of their 'value', *i.e.* communicative significance. As a first step, they may be presented as synonymous paraphrases. Sharwood Smith (1976) uses such intralingual forms as *It is very important that . . .*, which parallels Polish L1 *To jest bardzo wazne . . . .* Once the former is well-established, he can introduce the modal *must* via its paraphrase, without further recourse to the learner's L1.

One final word of warning: it is essential that there be an *authentic* L1 form with which to associate any given target L2 form. Some teachers have yielded to the temptation to create an artificial quasi-L1 form for learners to base L2 production on. Barrutia (1967: 161) cites and rightly disparages one such practice: "Telling the student that in order to say 'I like beer' [in Spanish] he must first put it into the form 'Beer is pleasing to me', which then gives him 'A mi me gusta la cerveza'." I call this the 'The pen of my aunt' syndrome. This practice is not only time-consuming, it involves gratuitous effort, since the learner who can perform this operation has learnt the target pattern anyway, and is merely doing tricks. That the practice I am decrying was widespread in teaching Classics is well known: learners got to *Dixit se felicem esse* by way of a pseudo-English* *He said himself to be happy.* The practice had no effect on Latin proficiency, but might explain the Classicist's predilection for using Latin forms in his English.

For the majority of foreign-language learners – especially the low-achievers in Britain's Comprehensive Schools – the interlingua will probably not have time to get naturalised, and will become fossilised. In fact, it is likely to be adequate, as a viable medium for basic communication in an L2, for those whose formal foreign-language education ends with school-leaving, as well as for those who have specialist or sporadic communicative needs in an L2. The minority – a second-language élite! – will need to proceed beyond the interlingua: those who will become professional foreign-language communicators, and those with literary, aesthetic, linguistic or pedagogic callings. I hope this does not appear undemocratic, but we must face the grim reality that possibly 90% of pupils in school foreign-language courses are under-achievers.

Most of what has been said here applies to the 'productive' command of the L2. It could be objected that I have not catered for the eventuality of learners being addressed by native speakers or having to read 'authentic' texts in the L2. While I have argued for *formal* criteria (L1:L2 isomorphism) being predominant in the early stages of L2 teaching for productive control, and functional considerations gradually taken over during the process of naturalisation, I think these priorities should be reversed for the teaching of comprehension. As Littlewood (1978) has argued, early work on comprehension should concentrate at inferring messages, *i.e.* on communicational receptivity, relying on mainly contextual cues rather than linguistic signalling devices. Progress in comprehension involves helping the learner to associate functions to forms with precision. To summarise, the following diagram is offered to clarify the relationships we have been discussing:

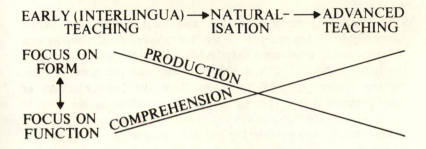

NOTES

1 Just as Catania (1973) recognises three branches of Psychology: "the psychologies of structure, function, and growth", there are likewise three branches of linguistics: structural, socio- and psycholinguistics.
2 It is significant that Hymes refers to one of the founders of CA (Weinreich) in this context.

7

Some Issues of
Contention

CA is not only problematic, but also fraught with controversy. Especially in the last ten years it has come under attack from several quarters, and its proponents have had to learn to live with a protracted 'crisis of confidence'. CA is very insecure and yet, paradoxically, remains highly vigorous, to judge from the large numbers of practitioners it enlists. This vigour manifests itself in several ways: in the number of CA Projects funded in the last ten years;[1] papers read at conferences[2] and published in journals; masters' dissertations; and postgraduate course component offerings in CA. It seems that CA has very high 'face validity', that is it seems the plausible and obvious thing that applied linguists ought to do, and yet at the same time there are these pangs of insecurity concerning its theoretical foundations. CA is sound practice in search of a sound theory. In this chapter, I wish to identify what appear to be the main sources of the insecurity and to summarise current opinion about each.

7.1 Criteria for Comparison

There are two facets of this issue: first, the question of whether different languages are comparable at all, beyond merely superficial observations such as 'French is melodic. German is gutteral', and the like; and second, if they are comparable in principle, by what criterion are they best compared?

The first question became a major dilemma for the Structuralists, since it was they who promoted CA, while at the same time structuralist orthodoxy insisted on the *uniqueness* of each language. They objected vigorously to the traditional practices of super-imposing the descriptive categories of the prestigious Classical languages on to modern vernaculars, and on insisting for example that prepositions precede and inflect the pronouns they govern, as in *with whom*? Di Pietro (1968: 66) states the Structuralists' dilemma in the face of CA thus:

"Even from the start, the limitations of Structural linguistics were evident with regard to CA. The insistence on defining phonological and grammatical categories solely in terms of individual languages made detailed contrastive statements laborious, if not theoretically impossible, to phrase."

This insistence that each language has its own unique genius reflects Bally's famous dictum that a language is "un système où tout se tient" or a system made up and defined by the sum of its constituent terms. According to this view the fact that English and German have phonemes which are conveniently represented by the same symbols /i/ and /ʃ/, for example in *queen, shoe, viel* 'much', *schön* 'pretty' should not be taken to imply that the English and German sounds are in any sense 'the same'. English /i/ and /ʃ/ are defined by the relationships they enter into with all the other sounds of English, and German /i/ and /ʃ/ by the relationships holding between them and the other sounds of German. These networks of relationships are different in the two languages, and therefore English /i/ and /ʃ/ have different *values* from those of German /i/ and /ʃ/. They have so little in common, apart from the trivial coincidence of their articulatory and acoustic make-up, that they are simply not comparable. To compare them would be tantamount to putting ten-ton lorries and banana skins into the same class on the grounds that neither ought to be left on footpaths!

Similarly, the fact that we use the labels 'tense' or 'articles' to refer to a certain grammatical category in two different languages should not be taken to mean that we are talking about the same thing. The fact that German and French nouns have inherent grammatical gender does not mean that 'masculine' in German has the same value as 'masculine' in French. In French 'masculine' is in contrast only with 'feminine' (French operating a two-term gender system) whereas in German 'masculine' contrasts with 'neuter' and 'feminine' in a three-term system: it follows that 'masculine' has a different value in each language. Or we might take the *article* systems of English and German to show the danger of regarding entities as comparable just because they are called by the same name. It seems that German and English (but not Russian) not only have article systems, but that the German and the English systems each have three terms: definite, indefinite, and 'zero' (Ø).

der Lehrer: *the* teacher

ein Lehrer: *a* teacher

Ø Lehrer (pl):   teachers

Ø Bier (sing):   beer

However, we discover that certain article + noun combinations occur in one of these languages but not the other. German uses the definite article with a singular mass noun and with a human proper noun:

Die Butter ist gesund = Ø Butter is wholesome

Der Fritz ist schlau = Ø Fred is smart

Since different combinations occur, so do different language-internal contrasts: (with singular mass nouns) there is a Ø vs *the* opposition in English but not in German. So Ø, and *the* have different values in the two languages.

I think these objections are, to a certain degree, answerable. *First*, one does not refer to categories by the same label unless they have *something* at least in common. One is ready to admit that certain categories are lacking in certain languages: nobody would wish to argue that Russian, for example, has articles, even though it does have means of indicating definiteness and indefiniteness. Moreover, it seems that bilinguals and language-learners do naturally equate entities across languages, and that these interlingual identifications often correspond to the ones linguists would make. Thus, Germans equate English *the* with the *der/die/das* of German, and Spaniards associate the English close front vowels /i/ and /ɪ/ with their own Spanish /i/. It may be that language learners are not always totally rigorous in the linguistic analyses they make and on which they base their interlingual identifications: their criteria are rather superficial ones, such as articulatory or acoustic similarity, or distribution. But since CA is concerned with learning by ordinary fallible humans, we had much better face behavioural reality, rather than pretend that the man in the street is a sophisticated linguistic analyst.

The second defence of the position that languages are *in principle* comparable is to insist that comparability does not presuppose absolute identity, but merely a degree of shared similarity. To refer to our example of English and German articles again: it is a sufficient basis for comparison that each language makes use of a small class of function words that occur in prenominal position and seem to indicate the specificness or genericness of the noun. We proceed from here to say exactly what the German and English categories have in common and what it is that distinguishes them. Interlingual identification is, in other words, the point of departure for CA, and identification is not meant to imply 'identity'.

So much then for the question of whether languages are comparable in principle. Assuming they are, the next question is how to set about the task. To answer this question, let us go back to first principles, asking ourselves: how does one set about comparing anything? The first thing we do is make sure that we are comparing like with like: this means that the two (or more) entities to be compared, while differing in some respect, must share certain attributes. This requirement is especially strong when we are *contrasting*, *i.e.* looking for differences, since it is only against a background of sameness that differences are significant. We shall call this sameness the *constant* and the differences *variables*. In the theory of CA the constant has traditionally been known as the *tertium comparationis* or TC for short.

In Chapter 4 we mentioned the TCs available for phonological and lexical CA. For phonology the IPA chart and vowel diagram seemed strong candidates, while for lexis the (probably universal) set of semantic components seemed useful. But we have so far failed to identify any such obvious TC for grammatical CA. Over the years three candidates have been proposed: surface structure, deep structure, and translation equivalence.

7.1.1 Surface Structure

A surface grammar, as we saw in Chapter 3, describes the overt signals or 'devices of form and arrangement' as Fries called them, which a language exploits. Stockwell et al. (1965: 2) identify four such devices: word order, intonation, function words and affixation. If these four were the only grammatical categories there would be just four possible CAs of any pair of languages, each having colossal scope and bearing such titles as: 'Word order in X and Y'. Fortunately, their scope can be limited in a number of ways. To see what these are, consider the following hypothetical titles of possible CAs using surface-structure categories as the TC.

> Order of attributes in the NP of X and Y
> Fall-rise intonation in X and Y
> Quantifiers in X and Y
> Passive constructions in X and Y etc. . . .

Notice that such CAs as these are possible only when each of the two languages has a grammatical category in common by virtue of broadly similar internal composition (constituency) and distribution. These are the two main dimensions of grammar recognised by the Structuralist. Only when the two are similar in constituency and distribution will the surface-structure contrastivist refer to them by the same labels: 'attribute', 'NP', 'fall-rise contour' or 'passive'. For example, we discover that in English and German there is a recurrence of the combination *Auxiliary* + *Past Participle*. Therefore the criteria of constituency and distribution are satisfied and we can take *Aux.* + *PP* as our TC. We may be tempted to cut corners here and say that since *Aux.* + *PP* is the formal manifestation of the category *Perfect*, our CA should properly be entitled: 'The Perfect in X and Y'. This, as Corder (1973: 234) points out, is a common but risky practice: we ought not to equate two grammatical categories interlingually merely because they go by the same name. As we saw in the case of segmental phonemes of German and English (p. 167), the two categories may have different *values* in X and Y anyway. And, in the case of grammatical categories, there is always the possibility that X and Y share a label simply because they had the prestigious categories of Latin imposed on them.

One might wish to argue that equating 'Perfect' of two languages is no less arbitrary than equating 'Auxiliary' and 'Participle', since the latter two are only equated on the basis of their identity of labels. This, I feel, is not likely to be true if the two language descriptions antecedent to the CA have been conducted independently, and, as was the ambition of the Structuralists, with absolute objectivity, constituency and distribution alone being the criteria for linguistic relevance.

Most of the CAs ever written have taken surface structure categories as the TC. This does not mean that they yield superior TCs. There are advantages as well as disadvantages.

First, there is no denying that it is surface structures which learners of an L2 are confronted with, and which they have to master in order to communicate. As Haugen (1956: 67) put it: "Interlingual identification occurs when speakers equate items in one language with items in another *because of their similarities in shape, distribution, or both*" (my italics). Moreover, their failures to do so are reflected in the surface structure of their erroneous FL utterances. As Jakobovits (1969: 73) observes: "... similarities and differences of surface features may be more relevant for the operation of transfer effects in second language learning than deep structure relations". In other words, learners naturally equate surface structures.

There are also disadvantages, however. First, as Stockwell et al. (*op. cit.*: 3) point out, surface grammar ". . . tells us little or nothing about the way in which sentences are formed. It is grammar conceived largely from the hearer's point of view". This is an interesting claim, inasmuch as it raises the issue of *directionality* touched on elsewhere, in this book: *cf.* p. 142 and James (1980).

The main objection to using surface structure as the TC is that it leads to interlingual equations that are superficial and insignificant. As Widdowson (1974) points out, we are hereby led to identify as sames, categories having very different *values* in the economy of the respective grammars, as well as different conditions for *use* in real-life settings. Thus, the surface-structure TC implies the equation of (the verb forms in) 1 and 2 whereas in situations of use (*i.e.* pragmatically) it is just as frequently 3, not 2, that is equivalent to 1.

1) The postman opened the door.
2) Le facteur ouvrit la porte.
3) Le facteur a ouvert la porte.

Such facts as this made Contrastivists receptive to the suggestion, voiced about a decade ago (James, 1969; Wagner, 1970) that *deep structure* would be a more satisfactory TC.

7.1.2 *Deep Structure*

It is possible for superficially dissimilar sentences of a language to be paraphrases of one another, *i.e.* they convey the same ideational content: in this case they are said to share the same deep structure. Examples are sentence-pairs a) and b):

a) ⎰ John is easy to please.
   ⎱ It's easy to please John.
b) ⎰ There's a hole in my bucket.
   ⎱ My bucket has a hole in it.

a) and b) are *intra*lingual paraphrases.

It is at least possible to argue that *inter*lingual paraphrases, that is pairs of sentences from two different languages having the same ideational content likewise derive from a common deep structure. Note that the idea of intralingual paraphrase implies that deep structure is language-specific, while that of interlingual paraphrase implies that it is language-independent.[3] If this is so, deep structure ought to serve as a viable TC.

So we are provided with the constant in the form of universal deep structure: what, then is the variable? To answer this question we must reiterate a point made earlier – that it is surface structure that has to be learnt and that learners are exposed to. Now, the relation between the two levels of deep and surface structure is made explicit in a Chomsky-type grammar by the transformations involved in converting the former into the latter (*q.v.* Chapter 3). The proposal is that, if shared deep structure is converted into language-specific surface structure by the sequential application of transformations, then the points in their transformational derivations at which equated deep structure representations of two languages begin to diverge, can be taken as a measure (or 'metric') of their differences: "the differences between languages must come at various levels of intermediate structure". (Di Pietro, 1971: 26). The 'earlier' they diverge, the greater the difference, the 'later' the less. In this way it is possible to describe degrees of equivalence between languages in terms of correspondences between the *rules* of their respective grammar: we gain the double advantages of quantification and explicitness.

Klima (1962) exemplified the approach through the transformational histories of two sentences in English and German.

> G: Er tut es, ohne daß sie ihn sehen.
> E: He does it without them/their seeing him.

G. Rules	*E. Rules*
1 S → er tut es ohne + [Complement]:	S → he does it wihout + [Comp]
2 Comp → sie sehen ihn:	Comp → they see him.
3 Embed 2 in 1 → er tut es ohne daß + [sie sehen ihn]:	Embed 2 in 1 → he does it without + [they see him]
4 End position of verb: Sie sehen ihn → sie ihn sehen.	N/A
5 N/A:	Replace Tense by Gerund marker – ING
6 N/A:	Convert subject pronoun of embedded sentence into Obj/Poss. form.

Note that R1–3 specify the two sentences as having deep structure identity. German requires but one more rule (R4), which is not applicable (N/A) to English, while English requires two more (R5–6) not applicable to German.

It seems indisputable, then, that the use of a deep structure TC, permitting as it does subsequent transformational treatment, is a useful approach. Some have gone further, to claim that certain differences between English and German can only be observed if transformational grammar is adopted as the theoretical framework for one's statements" (König, 1970: 45). He supports his claim with the following German–English pair of sentences:

> This bet won me a lot of money.
> Mit dieser Wette gewann ich viel Geld.

which have the shared deep structure:

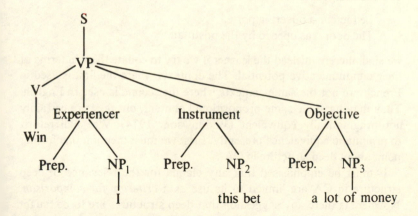

In each language, Subject is chosen by a transformation which adjoins one of the three NPs to the S node, deleting at the same time the case node which dominated the selected NP. In German only 'Experiencer' can be selected as Subject while in English either Experiencer or Instrumental can so function, allowing two realisations:

> *This bet* (Instrum.) won me a lot of money
> *I* (Experiencer) won a lot of money with this bet

The deep structure TC has both advantages and drawbacks. As to the former, its advantages, we need only remind ourselves of the purported universality of deep structure to see how convenient a TC it becomes in CA. In addition to this, there is growing evidence that learners, at least those left to their own devices to pick up an L2 in a natural way, instinctively return to deep structure. They lighten their learning burden by disregarding such semi-redundant and trans-formationally introduced features of surface structure as articles, inflections and the copula (Ferguson, 1971). In that case, the learner seems to endorse the linguist's return to deep structure. A third advantage of this TC lies in the possibilities it opens up of equating interlingually superficially very different structures: we have seen many examples of this.

As for its drawbacks, we must not lose sight of the fact that sentences – of the same or of different languages – with a common deep structure are not necessarily communicatively equivalent. In other words, even though we can demonstrate the common origin of two such sentences as:

> Le facteur a ouvert la porte.
> The door was opened by the postman.

we shall merely mislead the learner if we try to equate them in terms of their communicative potential. The contexts where the first is used in French are not the same contexts where the second is used in English. They may have the same propositional content, but they are certainly not pragmatically equivalent (Widdowson, 1974). We shall return to pragmatic equivalence presently. First we must mention one further point about deep structure in CA.

It must be emphasised that any claims for the relevance of deep structure in CA are limited to its use as a *criterion for comparison*. Nowhere is there any suggestion that deep structures are to be taught to learners. According to Denison (1973), contrastivists somewhere along the line since Chomsky have been suggesting that a return to deep structure by learners is a necessary step in the L2 learning process. He challenges the view that "the learner need only rediscover the lost perfection of his own L1 deep structure, move to the realisation that this is also L2 deep structure, and from there by the necessary transformations to a command of L2 surface structure" (*ibid.*: 237). Although I am unaware of any contrastivist who has ever drawn such a conclusion about the role of deep structure in CA, perhaps we should take Denison's remarks as a dire warning. As he rightly observes: "It is not the unscrambled egg [*i.e.* deep structure: CJ] which causes interference in L2, it is the total scrambled egg of surface structure with the ingredients arranged precisely as they are found" (*ibid.*: 242) of course, learners have to learn surface structure, not deep structure: they 'know' the latter anyway if it is universal. It is true that interference errors are a reflection of the surface-structure discrepancies between L1 and L2, but surely it is on the basis of deep structure identity that learners associate certain L1 patterns with certain communicative intentions in the first place. In other words, though superficial structural L1:L2 contrasts may explain the *form* of interference errors, they do not explain what sets transfer into motion: perhaps the explanation lies in deep structure identity. We can now move on to consider the third TC – translation equivalence.

7.1.3 *Translation Equivalence*

It has been standard practice in grammar CA to compare the formal features of translationally paired sentences: "one *constant* in grammatical comparison is presumably the meaning of a pair of sentences" (Stockwell et al., 1965: 282). It is for this reason that translation theorists and contrastivists have allied themselves in the pursuit of a common objective: the definition of translation equivalence (Wilss, 1977).

To the layman, translation equivalence is synonymous with sameness of meaning. According to this view, the contrastivist should equate pairs of sentences of L1 and L2 which 'mean the same'. Here he runs into a big problem, however: how to determine whether an L1 and an L2 sentence do mean the same. Even bilinguals who know the two languages very well will disagree about this. Therefore, the contrastivist and the translation theorist must seek some *objective* definition of translation equivalence.

One way to define translation equivalence is in terms of deep structure identity, since the deep structure of a sentence is a representation ". . . which incorporates all information relevant to the single interpretation of a particular sentence." (Chomsky, 1965: 16). This is a claim that deep structure equals meaning, which implies that identity of deep structure equals sameness of meaning. A reasonable conclusion to draw from all this is that "equivalent constructions have identical deep structures even if on the surface they are markedly different" (Krzeszowski, 1971: 38). To prove his point, Krzeszowski uses the set of arguments advanced by Lakoff (1968) to show that a) and b) have the same deep structure, *i.e.* c):

    a) Seymour sliced the salami with a knife.
    b) Seymour used a knife to slice the salami.
    c) Seymour used a knife. (Seymour sliced the salami)

       NP   V   NP (NP   V   NP) S

Note the absence of any instrumental NP in c): this is a surface structure option inserted into a) by a transformation.

The basis of Lakoff's conviction that a) and b) do have a common deep structure is that they are subject to the same selectional and co-occurrence restrictions (we shall explain these terms presently). That they mean the same or are *paraphrases* he takes on trust, it seems. Krzeszowski's thesis is that paraphrase is merely a special case of (intralingual) translation, and if he can somehow show that interlingual (Polish) translation equivalents of a) b) have the same deep structure as each other and as a) b) then he would indeed have sustained his hypothesis that translation equivalence implies deep structure identity. His Polish translation equivalents are d) and e):

d) Seymour pokrajał salami nożem.
e) Seymour użył noża aby pokrajać salami.

He now demonstrates that a) b) and d) e) must derive from a common deep structure since they are subject to the very same selectional and co-occurrence restrictions; namely:

1) In Polish and English the verb (slice/pokrajać) must be [+ Active].
2) NP_2 (salami) must not be coreferential with NP_3 (knife).
3) Questions derived from the Polish and English pairs are ambiguous in the same ways: the scope of interrogation can be either the instrumental NP or the whole predicate:

Did Seymour (slice the salami [with a knife])?
Czy Seymour (pokrajał salami [nożem])?

4) Negativised versions of all four sentences are ambiguous in the same ways: the scope of negation may be either the instrumental NP or the whole predicate. And so on.

So far so good. But several of Krzeszowski's assumptions are questionable. First, as Bouton (1976) has pointed out, verbal aspect is an integral part of deep structure representations, and Polish, a Slavonic language, marks aspect: in surface structure a choice must be made between two morphologically differentiated forms – perfective or imperfective. Krzeszowski's Polish sentences all contain perfective aspect forms, and thus carry the information that the work of cutting has been completed, whereas Lakoff's English sentences lack this information. How, then, can they be said to convey the same meaning or to have the same deep structure? There are further objections:

Chomsky (1969) has questioned Lakoff's contention that c) is the deep structure of a) and b), on the evidence of f):

  f) Seymour used a knife to slice the salami with.

The presence of *with* here suggests that *use* and an instrumental (albeit vestigial) can co-occur in surface structure, and casts doubt on Lakoff's claim that either the one or the other are alternative yet mutually exclusive reflexes of the same deep structure category. Chomsky then points to the force of the adverb *over and over again* in g) and h):

  g) John used the mallet over and over again to smash the statue.
  h) John smashed the statue over and over again with the mallet.

Here, g) implies that only one statue got smashed while h) suggests several different ones were. The difference in meaning is more than enough to suggest that *use . . . to smash* and *smash with*, and by extension *use . . . to slice* and *slice with* likewise do not derive from a common deep structure.

In the last few years the pendulum has swung away from the view that deep structure identity is a guarantee of translation equivalence, and vice-versa. Bouton (1976) advances two proofs. First, he challenges Di Pietro's claim that the translationally equated

  The wine was drunk by midnight.
        and
  On a bu le vin avant minuit.

are of common deep structure. This cannot be true, Bouton contends, since the English verb is passive while the French is active, and active and passive verbs are not subject to the same co-occurrence restrictions. In the same paper Bouton achieves a *reductio ad absurdum*. His data involve negative-polarity questions in English and Korean (Kim, 1962: 33). The English negative question *Didn't you go to school today*? will be answered *Yes* if the child did go, by *No* if he did not go. In Korean, the same question [je hakkyo-e an kanni]? is answered with *No* [anyo kasseyo] if he did, and with *Yes* [ne an kasseyo] if he did not. It follows that ". . . the English *yes* and the Korean *no*, and the English *no* and the Korean *yes* are translation equivalents". (Bouton, *ibid.*: 158). Surely this cannot be taken to imply that these responses of opposite polarity have identical deep structure, if indeed they can in any meaningful sense be said to have structure at all!

There is, however, a far simpler reason than those we have

explained why deep structure identity does not guarantee translation equivalence. This is that meaning, and equivalence of meaning, are of several types, and deep structure is predicated on but one of these, to the exclusion of the others. Deep structure is concerned with the propositional or 'ideational' (Halliday, 1970) meaning that single isolated sentences convey. There are at least two further kinds of meaning contained in sentences: 'interpersonal' and 'textual' meanings as Halliday (*ibid.*) calls them. For two sentences from different languages to be translationally equivalent they must convey the same ideational *and* interpersonal *and* textual meanings: deep structure identity takes care of only one of these, the ideational. The interpersonal meaning of a sentence determines what kind of speech act it performs for its user: to praise, condemn, refuse, agree, and so on. The textual meaning of a sentence determines what information it contributes to the message: how it helps maintain cohesion and coherence (*q.v.* Chapter 5). We might say, following Widdowson (1974), that there are two levels of translation – semantic and pragmatic – and that for CA we ought to equate L1 and L2 forms which, no matter how far they diverge superficially, are semantically and pragmatically equivalent. We conclude that translation equivalence, of this rather rigorously defined sort, is the best available TC for CA.

7.2 The Psychological Reality of CAs

In a sense, the contrastivist continually transcends his own competence, in that he is first and foremost a linguist, whose proper concern is with structure, and yet he presumes to draw conclusions about a mode of human behaviour, learning. He seems to act thus out of a conviction that his CAs possess some sort of *psychological reality*. One eminent psychologist of language has suggested that a stricter division of labour would be preferable, since "To find out what the structure is like, is the task of linguistic science; to find out how the structure functions and how it is acquired, is the task of psycholinguistics." (Hörman, 1971: 31).

And yet there is no denying that recent linguistic theory has had a great appeal for the psychologist (*cf.* Greene, 1972), an appeal based on the assumption that the rules of grammar written by the linguist must simultaneously govern the behaviour of the speaker or hearer. However, grammars of the kind that are written today, subject as they are to the limitations in our knowledge of brain mechanisms, contain no claims about the psychological operations involved in linguistic performance. Grammars are accounts of linguistic *knowledge*, that is of Competence, not of Performance: "not ... the processes which deploy that knowledge" (Bever, 1971: 161). To overlook this fact is to fall headlong into what Chesterman (1980) has termed the 'psycholinguistic fallacy', or "... to assume that the formal processes used by the grammar actually represented the productive and perceptive processes of language behaviour". Is the contrastivist, therefore, a victim of the fallacy? I wish to argue that this is not necessarily so.

There is a distinction to be drawn between 'psychological' reality on the one hand and 'mental' reality on the other. While grammars lack the former they can reasonably lay claim to the latter. Bever (1968: 15) seems to have had this distinction in mind when he wrote: "behavioral processes manipulate linguistically defined structures but do not mirror or simulate grammatical processes". Grammars are structural statements, *i.e.* they describe the principles on which languages must be organised and stored in the mind by humans. This is what we mean by saying they have mental reality. It is another thing altogether to say that a grammar describes the dynamic processes whereby utterances are synthesised and analysed. If they did, they would indeed possess *psychological* reality. But they do not: they aim only to reflect *mental* reality.

This distinction between 'mental' and 'psychological' reality is that which Aristotle drew between formal and efficient causes. And more recently, in the same tradition, Ryle (1973) has distinguished two modes of knowing: knowing *that* and knowing *how*. He sets out to show that behaviour reflects not only psychological processes (= efficient causes or knowing *how*) but also 'qualities of mind', that is, formal causes or knowing *that*: "there are many activities which directly display qualities of mind, yet are neither themselves intellectual operations nor yet effects of intellectual operations". This statement could vindicate CA of the charge of embracing the 'psycholinguistic fallacy'. Interference from L1, for example, can be viewed as resulting from conflict set up between the mental organisational *disposition* imposed by L1 and the mental organisational *demands* of the L2.

There are at least three important consequences of basing CAs on Competence accounts of language. First, Competence was conceived by Chomsky as a property of the individual. This is what distinguishes Competence from Saussure's *langue*, which has some collective status, in that it appeals to a society's consensus about its language norms. It is also Chomsky's concentration on the individual which has made his work largely unacceptable or uninteresting to the sociolinguist. Now CA is, for practical purposes, necessarily concerned with groups: one produces CAs with representative populations of L2 learners in mind and one cannot do a separate CA for each individual learner.

Secondly, Competence is neutral between speaker and hearer: "Actually, grammars of the form that we have been discussing are quite neutral as between speaker and hearer, between synthesis and analysis of utterances" (Chomsky, 1957: 48). He goes on to point out that the term 'generate' (as in Generative Grammar) is neutral in the same way. One wonders why Chomsky did not avoid the terms 'speaker' (which implies synthesis) and 'hearer' (which implies analysis) altogether, perhaps using a neutral term such as 'knower' (cf. German natürlicher Sprachträger). This neutrality carries the implication that the predictions emanating from CAs should be equally valid for productive and receptive control of the L2. Yet these two facets of language skill are rarely if ever symmetrical, as is well known. Corder (1973: 230) points out that 'speakers' of English may well be able to discriminate aurally between [k] and [x] as in Scots lock/loch or German leck ('leaky') lachen ('laugh'), yet remain incapable of producing the [x] themselves.

Connected to this dichotomy of modality (speaking vs. hearing) is the further dichotomy of directionality (cf. p. 142). The crucial question here is whether the learning of Lx by speakers of Ly as well as the learning of Ly by speakers of Lx will be handled by one and the same CA. Or are CAs essentially unidirectional, one CA being needed to cater for each direction? Filipović assumes that CAs need to be duplicated to cater for each directionality: he has produced two CAs, one for Serbo-Croatian learners of English and another for English learners of Serbo-Croatian (Filipović, 1975). My own view (James, 1980) is that CAs, as bilingual Competence grammars, are adirectional, since they are concerned with the mental organisation of knowledge rather than with how this knowledge is deployed. Any contrast identified by the CA has reciprocal implications. For example, a structural contrast between English and French exists in the system of possessive determiners. In English, it is the gender and number of the possessor that determines the form selected, whereas French selects according to the gender and number of the thing possessed. The CA predicts, therefore, that the English learner of French will produce

*Elle a vu sa grand' père

for the intended 'She's seen her grandpa' and at the same time, that the French learner of English will produce

*She's seen his grandfather

for the intended 'Elle$_1$ a vu son$_1$ grand' père. In other words, the contrastive statement is antecedent to interpretation for either directionality of learning. It is the interpretation of the CA which takes directionality into account.

Of course, the two directionalities may involve very different learning tasks: there is not always the kind of neat symmetry as implied by our last example. It may happen that one of the two languages lacks a category present in the other. A case in point is the article in English, which is lacking in Russian. The Russian learning English will have to learn to insert articles, while the Englishman learning Russian will have to get used to their absence. This is a performance factor, and, as Wilkins (1972: 194) observes "It seems to be far more difficult to remember to put things in than it does to leave them out."

The third property of Competence models is that they are idealised to the point of disregarding the constraints of time and memory that Performance is bounded by: "Part of the idealisation of competence from speech processes is the detachment of competence from time" (Cook, 1977: 24). A CA predicated on such an idealisation conceives of the L1 and the L2 meeting *in toto* and in an instant when the learner gains his first exposure to the L2. The arbitrariness of this assumption has been seized upon by Slama-Cazacu, who objects to this concept of CA *in abstracto*. She proposes a performance-based alternative CA, "... what we call 'contact analysis' – the analysis of the phenomena that arise, in the learner himself, from the contact of the two linguistic systems . . . involved in the process of foreign-language learning" (Slama-Cazacu, 1971: 63). My own view is that this performance-based and process-oriented approach to learning problems is more properly part of Error Analysis than of CA (*cf.* 7.4).

7.3 The Predictive Power of CAs

It is the ambition of any science to transcend observation and predict the unobserved. There are two possible bases for prediction: either one can predict by generalisation from observed instances, or, more ambitiously, one can predict one phenomenon on the basis of observation of some other phenomenon. The error analyst chooses the first path: having observed errors like *I must to go*, *I should to learn* he generalises to predict the likely occurrence of *I can to speak English*. The contrastivist prefers the second path: on the basis of an analysis of two related linguistic systems he predicts learners' behaviour. As we conceded in the previous section, he seems in this to transcend his competence as a linguist, for "All such predictions are outside the techniques and scope of descriptive linguistics" (Harris, 1963: fn. 24). We have discussed why prediction is essayed by contrastivists. Here we shall raise two related questions: WHAT it is that CAs are supposed to predict; and their SUCCESS in prediction.

In his *Preface*, Lado (1957) mentions ". . . the assumption that we can predict and describe the patterns that will cause difficulty in learning, and those that will not cause difficulty." He is using 'predict' here in the simplest sense of 'identify', and *not* in the sense of 'prognosticate'. What Lado's CA identifies, moreover, is just two categories of L2 items, the hard and the easy. Since Lado, the notion of prediction has been literally reinterpreted to a point where it bears only a tenuous relationship with what he intended. Closest to Lado's view is the psychological one that CAs identify the conditions conducive to two kinds of *transfer*, positive and negative. Going one step forward, since negative transfer is normally manifest in errors, we meet the claim that CAs predict *error*. And finally, since *errors* signal inadequate learning, there is the conclusion that CAs predict *difficulty*. So we now have at least three candidates as the objects of CA predictions. It is arguable that there is no justification for regarding errors and difficulty as relevant candidates.

Tran-Thi-Chau (1975: 127) posed the following question: "What is the degree of adequacy of CA in predicting and explaining learners' difficulties?" To answer it she asked L2 learners to say which parts of the L2 they found difficult and from their replies derived a measure she called SPD – Students' Perception of Difficulty. She also counted learners' errors. Low correlations were found to exist between CA predictions, SPD, and incidence of error. In a similar way Jackson and Whitman looked for correlations between CA predictions, difficulty and error incidence: "In order to test the gross capacity of a CA to predict difficulty, a variable E was derived from the mean percentage of grammatical responses, P, to represent gross occurrences of error" (Jackson and Whitman, 1971: 51). Their findings are embodied in a Report which concludes that CAs have hardly any predictive power at all.

Both Tan-Thi-Chau and Jackson and Whitman beg important questions in their assumption that difficulty and error should be correlated to one another and to CA predictions. After all, learners do not commit errors in order to minimise their experience of difficulty, and, as Kellerman (1977: 87) rightly points out "a highly erroneous sentence may cause the learner no difficulty at all". And conversely, we may find a low incidence of error in conditions where the learner is experiencing great difficulty. This phenomenon may be accounted for in terms of the learner's operation of an 'avoidance strategy'.

It was Dušková (1969: 29) who first noticed the avoidance phenomenon: her Czech learners of English committed hardly any errors involving items which were obviously – and predictably – very difficult, because they avoided that item and resorted to circumlocution to that end. Levenston (1971) was likewise talking of selective avoidance of difficulty when he used the term 'underrepresentation': learners underrepresent L2 items that are difficult by virtue of being exotic to their L1 and, conversely 'over-indulge' patterns that are similar. Schachter (1974) coined the term 'avoidance', it seems. She found that Chinese and Japanese learners of English made few errors over English relative clauses, contrary to an expectation that they would be very difficult based on the CA finding that relative clauses in these two Eastern languages are very different from English relative clauses. What these learners in fact did was resort to paraphrase, using a kind of co-ordination instead of the desired subordination: in place of *We put them into boxes which we call rice boxes* these students produced the semi-grammatical *We put them into boxes we call them rice boxes*. Kleinmann (1977) has shown that avoidance can occur without ignorance (*cf.* Chapter 2) and indeed must be independently operable by learners, since *true* avoidance implies being able to choose not to avoid, *i.e.* to use the form in question.

So much for what CAs are supposed to predict. Another issue is the *reliability* of these predictions. It seems that these predictions can fail in two possible ways, either in being indeterminate or in being wrong. Indeterminacy refers to the CA being unable to specify which of two or more structurally likely substitutions the learner will select. Wilkins' (1968) example of this is well-known: a CA can predict that French speakers will use either L1 /s/, /z/, or /t/, /d/ for English /θ/, /ð/, but not which. Baird (1967) and Denison (1966) point out that some Indian languages have a dental [t] and a retroflex [ḍ], either of which can be "predicted to substitute" for L2 English /t/. Denison concludes: "I challenge anyone accurately to predict the substitution phonemes actually selected." Other instances of this indeterminacy are: Yarmohammadi (1970), Nemser (1971b).

Cases of *false* CA predictions are again of two kinds: they may predict errors which fail to materialise, or, conversely, fail to predict those which do. Gradman (1971: 13) questions Lado's CA prediction that English learners will find the /ʒ/ difficult in word-initial position, as in *jamais, jaune*. "The problem in such an analysis is that it overlooks facts" taunts Gradman, having observed English speakers easily pronounce initial /ʒ/ in *Zhivago* in cinema queues. Kofi Sey (1973) in a book on Ghanaian English, exemplifies instances of 'errors' which would be predicted *not* to occur by a CA of English and Twi, Akan or Ewe. For example, the error with the Mass Noun *respect* in **The teachers will be given the respects they deserve* would have been avoided if L1 usage had been transferred, since this feature "is equally applicable to nouns in Ghanaian languages" (*ibid.*: 27). The fullest report on the 'unpredictability' of CAs – in fact of *four* extant CAs of Japanese and English – is that of Jackson and Whitman (1971). They administered two tests to 2500 Japanese learners of English and to a control group of 400 fourth grade American children. Their results were generally negative, as summed up in the following: "The main conclusion concerning the gross capacity of contrastive analyses to predict difficulty is that it hardly exists" (*ibid.*: 81). However, their test procedure must be said to contain certain weaknesses. The first emanates from the fact that the distractors in the test items were constructed not on the basis of errors which Japanese learners of English are likely to make, but on the basis of the native control group's errors: surely a test based on CA should reflect the responses typical of the population of which the CA is a model. Secondly, the Japanese group's performance on particular items was found to correlate most highly with the English L2 syllabus, that is, with whether or not the particular structure tested had been taught. Naturally, the whole CA hypothesis is predicated on the assumption that the learner has had the opportunity to learn what is tested. There is no point in drawing significance from the learner's ignorance of items he has had no exposure to.

7.4 Contrastive Analysis versus Error Analysis

We have just been discussing CA as a predictive device. Wardhaugh (1970) suggests that the 'CA Hypothesis' exists in two versions, a strong version and a weak version. While the two versions are equally based on the assumption of L1 interference, they differ in that the strong claims predictive power while the weak, less ambitiously, claims merely to have the power to diagnose errors that have been committed. The strong version is *a priori*, the weak version *ex post facto* in its treatment of errors.

Wardhaugh suggests that predictive CA is really a sham in that no contrastivist has ever really predicted solely on the basis of the CA, but has really relied on his and on teachers' knowledge of errors already committed. It is also, he claims, a 'pseudo-procedure', which is to say a procedure that could in theory be put to use, if enough time were available, but in reality never is resorted to because we like to take shortcuts. My own view is that CA is always predictive, and that the job of diagnosis belongs to the field of Error Analysis (EA).

According to Wardhaugh, using the weak version of CA means that "reference is made to the two systems only in order to explain actually observed interference phenomena" (*ibid.*: 127). We need go no further. Just consider what Wardhaugh's claim amounts to: it means that the analyst is capable of deciding, without first conducting a CA, which subset of the attested errors are attributable to L1 interference. Possessing such vital knowledge, he subsequently makes reference "to the two systems", or, in other words, conducts a CA, in order to "explain" these errors. Surely such explanation is gratuitous, since the source of these errors must already have been known for them to be consigned to the category of L1 causation in the first place! This seems to be a veritable 'pseudo procedure.'

Let us pursue this problem of error-identification without prior CA, or, as Richards calls it, "a non-contrastive approach to error analysis". (Richards, 1974). While recognising that some errors are the result of L1 interference, he lays emphasis on those which cannot be so accounted for. He collected samples of errors in L2 English produced by learners with a whole range of L1s: "speakers of Japanese, Chinese, Burmese, French, Czech, Polish, Tagalog, Maori, Maltese, and the major Indian and West African languages" (*ibid.*: 173). He identified common errors and categorised these by cause into four types, as caused by "overgeneralisation, ignorance of rule restrictions, incomplete application of rules, and the building of false systems or concepts" (*ibid.*: 181). His two assumptions are i) that if errors are 'universal' they cannot be interlingual, and ii) that the four error types listed exclude reference to L1. We can question both assumptions.

First, the fact that an error is committed by learners with many different L1s is no proof that it is a non-contrastive error: it is possible that *all* of the languages sampled contrast with English with respect to the particular structure involved. Certainly one would wish to see it as an idiosyncrasy of the 'genius' of English that it contrasts at this point with so many other languages, but that again does not imply that L1 interference did not occur. Richards was not the first to draw such an inference. French (1956), in a book devoted to common errors in L2 English committed by learners in regions thousands of miles apart, concludes: "if errors are due, as unmistakeably as the best authorities would have us believe, to cross-associations (*i.e.* L1-Interference) then the Japanese form of error should be one thing and the Bantu form quite another. But the plain fact is that Japanese and Bantu alike say *Yes, I didn't .. .*" (French, *ibid.*: 6). His example concerns ways of answering questions of negative polarity such as *Didn't you go*? There are two typological answer-types to such questions. English is one of the languages that answers such questions by an acceptance or rejection of the implied *facts* while the other language-type, including Japanese, Swahili, Akan (Chinebuah, 1975) and Korean (Bouton, 1976) base their answers on the *form* of the interrogative. Thus 'no' in the first type of language corresponds to 'yes' in the other, as is shown by the English and Sudanese answers to the question *Doesn't he go to school*?:

Sud. [æjwæ, mæ bɨmʃi]: [læ bɨmʃi]

Lit.: yes not go-he no go-he

Eng. No, he doesn't: yes, he does

Such evidence from linguistic typology shows that apparently 'universal' errors can indeed be plausible instances of interference errors.

There is a further problem of error-identification without prior CA. If it is true that CAs can predict errors which fail to materialise it is equally true that EA can fail to recognise errors which have materialised. In other words, without the expectancies generated by a prior CA, it is possible that real errors will go unnoticed. I am referring to what Corder (1971) calls *covert errors*, or forms produced by learners that are grammatical by the standards of the target language but do not mean to a native speaker what they mean to the learner. Some examples: A German learner of English produces a covert error in saying the well-formed *Will we go for a walk*? when, however, he intended, the invitation *Wollen wir spazieren gehen*? His English addressee will not notice any formal error here, but he will interpret the utterance as a request for prediction, not as an invitation. The

French learner of English may say *I visited her grandmother* while intending *I visit his grandmother*: applying the French rule of agreement between possessive pronoun and possessed headnoun has caused this covert error. Sometimes the context will signal the error to the Error Analyst, but not infallibly. But a CA can as confidently predict covert as it can overt errors.

I have no wish to vindicate CA at the expense of EA: each approach has its vital role to play in accounting for L2 learning problems. They should be viewed as complementing each other rather than as competitors for some procedural pride of place.

There seems to be little gain in adopting an exclusive 'either-or' approach, and the results of so doing can be positively debilitating. Take for example Walmsley's (1979: 113) suggestion for lesson plans: "that the traditional *Drill*-phase should be remodelled to function as a *Remedial*-phase, organised on the basis of the learner's actual errors". This is an approach via EA. It has some merit, but let us not throw out the baby with the bath water: learners' (not learner's) errors can often be predicted by a CA and dealt with in a *Drill*-phase. Let us have both *Drill* and *Remedial*-phases.

7.5 Scale of Difficulty

Members of various Diplomatic Corps throughout the world are encouraged, usually by financial incentives, to learn foreign languages. The reward is greater for learning 'hard' than for learning 'easy' languages. But which are which? Cleveland et al. (1960) supply an answer: English L1 speakers learn French, German, Romanian, Spanish and Italian in two-thirds the time they take to learn Russian, Greek and Finnish and in half the time needed for Chinese, Japanese and Vietnamese. Assuming learning time is a valid measure of difficulty, we see that for English learners it is the Oriental languages that are hardest. Such languages are sometimes called 'exotic' languages by Westerners. Mackey (1972) would say that the 'interlingual distance' between mutually exotic languages is great. 'Exotic' is of course a relative term since it usually means 'very different'. No language can be *inherently* exotic, and it seems that no language is inherently difficult, since children throughout the world master their native tongue in approximately the same time, by the age of five, no matter which language is involved.

This is not to say that there is no such thing as inherent, *i.e.* non-contrastive difficulty. There certainly is, and even accomplished native speakers of English do not find multiply embedded constructions easy to process.[4] German, French and Norwegian, as Pope (1973) points out, have special words for expressing positive disagreement, *Doch* and *Si* for the simple reason that positive disagreement is a 'semantically difficult' category. However, inherent difficulty is characteristically localised (as our examples show) and one would not wish to claim that any particular language was *overall* inherently more difficult than another. One might well say, on the other hand, that for the English speaker, Japanese is contrastively overall harder than French.

Lado (1957) viewed learning difficulty and difference as being directly and proportionally related. Of the L2 learner he wrote: "Those elements that are similar to his native language will be simple for him, and those elements that are different will be difficult" (Lado, *op. cit.*: 2). Some empirical confirmation of the correlation between language distance and learning difficulty is provided by Oller and Redding (1971). They confirmed that learners of English who had articles or article-like categories in their L1 performed significantly better on a test of English article usage than learners whose L1s were without articles: "it seems evident that speakers of languages which use articles experience positive transfer from their native languages when learning English" (*ibid.*: 94). Notice though that this finding is item-specific, in referring only to articles: there is no claim for the *global* facilitative effect of language proximity.

The suggestion that there is a constant relation between difference and difficulty has been challenged. Whitman and Jackson (1972: 40) conclude, from their study of the errors produced by Japanese learners of English that "relative similarity, rather than difference, is directly related to levels of difficulty". Perhaps, then, a facile equation of difference with difficulty is what Gilbert Ryle would call a 'category mistake'. Another who has challenged this assumption is Lee (1968) who reported that when he started to learn what was for him an exotic language (Chinese), he experienced very little L1 interference: his explanation was that his L1 and Chinese were so far apart that he was lifted into a new orbit of non-interference. One might have expected Lee to have paid a price for this removal of negative transfer potential, however: there would have been no positive transfer either, in this new orbit.

In fact, psychologists have for over fifty years been aware of what is called the 'similarity paradox' in human learning (Osgood, 1949). It is a paradox which impinges on all forms of learning – not only L2 learning – when one learning task is followed by another. This is the paradox: if interference increases with the similarity of the two learning tasks, then when the two tasks are *identical*, interference ought to be at its most potent! As Osgood puts it: "Ordinary learning, then, is at once the theoretical condition for maximal interference but obviously the practical condition for maximal facilitation" (Osgood, *ibid.*: 132). 'Ordinary learning' occurs with task identity. Osgood's resolution of the paradox confirms a hypothesis advanced in 1927 by Skaggs and Robinson. It states that facilitation is greatest when the successive tasks are identical (ordinary learning, (A)); interference is maximal and difficulty greatest when there is a certain degree of similarity (B); and there is moderate ease of learning when the tasks have what Osgood terms 'neutral' resemblance (C). This scale is of the form:

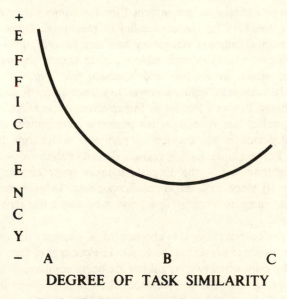

DEGREE OF TASK SIMILARITY

Fig. 3: The Skaggs-Robinson Hypothesis

That this hypothesis is still attractive as a proposition concerning L2 learning is evident from the words of Corder (1978b: 11):

> "the second languages that we may be least likely to master satisfactorily are those which are either the closest to, or the most distant from, our mother tongue. The first because we really never need to make the journey at all, and the second because the journey is too long ever to complete."

We have now begun to specify more closely the relationship between difference and difficulty: starting with Lado's position, which recognised two terms (easy/hard), we have moved to a point where we begin to discern points on a *scale* of difficulty.

The most well-known scale of difficulty in CA is that proposed by Stockwell and Bowen (1965) for phonology and elaborated to embrace grammar in Stockwell, Bowen and Martin (1965). The scale is based on types of relationship existing between comparable rules of L1 and L2. There are three sorts of relationship:

i) L1 has a rule and L2 an equivalent one.
ii) L1 has a rule but L2 has no equivalent.
iii) L2 has a rule not matched by L1.

Next, the two languages are matched for the *choices* they offer their respective speakers for the expression of meanings. There are three types of choice: optional, obligatory and zero (∅). An optional choice in phonology "refers to the possible selection among phonemes": one is free to select, in English and Spanish, /m/, /n/, /t/ – as the word-initial consonant before a vowel. In grammar, for Russian, one is free to choose between Perfect or Imperfective Aspect. An obligatory phonological choice is made when phonetic environment determines which allophone is to represent a phoneme which one has freely selected. For example, having chosen /l/ rather than /n/ – *i.e.* to say *lip* rather than *nip* – the English speaker *must* choose its clear allophone [l] since it is in prevocalic position. In grammar, having chosen the category Proper Noun, one must select the zero article in most cases.

Zero choice refers to the absence of a category in one of the languages which is present in the other. The concept of zero choice "is meaningful only when two languages are being compared" (Stockwell and Bowen, *op. cit.*: 10). For example, there is zero choice in Russian – *vis-à-vis* English – when it comes to articles.

These different available choices or nonchoices can be ranged in pairs (L1:L2) to identify eight possible types of cross-language relationships on the level of phonology. This eight-point scale becomes a sixteen-point scale on the scale of grammar, where the semantic congruity or lack of it between pairs adds another dimension. And finally, the eight possibilities can be ordered in difficulty. The scale is for convenience reduced to a three-point scale of difficulty by coalescing categories. Here is the Stockwell and Bowen scale:

Comparison

Order of Difficulty			L1	L2
I	1	MOST	∅	Ob(ligatory)
	2	↑	∅	Op(tional)
	3		Op	Ob
II	4		Ob	Op
	5		Ob	∅
	6		Op	∅
III	7	↓	Op	Op
	8	LEAST	Ob	Ob

The proposed scale is highly controversial. Tran-Thi-Chau (1975: 130–134) criticises it on several counts. First, she questions the assumption that categories *absent* in L1 but present in L2 are going to be the main source of difficulty: in her data, absent categories carry a relatively low error index. It is probably the case that sounds or structures of L2 nonexistent in the L1 are not difficult once they have been identified to be learnt, but until they are, they will continue to be overlooked: this should not, however, be interpreted so much as their constituting a *learning* as a *recognition* difficulty. To defend Stockwell et al. recall Brière's (1968: 73) finding that for Americans, /R/, /γ/ and /ḥ/, which do not exist in L1, were more difficult than sounds with close L1 equivalents.

Tran-Thi-Chau objects also to the scale placing verb form concord on the same level of difficulty as the Imperfective vs. Perfective contrast in Spanish. The former, she argues, "requires only memorisation" whereas the latter calls for detailed knowledge of the contextual determinants of each choice.

Nickel (1971b: 188) objects to the fact that "the scale . . . is much too broad since it ignores the phenomenon of *partial* agreement between constructions". For example, there seem to be times when the English and German Perfect correspond, and times when they do not:

Kolumbus entdeckte Amerika im Jahre 1492.
Columbus discovered America in 1492.

as against

Gutenberg hat die Buchdruckerei entdeckt.
Gutenberg invented printing.

(Stopp, 1957: 171)

And finally, there is the objection that the scale overlooks the different orders of difficulty that arise for encoding and decoding language: "divergence is probably more important for the language learner as a speaker while convergence is more critical for him as a hearer" (Nickel and Wagner, 1968: 252). We have already discussed this Performance issue in an earlier section.

There is undoubtedly substance in all of these criticisms of the scale of difficulty. But all of them can be answered to some extent without totally abandoning the conceptual framework it is based on.

In this chapter I have shown that CA is in no way a *fait accompli*, and that very much more research is needed to resolve the many issues of contention. This research will be conducted on two fronts, the empirical and the theoretical. While some parts of the issues can be resolved if more facts are available, there is also a need for more clear thinking about the theoretical bases of CA. It is hoped that some readers of this book will be stimulated to proceed far beyond its limited confines.

NOTES

1 These projects are listed in the Appendix.
2 The largest of these serving applied linguistics, the AILA Congress, has a section devoted to CA.
3 These two views of deep structure correspond to the terms language-specific *'infrastructure'* and *'universal'* profound structure in Birnbaum (1970).
   And Chomsky (1967: 80): "It seems to be true that the underlying deep structures vary slightly, at most, from language to language . . . .. It is pleasant to discover that they do not vary much from language to language". In C. H. Millikan and F. L. Darley, *Brain Mechanisms underlying Speech and Language*, N.Y. Grune & Statton.
4 It is uncertain to what degree learning difficulty and processing difficulty are related *cf.* Cook (1977).

References

Agard, F. B. and Di Pietro, R. J., *The Grammatical Structures of English and Italian*, University of Chicago Press, 1966.

Alatis, J. E., ed., *Monograph Series on Languages and Linguistics*, No. 22. Georgetown University Press, Washington, 1969.

Austin, J. L., *How to Do Things with Words*, Oxford University Press, 1962.

Bach, E., "The order of elements in a transformational grammar of German." *Language*, Vol. 38, pp. 263–269, 1962.

Baddeley, A. D., "Human memory." In P. C. Dodwell, ed.: *New Horizons in Psychology*, Vol. 2, Penguin, 1972.

Baird, A., "Contrastive studies and the language teacher." *ELT*, Vol. 21, pp. 130–135. 1967.

Bančila, F., "Some remarks on the semantic field of terms for physical pain in English and Romanian." *The Romanian–English CA Project*, Bucharest, pp. 265–276, 1974.

Barrutia, R., "Dispelling the myth." *MLJ*, Vol. 51, No. 1, 1967.

Berlin, B. and Kay, P., *Basic Color Terms: Their Universality and Evolution*, Berkeley, 1969.

Bever, T. G., "A survey of some recent work in psycholinguistics." In W. J. Plath, ed.: *Specification and Utilization of Transformational Grammar*, IBM Corporation, New York, pp. 1–66, 1968.

Bever, T. G., "The integrated study of language behavior." In J. Morton (ed.): *Biological and Social Forces in Psycholinguistics*, Logos Press, London 1971.

Bidwell, C. E., *The Structure of Russian in Outline*, University of Pittsburgh Press, 1969.

Birnbaum, H., *Problems of Typological and Genetic Linguistics viewed in a Generative Framework*, Mouton, The Hague, 1970.

Bloomfield, L., *Language*, Allen & Unwin, 1933.

Boas. H. U.. "Some remarks on case grammars as bases for contrastive analysis." *PSiCL*, Vol. 7, pp. 21–32, 1977.

Bosco, F. J. and Di Pietro, R. J., "Instructional strategies: their psychological and linguistic bases." *IRAL*, Vol. 8, No. 1, pp. 1–19, 1970.

Bouton, L. F., "The problem of equivalence in contrastive analysis." *IRAL*, Vol. 14, No. 2, pp. 143–163, 1976.

Briere, E. J., *A Psycholinguistic Study of Phonological Interference*. Mouton. The Hague, 1968.

Brooks, N., "The meaning of audiolingual'." *MLJ*, Vol. 59, Nos. 5–6, pp. 234–240, 1975.

Brown. P. and Levinson. S.. "Universals in language usage: politeness phenomena." In E. Goody. ed.: *Questions and Politeness.* Cambridge University Press. 1978.

Brown, R., *A First Language: The Early Stages*, Harvard University Press, 1973.

Brown, R. and Gilman, A., "Pronouns of Power and solidarity." In T. A. Sebeok, ed.: *Style in Language*, M.I.T. Press, Cambridge, 1960.

Brumfit, C. J., Review of D. A. Wilkins: *Notional Syllabuses*, Oxford University Press, 1976. *BAAL Newsletter*, No. 5, pp. 1–9, 1978.

Bryzgunova, E. A., *Prakticheskaya Fonetika i Intonatsiya Russkovo Yazika*, Moscow University Press, 1963.

Burgschmidt, E. and Götz, D., *Kontrastive Linguistik, Deutsch-Englisch: Theorie und Anwendung*, Hueber, Munich, 1974.

Carroll, J. B., "The contribution of psychological theory and educational research to the teaching of foreign languages." *MLJ*, Vol. 49, pp. 273–281, 1965.

Carton, A. S., "Inferencing: a process in using and learning language." In P. Pimsleur & T. Quinn, eds.: *The Psychology of Second Language Learning*, Cambridge University Press, 1971.

Catania, A. C., "The psychologies of structure, function and development." *American Psychologist*, Vol. 28, No. 5, pp. 434–443, 1973.

Catford, J. C., *A Linguistic Theory of Translation*, Oxford University Press, 1965.

Chesterman, A., "Contrastive generative grammar and the psycholinguistic fallacy." *PSiCL*, Vol. II, pp. 17–24, 1980.

Chinebuah, I., "Grammatical deviance and first language interference." Mimeo. Institute of African Studies, University of Ghana, Legon, 1975.

Chomsky, N., *Syntactic Structures*, Mouton, The Hague, 1957.

Chomsky, N., "Review of B. F. Skinner, *Verbal Behavior.*" *Language*, Vol. 35, pp. 26–58, 1959.

Chomsky, N., *Current Issues in Linguistic Theory*, Mouton, The Hague, 1964.

Chomsky, N., *Aspects of the Theory of Syntax*, M.I.T. Press, Cambridge, 1965.

Chomsky, N., "Linguistic theory." In R. C. Mead, ed.: *Northeast Conference Working Committee Report*, M.L.A., New York, 1966.

Chomsky, N., "The general properties of language." In C. H. Millikan and F. L. Darley, *Brain Mechanisms Underlying Speech and Language*, Grune & Stratton, New York, pp. 73–88, 1967.

Chomsky, N., "Deep structure, surface structure and semantic interpretation." Indiana University Linguistics Club, 1969.

Chomsky, N. and Halle, M., *The Sound Pattern of English*, Harper & Row, New York, 1968.

Christophersen, P., *Second Language Learning*, Penguin, 1973.

Cleveland, H., Mangone, G. J. and Adams, J. C., *The Overseas Americans*, McGraw Hill, New York, 1960.

Cook, V. J., "Cognitive processes in second language learning." *IRAL*, Vol. 15, No. 1, pp. 1–20, 1977.

Corder, S. P., "The significance of learners' errors." *IRAL*, Vol. 5, pp. 161–170, 1967.

Corder, S. P., "Idiosyncratic dialects and error analysis." *IRAL*, Vol. 9, No. 2, pp. 147–160, 1971.

Corder, S. P., *Introducing Applied Linguistics*, Penguin, 1973.

Corder, S. P., "Problems and solutions in Applied Linguistics." *Proceedings of IIIrd AILA Congress*, Vol. 3, Julius Groos, Heidelberg, 1974.

Corder, S. P., "The language of second-language learners: the broader issues." *MLJ*, Vol. 59, No. 8, pp. 409–413, 1975.

Corder, S. P., "Language continua and the interlanguage hypothesis." In S. P. Corder & E. Roulet, eds.: *The Notions of Simplification, Interlanguages and Pidgins and their Relation to Second Language Pedagogy*, Droz, Geneva, pp. 11–17, 1977a.

Corder, S. P., "Simple codes and the source of the second language learner's initial heuristic hypotheses." *Studies in Second Language Acquisition*, Vol. 1, No. 1, Indiana University, pp. 1–11, 1977b.

Corder, S. P., "Language distance and the magnitude of the language learning task." *Proceedings VIIth Colloquium on Applied Linguistics*, University of Berne, 1978a.

Corder, S. P., "Learner language and teacher talk." *AVLA Journal*, Vol. 16, No. 1, pp. 5–13, 1978b.

Coulthard, M., *An Introduction to Discourse Analysis*, Longman, 1977.

Crothers, E. and Suppes, P., *Experiments in Second Language Learning*, Academic Press, New York, 1967.

Dagut, M. B., "Incongruencies in lexical gridding." *IRAL*, Vol. 15, No. 3, pp. 221–229, 1977.

Dakin, J., *The Language Laboratory and Language Teaching*, Longman, 1973.

Davies, A., ed., *Language Testing Symposium*, Oxford University Press, 1968.

Delattre, P., *Comparing the Phonetic Features of English, German, Spanish and French*, Julius Groos, Heidelberg, 1965.

Denison, N., "The nature and diagnosis of interference phenomena." *Philippine Journal for Language Teaching*, Vol. 4, Nos. 3–4, pp. 1–16, 1966.

Denison, N., "Observations on 'deep structure' in contrastive linguistics." In R. R. K. Hartmann, ed.: *German Linguistics: Papers from the Nottingham BAAL Seminar*, Langenscheidt, Tübingen, 1973.

Derwing, B. L., *Transformational Grammar as a Theory of Language Acquisition*, Cambridge University Press, 1973.

Deyes, A. F., "Towards a linguistic definition of functional varieties of written English." *IRAL*, Vol. 16, No. 4, pp. 313–329, 1978.

Diebold, A. R., "Incipient Bilingualism." *Language*, Vol. 37, pp. 97–112, 1961.

Di Pietro, R. J., "Contrastive analysis and the notions of deep and surface grammar." In J. E. Alatis, ed.: *Monograph Series on Language and Linguistics*, Vol. 21, Georgetown University Press, 1968.

Di Pietro, J. R., *Language Structures in Contrast*, Newbury House, Rowley, Mass., 1971.

Dodson, C. J., *Language Teaching and the Bilingual Method*, Pitman, 1967.

Dulay, H. C. and Burt, M., "You can't learn without goofing." In J. C. Richards, ed.: *Error Analysis*, Longman, pp. 95–123, 1974.

Dušková, L., "On sources of errors in foreign language learning." *IRAL*, Vol. 7, No. 1, pp. 11–36, 1969.

Edmundson, W., "Gambits in foreign language teaching." In H. Christ and H. E. Piepho, eds.: *Proceedings VIIth Colloquium of the Giessen Foreign Language Teachers' Association*, 1976.

Ellis, H. C., *The Transfer of Learning*, Macmillan, New York, 1965.

Ellis, J., *Towards a General Comparative Linguistics*, Mouton, The Hague, 1966.

Fedorowicz-Bacz, B., "Against Ross' hypothesis that adjectives are higher NPs – An exercise in extrapolated argumentation." *PSiCL*, Vol. 14.

Feigenbaum, I., "Using foreign language methodology to teach standard English." *Florida Foreign Language Reporter*, Vol. 7, No. 1, pp. 116–122, 1969.

Ferguson, C. A., "Absence of copula and the notion of simplicity." In D. Hymes, ed.: *Pidginization and Creolization of Languages*, Cambridge University Press, pp. 141–150, 1971.

Filipović, R., ed., *Contrastive Analysis of English and Serbo-Croatian*, Institute of Linguistics, Zagreb, 1975.

Fillmore, C. J., "The problem of embedding transformations in a grammar." *Word*, Vol. 19, pp. 208–231, 1963.

Fillmore, C. J., "The case for case." In E. Bach and R. T. Harms, eds.: *Universals of Linguistic Theory*, Holt, Rinehart and Winston, New York, 1968.

Fillmore, C. J., "Types of lexical information." In D. Steinberg and L. A. Jakobovits, eds.: *Semantics; An Interdisciplinary Reader in Philosophy, Linguistics and Psychology*, Cambridge University Press, pp. 370–393, 1971.

Firbas, J., "Thoughts on the communicative function of the verb in English, German and Czech." *Brno Studies in English*, Vol. 1, pp. 39–63, 1959.

Firth, J. R., *Papers in Linguistics, 1934–51*, Oxford University Press, 1951.

Fishman, J., "'Standard' vs. 'dialect' in bilingual education." *MLJ*, Vol. 61, No. 7, pp. 315–324, 1977.

Fisiak et al., *An Introductory English–Polish Contrastive Grammar*, Panstwowe Wydawnictwo Naukowe, Warsaw, 1978.

Fowler, R., *An Introduction to Transformational Syntax*, Routledge & Kegan Paul, 1971.

French, F.G., *Common Errors in English: Their Cause, Prevention and Cure*, Oxford University Press, 1956.

Fries, C. C., *Teaching and Learning English as a Foreign Language*, University of Michigan Press, 1945.

Fries, C. C., *The Structure of English*, Longman, 1952.

George, H. V., *Common Errors in Language Learning*, Newbury House, Rowley, Mass., 1972.

Goffman, E., "Replies and responses." *Language in Society*, Vol. 5, pp. 257–313, 1976.

Goodenough, W. H., "Componential analysis and the study of meaning." *Language*, Vol. 32, pp. 195–216, 1956.

Gradman, H., "The limitations of contrastive analysis predictions." *PCCLLU Papers*, University of Hawaii, pp. 11–16, 1971.

Grauberg, W., "An error analysis in German of first year university students." In G. E. Perren and J. L. M. Trim, eds.: *Applications of Linguistics*, Cambridge University Press, 1971.

Greene, J., *Psycholinguistics: Chomsky and Psychology*, Penguin, 1972.

Grice, H. P., "Logic and conversation." In P. Cole and J. L. Morgan, eds.: *Syntax and Semantics, Vol. III: Speech Acts*, Academic Press, New York, pp. 41–58, 1975.

Hadlich, R., "Lexical contrastive analysis." *MLJ*, Vol. 49, No. 2, pp. 426–429, 1968.

Halle, M., *The Sound Pattern of Russian: A Linguistic and Acoustical Investigation*, Mouton, The Hague, 1971.

Halliday, M. A. K., "Categories of the theory of grammar." *Word*, Vol. 17, No. 3, pp. 241–292, 1961.

Halliday, M. A. K., "Language structure and language function." In J. Lyons, ed.: *New Horizons in Linguistics*, Penguin, 1970.

Halliday, M. A. K. and Hasan, R., *Cohesion in English*, Longman, 1976.

Halliday, M. A. K., McIntosh, A. and Strevens, P. D., *The Linguistic Sciences and Language Teaching*, Longman, 1964.

Hammerly, H., "The correction of pronunciation errors." *MLJ*, Vol. 57, No. 3, pp. 106–110, 1973.

Harbrace (*Harbrace College Handbook* 8th Edition), by J. C. Hodges & M. E. Whittan. Harcourt, Brace and Jovanovich, New York, 1977.

Harris, D. P., "The linguistics of language testing." In A. Davies, ed., *Language Testing Symposium*, Oxford University Press, pp. 36–45, 1968.

Harris, Z. S., "Transfer Grammar." *IJAL*, Vol. 20, No. 4, pp. 259–270, 1954.

Harris, Z. S., *Structural Linguistics*, University of Chicago Press, 1963.

Hartmann, R. R. K., "Über die Grenzen der Kontrastiven Lexikologie." *Jahrbuch des Instituts für deutsche Sprache*, Vol. 39, Schwann, Düsseldorf, pp. 181–199, 1975.

Hartmann, R. R. K., "Contrastive textology in descriptive and applied linguistics." *Sophia Linguistica* (Tokyo), Vol. IV, pp. 1–12, 1978.

Haugen, E., *Bilingualism in the Americas*, The American Dialect Society, 1956.

Hetzron, R., "Phonology in Syntax." *JL*, Vol. 8, No. 2, pp. 251–265, 1972.

Higa, M., "The psycholinguistic concept of 'difficulty' and the teaching of foreign language vocabulary." *Language Learning*, Vol. 15, pp. 167–179, 1966.

Hockett, C. F., "Two models of grammatical description." *Word*, Vol. 10, pp. 210–233, 1954.

Hok, R., "Cognitive and S-R learning theories reconciled." *IRAL*, Vol. X, No. 3, pp. 263–269, 1972.

Hörmann, H., *Psycholinguistics: An Introduction to Research and Theory*, Springer, Berlin, 1971.

House, J., "Interaktionsnormen in deutschen und englischen Alltagsdialogen." Paper to the GAL Conference, University of Mainz, 1977.

Huber, W. and Kummer, W., *Transformationelle Syntax des Deutschen I*, Fink, Munich, 1974.

Hymes, D., "On communicative competence." In J. B. Pride and J. Holmes, eds.: *Sociolinguistics*, Penguin, pp. 269–293, 1972.

Hymes, D., "Ways of speaking." In R. Bauman and J. Scherzer, eds.: *Explorations in the Ethnography of Speaking*, Cambridge University Press, pp. 433–452, 1974.

Jackson, K. L. and Whitman, R. L., *Evaluation of the Predictive Power of Contrastive Analyses of Japanese and English*. Final Report; Contract No. CEC-0-70-5046 (-823), U.S. Office of Health, Education & Welfare, 1971.

Jacobs, R. A. and Rosenbaum, P. S., *English Transformational Grammar*, Ginn and Co., Waltham, Mass., 1968.

Jakobovits, L. A., "Second language learning and transfer theory." *LL*, Vol. 19, pp. 55–86, 1969.

Jakobovits, L. A., *Foreign Language Learning: A Psycholinguistic Analysis of the Issues*, Newbury House, Rowley, Mass., 1970.

James, C., "Deeper contrastive study." *IRAL*, Vol. 17, No. 2, pp. 83–95, 1969.

James, C., "The exculpation of contrastive linguistics." In G. Nickel, ed.: *Papers in Contrastive Linguistics*, Cambridge University Press, pp. 53–68, 1971.

James, C., "Foreign language learning by dialect expansion." *Papers from the International Symposium on Applied Contrastive Linguistics*, Cornelsen-Velhagen & Klasing, pp. 1–11, 1972.

James, C., "The transfer of communicative competence." In J. Fisiak, ed.: *Contrastive Linguistics and the Language Teacher*, Pergamon Press, pp. 57–69, 1981.

James, C., "Directionality in contrastive analysis." In W. Wilss, ed.: *Kontrastive Linguistik und übersetzungswissenschaft*, Fink, Munich, 1980.

Jespersen, O., *Language: Its Nature, Development and Origin*, Allen and Unwin, 1947.

Johansson, F. A., "Multiple contact analysis." In J. Svartvik, ed.: *Errata: Papers in Error Analysis*, Gleerup, Lund, pp. 48–54, 1973.

Johansson, S., *Papers in Contrastive Linguistics and Language Testing*, Gleerup, Lund, 1975.

Johnson, F. C., "The failure of the discipline of linguistics in language teaching." *LL*, Vol. 19, pp. 235–244, 1970.

Kalisz, R., "On kinship terms in English and Polish." *PSiCL*, Vol. 5, pp. 257–270, 1976.

Kaplan, R. B., *The Anatomy of Rhetoric: Prolegomena to a Functional Theory of Rhetoric*, Center for Curriculum Development, Philadelphia, 1972.

Kasper, G., "Pragmatische Defizite im Englischen deutscher Lerner." Paper to the G.A.L. Conference, University of Mainz, 1977.

Katz, J. J., *The Philosophy of Language*, Harper and Row, New York and London, 1966.

Kellerman, E., "Towards a characterisation of the strategy of transfer in second language learning." *ISB*, Vol. 2, No. 1, Utrecht, pp. 58–146, 1977.

Kempson, R. M., *Presupposition and the Delimitation of Semantics*, Cambridge University Press, 1975.

Kim, S. H. P., "The meaning of 'yes' and 'no' in English and Korean." *LL*, Vol. 12, No. 1, pp. 27–46, 1962.

Kirkwood, H., "Translation as a basis for contrastive linguistic analysis." *IRAL*, Vol. 4, No. 3, pp. 175–182, 1966.

Kirstein, B. H. J., "Reducing negative transfer: two suggestions for the use of translation." *MLJ*, Vol. 56, No. 2, pp. 73–78, 1972.

Kleinmann, H. H., "Avoidance behavior in adult second-language acquisition." *LL*, Vol. 27, No. 1, pp. 93–107, 1977.

Klima, E., "Correspondence at the grammatical level", Research Laboratory of Electronics, M. I. T., 1962 mimeo.

Koestler, A., *The Act of Creation*, Hutchinson, 1964.

Kohler, K., "On the adequacy of phonological theories for contrastive analysis." In G. Nickel, ed.: *Papers in Contrastive Linguistics*, Cambridge University Press, pp. 83–88, 1971.

König, E., "Transformational grammar and contrastive analysis." *PAKS Report No. 6*, University of Stuttgart PAKS Project, pp. 43–59, 1970.

König, E., *Adjectival Constructions in English and German – A Contrastive Analysis*, Julius Groos, Heidelberg, 1971.

König, E., "Major and minor differences betwen languages." *Papers from the International Symposium on Applied Contrastive Linguistics*, Cornelsen-Velhagen & Klasing, pp. 51–66, 1972.

Krashen, S. D., "Formal and informal linguistic environments in language acquisition and language learning." *TESOL Qtly*, Vol. 10, No. 2, pp. 157–168, 1976.

Kress, G., "Sentence complexity in contrastive linguistics." In G. Nickel, ed.: *Papers in Contrastive Linguistics*, Cambridge University Press, pp. 97–102, 1971.

Krzeszowski, T. P., "Equivalence, congruence, and deep structure." In G. Nickel, ed.: *Papers in Contrastive Linguistics*, Cambridge University Press, pp. 37–48, 1971.

Krzeszowski, T. P., *Contrastive Generative Grammar: Theoretical Foundations*, Łodż University Press, 1974.

Krzeszowski, T. P., "Interlanguage and Contrastive Generative Grammar." *ISB*, Utrecht, Vol. 1, No. 1, pp. 58–78, 1976.

Kufner, H. L., *The Grammatical Structures of English and German*, University of Chicago Press, 1962.

Kuhn, T. S., *The Structure of Scientific Revolutions*, University of Chicago Press, 1962.

Kuno, S., *The Structure of the Japanese Language*, M.I.T. Press, 1973.

Labov, W., "The Study of language in its social context." *Sociolinguistic Patterns*, University of Pennsylvania Press, 1972.

Lado, R., "Survey of tests in English as a foreign language." *LL*, Vol. 3, Nos. 1–2, pp. 51–66, 1950.

Lado, R., *Language Testing: The Construction and Use of Foreign Language Tests*, Longman 1961.

Lado, R., *Linguistics across Cultures*, University of Michigan Press, Ann Arbor, 1957.

Lado, R., "Contrastive linguistics in a mentalistic theory of language learning." *GURT*, No. 21, Georgetown University Press, 1968.

Lakoff, G., "Instrumental adverbs and the concept of deep structure." *FL*, Vol. 4, pp. 4–29, 1968.

Lakoff, R., "The logic of politeness; or minding your p's and q's." *Papers from the 9th Regional Meeting*, Chicago Linguistics Society, pp. 292–305, 1973.

Lamendella, J. T., "On the irrelevance of transformational grammar for second-language pedagogy." *LL*, Vol. 19, Nos. 3–4, pp. 255–270, 1970.

Laver, J., "Communicative functions of phatic communion." In A. Kendon, R. M. Harris and M. R. Key, eds.: *Organisation of Behavior in Face-to-Face Interaction*, Mouton, The Hague, 1975.

Lee, W. R., "Thoughts on contrastive linguistics in the context of language teaching." *MSLL*, No. 21. Georgetown University Press, 1968.

Lee, W. R., "How can contrastive linguistic studies help foreign-language teaching?" The Serbo-Croatian–English Contrastive Project, *B Studies*, Zagreb University, pp. 57–66, 1972.

Leech, G., *Semantics*, Penguin, 1974.

Lehmann, D., "A confrontation of *say, speak, talk, tell* with possible German counterparts." *PSiCL*, Vol. 6, pp. 99–109, 1977.

Lehrer, A., "Semantic cuisine." *JL*, Vol. 5, No. 1, pp. 39–55, 1969.

Levelt, W. J. M., "Skill theory and language teaching" *SSLA* Vol. 1, No. 1, Indiana University, 1970.

Levenston, E. A., "Over-indulgence and under-representation – aspects of mother-tongue interference." In G. Nickel, ed.: *Papers in Contrastive Linguistics*, Cambridge University Press, pp. 115–121, 1971.

Lewis, E. G., *Linguistics and Second Language Pedagogy – A Theoretical Study*, Mouton, The Hague, 1974.

Littlewood, W. T. "Gastarbeiterdeutsch and its significance for German teaching." *AVLJ*, Vol. 14, No. 3, pp. 155–158, 1977.

Littlewood, W. T., "Receptive skill as an objective for slow learners." *Fremdsprachlicher Unterricht*, Vol. 2, pp. 11–20, 1978.

Lounsbury, F. G., "A semantic analysis of Pawnee kinship usage." *Language*, Vol. 32, pp. 158–194, 1956.

Lyons, J., *Introduction to Theoretical Linguistics*, Cambridge University Press, 1968.

Lyons, J., "Human language". In R. A. Hinde, ed.: *Non-Verbal Communication*, Cambridge University Press, 1972.

MacCorquodale, K., "On Chomsky's review of Skinner's 'Verbal Behavior'." *Jnl. Exptl. Anal. Beh.*, Vol. 13, No. 1, 1970.

Mackey, W. F., *La Distance Interlinguistique*, Laval University Press, 1972.

Makkai, V. B., "Transfer grammar as the end-product of contrastive analysis." *PCCLLU Papers*, University of Hawaii, pp. 165–172, 1971.

Malmberg, B., "Applications of linguistics." In G. E. Perren and J. L. M. Trim, eds.: *Applications of Linguistics*, Cambridge University Press, pp. 3–18, 1971.

Martin, E., "Verbal learning and the independent retrieval phenomenon." *Psych. Review*, Vol. 78, pp. 314–332, 1971.

Martin, W. and Weltens, J., "A frequency note on the expression of futurity in English." *Z.f.A. u A.*, Vol. 21, No. 3, pp. 289–298, 1973.

Marton, W., "Equivalence and congruence in transformational contrastive studies." *Studia Anglica Poznaniensa*, Vol. 1, Nos. 1–2, pp. 53–62. 1968.

Marton, W., "Some remarks on the formal properties of contrastive pedagogical grammars." In G. Nickel, ed.: *Proc. III AILA Congress*, Vol. 1, Julius Groos, Heidelberg, 1974.

Mel'chuk, I. A., "Machine translation and linguistics." In O. S. Akhmanova et al.: *Exact Methods in Linguistic Research*, University of California, Berkeley, pp. 44–79, 1963.

Miles, T. R., *Helping the Dyslexic Child*, Methuen, 1970.

Moulton, W. G., *The Sounds of English and German*, University of Chicago Press, 1962.

Muir, J., *A Modern Approach to English Grammar: An Introduction to Systemic Grammar*, Batsford, 1972.

Mukattash, L., *Problematic Areas in English Syntax for Jordanian Students*, University of Amman, Jordan, 1977.

Nemser, W., "Approximative systems of foreign-language learners." *IRAL*, Vol. 9, No. 2, pp. 115–123, 1971a.

Nemser, W., "The predictability of interference phenomena in the English speech of native speakers of Hungarian." In G. Nickel, ed.: *Papers in Contrastive Linguistics*, Cambridge University Press, pp. 89–96, 1971b.

Nemser, W. and Vincènz, I., "The indeterminacy of semantic interference." *The Romanian–English CA Project*, Vol. III. Bucharest University, 1972.

Neumann, G., *Ein Skizzenbuch von Berlin*, Sudwest Verlag, Munich, 1971.

Newmark, L. D., "How not to interfere with language learning." In M. Lester, ed.: *Readings in Applied Transformational Grammar*, Holt, Rinehart & Winston, pp. 219–227, 1970.

Newmark, L. and Reibel, D. A., "Necessity and sufficiency in language learning." *IRAL*, Vol. 6, No. 3, pp. 145–164, 1968.

Newsham, G., *The Paragraph in French and English*, Unpubl. Ph.D. Thesis, Faculté des Sciences et de l'Education, Université de Montreal, 1977.

Nickel, G., "Contrastive linguistics and foreign language teaching." In G. Nickel, ed.: *Papers in Contrastive Linguistics*, Cambridge University Press, pp. 1–16, 1971a.

Nickel, G., "Variables in a hierarchy of difficulty." *PCCLLU Papers*, University of Hawaii, pp. 185–194, 1971b.

Nickel, G. and Wagner, K. H., "Contrastive linguistics and language teaching." *IRAL*, Vol. 6, No. 3, pp. 233–255, 1968.

Nida, E. A., *Towards a Science of Translating*, Brill, Leiden, 1964.

Nida, E. A., *Componential Analysis of Meaning: An Introduction to Semantic Structures*, Mouton, The Hague, 1975.

Nowakowski, M., "The lexicon and contrastive linguistic studies." *PSiCL*, Vol. 6, pp. 25–42, 1977.

O'Connor, D. J., *Phonetics*, Penguin, 1973.

Oller, J. W., "Difficulty and predictability." *PCCLLU Papers*, University of Hawaii, pp. 79–98, 1971.

Oller, J. W. and Redding, J., "Article usage and other language skills." *LL*, Vol. 21, No. 1, 1971.

Osgood, C. E., "The similarity paradox in human learning: a resolution." *Psych. Review*, Vol. 56, pp. 132–143, 1949.

Palmer, F. R., *A Linguistic Study of the English Verb*, Longman, 1965.

Peters, P. S. and Ritchie, R. W., "A note on the universal base hypothesis." *JL*, Vol. 5, No. 1, pp. 150–152, 1969.

Pimsleur, P. and Quinn, T., *The Psychology of Second Language Learning*, Cambridge University Press, 1971.

Politzer, R. L., "An experiment in the presentation of parallel and contrasting structures." *LL*, Vol. 18, Nos. 1–2, 1968.

Politzer, R. L., *Linguistics and Applied Linguistics: Aims and Methods*, Center for Curriculum Development, Philadelphia, 1972.

Pomerantz, A., "Compliment responses: notes on the co-operation of multiple constraints." In J. Schenkein, ed.: *Studies in the Organisation of Conversational Interaction*, Academic Press, New York, pp. 79–112, 1978.

Pope, E., "Question-answering systems." *Papers from 9th Regional Meeting*, Chicago Linguistics Society, pp. 482–492, 1973.

Pul'kina, I. M., *A Short Russian Reference Grammar*, Russian Language Publishers, Moscow, 1975.

Quirk, R., *The Use of English*, Longman, 1962.

Quirk, R. et al., *A Grammar of Contemporary English*, Longman, 1972.

Reibel, D. A., "Language learning analysis." *IRAL*, Vol. 7, No. 4, pp. 284–294, 1969.

Reiss, K., *Möglichkeiten und Grenzen der Übersetzungskritik*, Hueber, Munich, 1971.

Richards, J. C., "Error analysis and second language strategies" *Language Sciences* Vol. 17, pp. 12–22, 1971.

Richards, J. C., ed., *Error Analysis: Perspectives on Second Language Acquisition*, Longman, 1974.

Richards, J. C., "Simplification: a strategy in the adult acquisition of a foreign language: an example from Indonesian/Malay." *LL*, Vol. 25, No. 1, pp. 115–126, 1975.

Richterich, R., "The analysis of language needs." *Modern Languages in Adult Education*, Council of Europe Committee for Out of School Education, Strassbourg, pp. 12–20, 1974.

Riley, P., "Towards a contrastive pragmalinguistics." *PSiCL*, Vol. 10, pp. 90–115, 1979.

Rodgers, T., "On measuring vocabulary difficulty – an analysis of item-variables in learning Russian:English vocabulary pairs." *IRAL*, Vol. 7, pp. 327–343, 1969.

Roos, E., "Contrastive collocational analysis." *PSiCL*, Vol. 5, pp. 65–74, 1976.

Ross, J. R., "Adjectives as nominal phrases." In D. A. Reibel and S. Schane, eds.: *Modern Studies in English: Readings in Transformational Grammar*, Prentice Hall, Englewood Cliffs, 1969.

Ryle, G., *The Concept of Mind*, Penguin, 1973.

Sampson, G., *The Form of Language*, Weidenfeld & Nicholson, 1975.

Sapon, S., "On defining a response – a crucial problem in verbal behavior." In P. Pimsleur and T. Quinn, eds.: pp. 75–85, 1971.

Saussure, F. de, *Course in General Linguistics*, McGraw Hill, New York, 1959.

Schachter, J., "An error in error analysis." *LL*, Vol. 24, No. 2, pp. 205–214, 1974.

Scherzer, J., "The ethnography of speaking: a critical appraisal." In M. Saville-Troike, ed.: *GURT*, University of Georgetown Press, pp. 43–58, 1977.

Schubiger, M., "English intonation and German model particles – a comparative study." *Phonetica*, Vol. 12, pp. 65–84, 1965.

Schwarze, C., "Grammatiktheorie und Sprachvergleich." *Ling. Berichte*, Vol. 21, pp. 15–30, 1972.

Sciarone, A. G., "Contrastive analysis: possibilities and limitations." *IRAL*, Vol. 8, No. 2, 1970.

Searle, J. R., *Speech Acts*, Cambridge University Press, 1969.

Searle, J. R., "Indirect speech acts." In P. Cole and J. L. Morgan, eds.: *Syntax and Semantics, Vol. III: Speech Acts*, Academic Press, New York, pp. 58–82, 1975.

Selinker, L., "Interlanguage." *IRAL*, Vol. 10, No. 3, 1972.

Selinker, L., Trimble, L. and Vroman, R., "Presupposition and technical rhetoric." *ELT*, Vol. 21, No. 1, 1974.

Sey, K. A., *Ghanaian English*, Macmillan, 1973.

Sharwood Smith, M., "Interlanguage and intralanguage paraphrase." *PSiCL*, Vol. 4, pp. 297–301, 1976.

Sharwood Smith, M., "Applied Linguistics and the psychology of instruction." *Studies in Second Language Acquisition*, Vol. 1, No. 2, Indiana University, 1978.

Shaumjan, S. K., *Strukturnaja Lingvistika*, Izdatel'stvo Nauka, Moscow, 1965.

Skinner, B. F., *Verbal Behavior*, Appleton-Century-Crofts, New York, 1957.

Slama-Cazacu, T., "Contrastive study *in abstracto*." *Reports & Studies*. The

Romanian–English CA Project, Bucharest University, pp. 57–70, 1971.

Slobin, D. I., *The Ontogenesis of Grammar*, Academic Press, New York, 1971.

Southworth, F. C. and Daswani, C. J., *Foundations of Linguistics*, The Free Press, New York, 1974.

Spock, B., *Baby and Child Care*, New English Library, 1973.

Stalnaker, R. C., "Pragmatics." In D. Davidson and G. Harman, eds.: *Semantics of Natural Language*, Reidel, Dordrecht, pp. 380–397, 1972.

Stockwell, R. P., Bowen, J. D. and Martin, J. W., *The Grammatical Structures of English and Spanish*, University of Chicago Press, 1975a.

Stockwell, R. P. and Bowen, J. D., *The Sounds of English and Spanish*, University of Chicago Press, 1965a.

Stopp, F. J., *Manual of Modern German*, University Tutorial Press, London, 1957.

Strevens, P. D., *Some Observations on the Phonetics and Pronunciation of Modern Portuguese*, University of Coimbra, 1954.

Strevens, P. D., *British and American English*, London, 1972.

Terrace, H. S., "Errorless transfer of discrimination across two continua." *Jnl. Exptl. Anal. Beh.*, Vol. 6, pp. 223–232, 1963.

Thorne, J. P., "On hearing sentences." In J. Lyons and R. Wales, eds.: *Psycholinguistics Papers*, University of Edinburgh Press, 1966.

Tran-Thi-Chau, "Error analysis, contrastive analysis, and students' perception: a study of difficulty in second-language learning." *IRAL*, Vol. 13, No. 2, pp. 119–143, 1975.

Underwood, B. J., "Interference and forgetting." *Psychol. Review*, Vol. 64, pp. 49–60, 1957.

Underwood, B. J. and Postman, L., "Extra-experimental sources of interference in forgetting." *Psychol. Review*, Vol. 67, 1960.

Valdman, A., "The 'Loi de Position' as a pedagogical norm." In A. Valdman, ed.: *Papers to the Memory of Pierre Delattre*, Mouton, The Hague, 1972.

Valdman, A., "Error analysis and grading in the preparation of teaching materials." *MLJ*, Vol. 59, No. 8, 1975.

Van Dijk, T. A., "New developments and problems in textlinguistics." *AILA Bulletin*, No. 1, pp. 13–26, 1978.

Wagner, K. H., "The relevance of the notion 'deep structure' to contrastive analysis." *PAKS Report*, No. 6, University of Stuttgart, 1970.

Walmsley, J. B., "Phase and phase-sequence." *MLJ*, Vol. 63, No. 3, pp. 106–116, 1979.

Wandruszka, M. W., *Interlinguistik: Umrisse einer neuen Sprachwissenschaft*, Piper, Munich, 1971.

Wardhaugh, R., "The contrastive analysis hypothesis." *TESOL Qtly*, Vol. 4, No. 2, pp. 123–130, 1970.

Weinreich, M., *Languages in Contact*, Linguistics Circle of New York, 1953.

Whinnom, K., "The origin of the European-based creoles and pidgins." *Orbis*, Vol. 14, pp. 509–527, 1965.

Whitman, R. L., "Contrastive analysis: problems and procedures." *LL*, Vol. 20, No. 2, 1970.

Whitman, R. L. and Jackson, K. L., "The unpredictability of contrastive analysis." *LL*, Vol. 22, No. 1, pp. 29–41, 1972.

Widdowson, H. G., "The deep structure of discourse and the use of translation." In S. P. Corder and E. Roulet, eds.: *Linguistic Insights in Applied Linguistics*, Didier, Paris, pp. 129–142, 1974.

Widdowson, H. G., "Linguistic insights and language teaching principles." In C. Gutknecht, ed.: *Forum Linguisticum, Vol. III – Communicative Linguistics*, Lang, Geneva, pp. 1–28, 1975.

Widdowson, H. G., "The significance of simplification." *Studies in Second Language Acquisition*, Vol. 1, No. 1, Indiana University, pp. 11–20, 1977.

Widdowson, H. G., *Teaching Language as Communication*, Oxford University Press, 1978.

Wilkins, D. A., Review of A. Valdman: *Trends in Language Teaching*, McGraw Hill, New York, *IRAL*, Vol. 6, No. 1, 1968.

Wilkins, D. A., *Linguistics in Language Teaching*, Arnold, 1972.

Wilkins, D. A., *Notional Syllabuses*, Oxford University Press, 1976.

Wilss, W., *Übersetzungswissenschaft: Probleme und Methoden*, Klett, Stuttgart, 1977.

Winter, E., "Connection in science material." *Science and Technology in a Second Language*, CILT, London, 1971.

Wolfe, D. L., "Some theoretical aspects of language learning and language teaching." *LL*, Vol. 17, 1967.

Wonderly, W. L., *Bible Translations for Popular Use*, United Bible Societies, London, 1968.

Yarmohammadi, L., "A note on contrastive analysis." *ELT*, Vol. 25, No. 1, 1970.

Yngve, V. H., "Human linguistics in face-to-face interaction." In A. Kendon, R. M. Harris and M. Ritchie Key, eds.: *Organisation of Behavior in Face-to-Face Interaction*, Mouton, The Hague, pp. 47–62, 1975.

Zimmermann, R., "Some remarks on pragmatics and contrastive analysis." In G. Nickel, ed.: *AILA Proceedings, Vol. I: Applied Contrastive Linguistics*, Julius Groos, Heidelberg, pp. 297–307, 1972.

Appendix

CA PROJECTS (One of the two languages is English)

NAME OF PROJECT	PLACE	DIRECTOR(S)
German–English PAKS	Kiel, later Stuttgart	Prof. Gerhard Nickel (project expired)
Polish–English	Poznan	Prof. Jacek Fisiak
Finnish–English	Jyväskylä	Prof. Kari Sajavaara and Jaakko Lehtonen
Swedish–English	Lund	Prof. Jan Svartvik (project expired)
Danish–English	Copenhagen	Dr. Claus Faerch
Romanian–English	Bucharest	Prof. Dumitru Chitoran
Serbo-Croat–English	Zagreb	Prof. Rudolf Filipović
Hungarian–English	Budapest and Debrecen	Prof. Laszlo Dezsö
French–English	several Belgian universities	Prof. René Dirven and others
Centre d'Études, Anglaises, Université Catholique de Louvain, Belgium.		J. van Roey
Dutch–English	Utrecht	Dr. Michael Sharwood Smith

Index